It is customary in the Tibetan tradition to recognize the teachings that have shaped one's life and beliefs. In that spirit, I pay homage to the Three Jewels and to my respected teachers. I thank my lineage of predecessors for their teachings and contributions to Buddhism, and I am grateful for the Tibetan and Mongolian cultures.

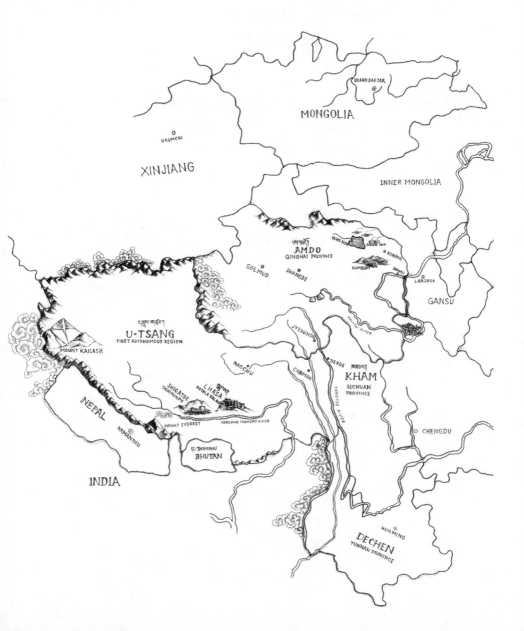

CONTENTS

FOREWORD

In 1998, I learned that Arjia Rinpoche, abbot of the renowned Kumbum monastery in Tibet, had come to the United States from Guatemala as a political exile. At the time, I was in New York to give a talk. It had been almost 40 years since I, too, had left Tibet, seeking freedom in exile, but even longer since I was last in Kumbum, where my own monastic life began. Now, here in front of me, was the abbot of my monastery.

Kumbum is the birthplace of Je Tsong Khapa, the founder of the Gelug tradition of Tibetan Buddhism to which I belong. For the first 200 years of its existence, Kumbum was a small pilgrimage site; then, in the sixteenth century, the Third Dalai Lama, Sonam Gyatso, transformed it into a great monastic university.

The monastery was located not far from where I was born, and I spent some time there in the mid-1950s, when Arjia Rinpoche was still a child. I have happy memories of Kumbum as it used to be, its beautiful, majestic buildings nestled into green hills. But recalling, too, what had happened to so many monasteries at the hands of the Communist Chinese, and what the Kumbum monks must have suffered, I was eager to hear what Arjia Rinpoche had to say about the monastery and how Tibetans in the vicinity were faring.

Rinpoche and I had a very warm meeting. So much had happened to both of us, and the way our lives have unfolded has been so different; but we both continue to share a concern for the welfare of the people of Tibet. Given his experience of working with the Chinese authorities, as well as his having met the president of China, Jiang Zemin, I hoped he might be able help us improve our dialogue with the Chinese. With that in mind, I asked him to write to President Jiang Zemin.

In due course, Arjia Rinpoche established the Tibetan Center for Compassion and Wisdom in Mill Valley, California, which did very well. Later, when my elder brother Tagtser Rinpoche fell ill and could no longer manage the Tibetan Cultural Center he had set up in Bloomington, Indiana, I thought of Arjia Rinpoche. He had the experience to take it on, and I felt he could restore and manage this important center.

As always, Arjia Rinpoche accepted the challenge. Another connection that seemed to make him the appropriate person to come to Bloomington was that, like him, my brother had also been abbot of Kumbum. Consequently, the center is now sometimes thought of as representing the Kumbum tradition in the West. Bearing in mind that Arjia Rinpoche comes from a Mongolian family, I also thought it would be fitting if the focus of the center could be extended to include Mongolian Buddhists. The result is that the center now serves not only the Tibetan community in America, but the Mongolian communities too, and has been renamed the Tibetan Mongolian Buddhist Cultural Center to reflect this.

Taking advantage of his newfound freedom of expression, Arjia Rinpoche, former abbot of the great monastic university of Kumbum, has compiled his memoirs in this book, *Surviving the Dragon*. He writes candidly about both the joys and the horrors of his life in Tibet: how he survived famine, how he rose through the ranks of lamas to work closely with the late Panchen Lama, and how he negotiated the political perils of life in Tibet to serve the Tibetan people under Chinese rule.

Whereas others have written only about their terrible experiences of incarceration and punishment under Communist rule, Arjia Rinpoche is an insider who was elevated to the top of the religious hierarchy and understood its workings from within. Nevertheless, when events following the death of the Tenth Panchen Lama and the controversial selection of the Eleventh threatened to oblige him to compromise his principles, he chose instead to go into exile.

In order to understand what is really happening in a country where the press is neither open nor free and people live in a state of constant fear and suspicion, we must rely on the reports of individuals like Arjia Rinpoche, who can now write without restraint about what he has seen, heard, and experienced in Tibet. I believe that what he has to say will be of great interest to the many people in the world who have the compassion to find common cause with fellow humans like the peoples of Tibet, Inner Mongolia, and East Turkestan who are currently living under such critical circumstances. I hope that in creating a better understanding of what is going on there, this book will contribute to bringing about peaceful change in Tibet, where an ancient people and their valued religion and culture are struggling to survive.

—*His Holiness the Dalai Lama*
July 20, 2009

INTRODUCTION

*"Very soon in this land [with a harmonious blend of religion and poli-
tics] deceptive acts may occur from without and within. At that time, if
we do not dare to protect our territory, our spiritual personalities,
including the Victorious Father and Son [Dalai Lama and Panchen
Lama] may be exterminated without trace, the property and authority
of our Lakangs [residences of reincarnated lamas] and monks may be
taken away. Moreover, our political system, developed by the Three
Great Dharma Kings [Tri Songtsen Gampo, Tri Songdetsen, and Tri
Ralpachen] will vanish without anything remaining. The property of
all people, high and low, will be seized and the people forced to become
slaves. All living beings will have to endure endless days of suffering
and will be stricken with fear. Such a time will come."*

—The Thirteenth Dalai Lama

Modern Chinese history can be characterized as a "Tale of Three Fish."
Taiwan is still swimming in the ocean: No one has caught that fish—at least
not yet. Hong Kong is alive but on display in a Chinese aquarium. Tibet, the
third fish, is broiled and on the table, already half devoured: Its language, its
religion, its culture, and its native people are disappearing faster than its gla-
cial ice. However, although its body may be disappearing, the spirit of Tibet
is still present. Hope is not yet lost.

Tibetans are not naïve, nor do they have a superstitious belief in deliverance
by some supernatural power. Instead they have a practical wisdom acquired from
their centuries of experience with invaders who have swept in, established themselves for a short time, and then disappeared. It was common practice at my home
monastery, Kumbum, that when a powerful warlord came to the gates the abbot
would give him gifts such as horses, rich brocades, and rugs, so that the monastery would be spared. This was just another indignity to endure, another page in
history to turn, another sign of the fundamental truth of impermanence.

Tibetan attitudes must be understood in the light of this history. Armed with pragmatism and Buddhist understanding of the nature of change, Kumbum survived. So when the Chinese Communists came on the scene in 1949, calling their occupation "liberation," Tibetans thought this intruder was just another gang of bandits pounding at their door. Tibetans assumed that if treated with proper diplomacy, these invaders, too, would leave; therefore the people of Tibet showed the Chinese dragon a smiling face.

But the Communists mistook these smiles as indications that Tibetans were happy to be freed from their "feudal serfdom." This misunderstanding must be clarified. Tibet's limited experience of the outside world left it poorly prepared for the late 1950s. Tibetans still saw the world through local, even feudal, eyes. A totalitarian society equipped with massive military power, rigid ideology, and instant communications was beyond Tibet's historic experience—and Communist China's interest in Tibet was no passing fancy.

Each emperor of China has been a fearsome master, sitting upon his throne of intricately carved dragons protecting his person and his realm. The table in front of him was supported by dragon claws; he wore on his robe an elaborately embroidered dragon. And at the seat of power was the Dragon Emperor himself. His was the energy that drove the known universe under the Mandate of Heaven—for good and for ill.

When the Communists came to power in China, the dragon fit neatly into their new agenda. In a traditional Chinese New Year's parade, the director choreographs the dragon's every step—when to lower his head and prance this way, and when to raise his head and prance that way—and China's Communist rulers have led the people in the same manner. Those who have lived under Communist rule—Han, Tibetan, Muslim, Mongolian, and Manchurian—have danced to the dragon's tune on the world stage.

Now China is modern, but it is only on the surface that the system has changed. Communist China has developed economically, but its lack of pluralism remains constant. No legislative or judicial branch has meaningful authority over the ruling elite, which prizes economic and military growth only as the means to enhance its power, to justify its rule, and to carve its image in history. There is a Chinese saying, "Everyone can see a symbol," and the 2008 Beijing Olympics provided such a dramatic symbol of the nation. But I fear that the modern rulers of Communist China will never progress beyond mere symbolism. Until they do, they can never address the substantive problems of what they still see as an expanding Chinese empire.

My life in Tibet spanned the five decades that Mao Zedong and Deng Xiaoping were in power. Although these two autocrats had different personalities—one was a fierce tyrant and the other a "free-market liberal"—both were alpha dogs at the head of an obedient pack. I have met their successor, Jiang Zemin, and I have had some interaction with Hu Jintao, the current president. I am disappointed to see that even into its third generation, Communist China's leadership lacks the moral authority to lead its people with ideas, inspiration, and example, rather than control them through fear and the exercise of brute force.

What you will read in the following pages is my attempt to convey an account of my own life, unimportant in itself but an interesting lens through which to see larger events in Tibet and China. I was born in 1950, and my life can be viewed as a series of eight-year cycles of crisis and resolution, much like that same period in Tibet and China.

Two years after my birth, a search committee from powerful Kumbum Monastery decided that I was the reincarnation of its beloved abbot and brought me to the monastery to be raised by monks. Although Chairman Mao Zedong's People's Republic of China had already "liberated" Tibet, monastic life still functioned under centuries-old traditions. Wherever I went at Kumbum, people bowed and prayed to me, for though still a child, I was also Arjia Rinpoche, the monastery's spiritual leader. As the years passed I took for granted my elevated status, which was reinforced by my tutor, my housekeeper, my servants, and even my playmates. At Kumbum I felt loved, honored, and totally cared for. Then, eight years after my birth, on October 15, 1958, the world turned upside down.

On that day Chinese Communist soldiers arrested, humiliated, and tortured hundreds of monks from our monastery under a new official policy that had shifted from reconciliation to occupation. The dragon was set loose on Tibet. The beloved members of my household were bound, thrown into trucks, and driven off to prison, leaving me alone and completely at a loss. Even the monk's robes that gave me some small sense of normalcy would soon be forbidden.

In the next eight-year cycle, which was marked by famine and humiliation, I learned to survive as a reviled elitist under the Communist system. Then, in 1966, things got worse: The dragon's breath of Mao's Cultural Revolution scorched all the lands under China's rule in an effort to eradicate all religion and culture. It nearly succeeded. In Tibet, thousands of monasteries were attacked, their buildings, ancient scriptural texts, and religious art damaged or destroyed by a system gone mad. The Red Guard tortured Tibetans, other ethnic groups, and the Chinese as well in a chaotic political environment that pitted Communist against Communist. Fortunately for me, I had a way to put these terrible events into perspective. My precious teachers helped me see them as examples of a basic Buddhist premise: Suffering is part of life, and actions based on compassion are the key to finding peace.

I held this lesson close during the following eight years, during which signs of renewal could be observed in China and Tibet after the death of Mao. Freed from my physical labors and the crippling stigma of elitism, I was able to return to my life as a rinpoche and attend university. I relished my newfound freedom, but my teachers did not let me forget the lessons of the past 16 years. They helped me resist the growing temptations of material comfort and enabled me to rededicate myself to my life as a monk and my responsibilities as an abbot.

By 1982, during the next eight-year cycle, my life was filled with hope. A delegation from His Holiness the Dalai Lama visited Tibet, and with the guidance and friendship of the Tenth Panchen Lama, I was becoming involved with politics. Beginning in 1990, I rose higher and higher within the political and religious hierarchy of the national Communist system. Materially I had become well off, but the emotional and spiritual price of this success began to take its toll. By 1998, due to the Chinese selection of a counterfeit Eleventh Panchen Lama, my own political ascent, and the role I was increasingly forced to play in the Communist charade, I could no longer ignore the conflict between the government's interests and my own religious vows. Rather than betray my faith, I chose to leave my homeland, my friends, and my beloved monks at Kumbum Monastery. I chose a life of exile.

This is my story.

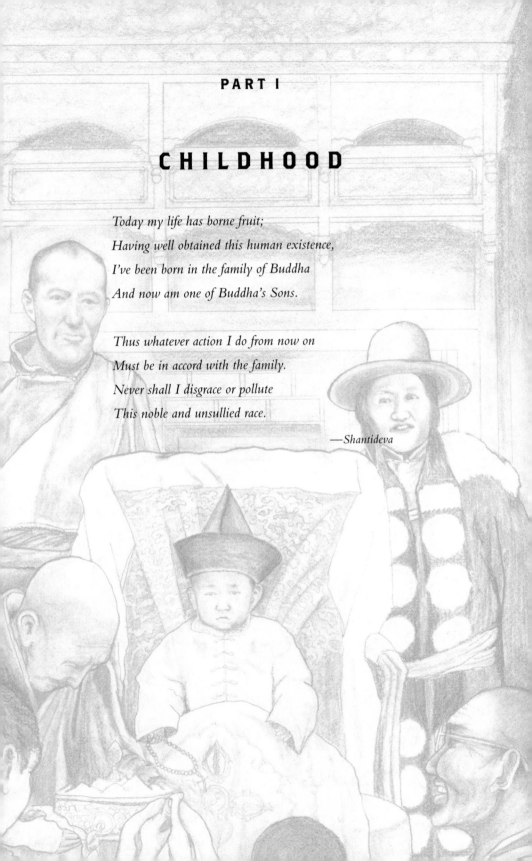

PART I

CHILDHOOD

Today my life has borne fruit;
Having well obtained this human existence,
I've been born in the family of Buddha
And now am one of Buddha's Sons.

Thus whatever action I do from now on
Must be in accord with the family.
Never shall I disgrace or pollute
This noble and unsullied race.

—*Shantideva*

CHAPTER 1

MY MOTHER HAS
A PROPHETIC DREAM

My life as a reincarnate lama began on a peaceful midsummer day in 1952, when I was two years old. A search committee of 10 monks had set out from one of Tibet's great monasteries, Kumbum, to bring back the reincarnation of the late Seventh Arjia Rinpoche, the monastery's hereditary abbot. Mounted on sturdy horses, the monks traveled swiftly across the Dolon Nor steppe in northeastern Tibet, intent on their mission. Occasionally the colorful wild-flowers of summer gave way to *gers* of nomad herdsmen, sprouting like clusters of small, white mushrooms from the boundless carpet of the steppe. Large flocks of white Tibetan sheep grazed in the distance; in smaller herds, young yaks played happily near their mothers. From time to time the monks passed nomad herdsmen and herds-women traveling on horses loaded with bags of goods to sell or trade at a crossroads market.

For a full year the monks had been sitting over tea with tribal leaders and local gossips, looking for boys who had special talents, or around whom auspicious events had occurred. Each monk had played his part: One looked for favorable signs, such as a rainbow over the home of a pregnant woman, or a prophecy; another watched a child's behavior as he interacted with monks who had been special friends of the deceased Arjia Rinpoche, or observed carefully as the child was presented with the Rinpoche's personal prayer

3

beads, spectacles, and utensils. Did any of them seem familiar? Two families in our tribe, my own and another, had been interviewed and tested by the search party in its quest to find the new abbot of Kumbum Monastery.

Before my birth, my mother had a prophetic dream: She was with her family; it was summer; storm clouds gathered and the sky darkened. With a big clap of thunder, a dragon suddenly appeared before her, startling her so much that she awoke from the dream. She interpreted it to mean that someday a person of great importance would come to her, but because it seemed boastful she didn't tell anyone about the dream for a long time.

Seven days after I was born, an itinerant monk came to our home and asked the exact time of my birth. He told my parents that my birth was very unusual and auspicious because I was born not only in the tiger year, but also on the tiger day, and at the tiger hour. To Tibetans and Mongolians, the tiger is the most powerful and majestic of animals, the king among great beasts. Thus, I had been thrice blessed. Again and again the monk asked my parents to take special care of me. He warned them not to allow impure things near me and asked that I be given my own special cup from which to drink and that my dishes be purified with incense. He requested that the same be done with my clothes and the place where I slept. He considered my birth to be a sacred event.

Now, two years later, the monks riding in the distance grew closer. Their golden hats shimmered, and on their backs brocade-covered cylinders held the promise of important messages. As the riders reached the outskirts of our tribe, the excitement became electric. Had the selection been made? At whose home would they stop? My parents peered through the small openings above the door of our traditional Mongolian tent, or *ger*. My mother had set aside special delicacies for the guests who would be visiting if her child was chosen as the reincarnation of Arjia Rinpoche.

Our furiously barking dogs gave my parents an excuse to go outside and look more closely at the arriving party. The search committee slowed and then stopped. My father advanced to their horses and held the reins as the maroon-robed travelers dismounted. Perhaps it wasn't the search committee after all! My nervous mother offered the monks tea and modest treats, reserving the delicacies while polite conversation was exchanged. My brothers found me where I was playing nearby and brought me back to the family tent.

At last the senior monk rose, placed white, hand-loomed scarves, or *khatas,* around my parents' necks, and offered them congratulations for having given birth to Arjia Rinpoche, eighth incarnation of the father of Lama Tsong Khapa, founder of the Gelug tradition of Tibetan Buddhism. My family prostrated before the monks in gratitude for this extraordinary honor; in her joy my mother wept.

Before my predecessor, the Seventh Arjia Rinpoche, died, he left important clues regarding his reincarnation. Arjia Rinpoche had told his followers that he especially liked the location of Dolon Nor. After his death, hundreds of monks gathered around the sealed clay oven in which his body lay. Chanting and praying, they went through the elaborate funeral rituals for such an important person. From time to time a monk would lean forward and pour oil into a metal gutter that funneled into the clay fire chamber, fueling the flames until nothing was left but ashes. Always they kept watchful eyes on the behavior of the smoke, which rose and coincidentally drifted toward Dolon Nor and the Golden Temple that housed Lama Tsong Khapa's shrine (*stupa*). As if to pay its final respects, the smoke swirled once in the sky above the temple, and then headed northwest. At that moment an old monk said tearfully, "Rinpoche is going to his favorite place, the Dolon Nor steppe."

Before setting out to find Rinpoche's reincarnation, the monks sought the advice of the Tenth Panchen Lama. Although he was only 12 years old at the time, he meditated for a moment on what had occurred, then spoke decisively. He ordered the seekers to "follow the direction of the first smoke."

In keeping with Tibetan custom, a year later the search began in earnest for a male child conceived within 49 days of Arjia Rinpoche's death. The region where the smoke had gone was sparsely inhabited, so the monks knew they would have a small pool of candidates—perhaps 10—to choose from; in a more populated area as many as 100 boys might be selected.

The searchers traveled through the countryside without revealing the true purpose of their journey. They stopped at camps and villages, casually conversing with locals, looking for any unusual signs that could indicate where a suitable boy might be found. Nearly a year later, when the final list was brought to the attention of the Panchen Lama, he saw my name and immediately pointed to it, saying, "Yes, this is the one." In the Gelug branch of Tibetan Buddhism, the largest branch, the Dalai Lamas and the Panchen Lamas stand together at the top of a hierarchical system of incarnations. For centuries they have provided a lineage of Buddhist wisdom and practice, and are revered not only for their status, but also because of the rigorous training they undergo.

Tibetan Buddhist hierarchy is not defined as strictly as it is in many Western religions, such as Catholicism. For example, the Dalai Lama is supreme in his secular role of political leader, but when it comes to religious authority, he and the Panchen Lama are equals. Then come the leaders of each of the four Tibetan spiritual traditions: Nyingma, Sakya, Kagyu, and Gelug. After this, the hierarchy gets hazy. Certainly the abbots of the major monasteries are high ranking. Others are highly regarded because of the contributions and achievements of their predecessors. Still others have achieved prominence in this lifetime.

Ordinarily, the Panchen Lama's selection of my name from the list of candidates would have been strictly followed. However, the young Panchen Lama's decision was not immediately accepted by my uncle Gyayak Rinpoche, who had a great deal of influence because he was the Panchen Lama's teacher, spiritual mentor, and constant companion. As I learned many years later, my uncle worried that if I, his nephew, were selected, people would doubt the legitimacy of the choice; they would suspect nepotism. Therefore Gyayak Rinpoche suggested that all 10 boys be examined, tested, and finally selected in the traditional way: using a *tsampa* ball.

For this ceremony, tsampa, the traditional Tibetan dough made from water, barley flour, and butter, is formed into balls. The name of each candidate is written on a strip of paper and inserted into a hole in each ball. Great care is taken to make sure the balls are then rolled into identical spheres and placed into a porcelain goblet decorated with the eight auspicious symbols of Tibetan Buddhism.

The selection ceremony for the Eighth Arjia Rinpoche took place in the most sacred space in Kumbum Monastery, the Great Hall of Golden Tiles (*Serdong Chenmo*), on the very spot where founder Lama Tsong Khapa was born. Inside the Golden Hall is a spectacular shrine covered in silver, embossed with snow lions, and encrusted with precious stones. On the massive structure stands a life-size statue of Lama Tsong Khapa, founder of the Gelug tradition, framed by an elaborately worked silver aura encrusted with gems. A large, mystical bird called a garauda is depicted flying above a giant polished turquoise stone, crowning the statue.

An open area surrounds the statue at the raised level of the shrine. During special occasions, such as the selection of an important reincarnation, high lamas sit around the shrine chanting prayers for guidance under the soft light of butter lamps. Incense permeates the air while ritual offerings of flowers, incense, fruit, and barley are made. The monks chant, *"Cho-kyi gyal-po kun-khen lo-zang-drag. Say-dang che-pa ney-dir sheg-su-sol"* ("All Buddhas and bodhisattvas, please come here, together with your offspring").

During this solemn ceremony, all eyes were on the Panchen Lama. He held the goblet containing the 10 tsampa balls and swirled it so that the balls circled upward toward the brim. As he continued to do so, one ball gained enough momentum to fly out of the bowl. Four monks held the corners of a large, golden silk cloth to catch the tsampa. The first ball was set aside. Two more balls flew out of the bowl and were set aside. Inside these three tsampa balls were hidden the names of the final candidates; each would be honored, as each represented an aspect of Arjia Rinpoche's qualities: his body, his speech, and his mind. The remaining seven balls, and the names contained within, were removed from contention.

After more prayers, the three balls were placed back into the goblet. Once more the swirling began, until one jumped out. The Panchen Lama opened

7

it and read aloud the words inscribed: Yung Drung Dorje. This was my infant name.

The region that the Seventh Arjia Rinpoche loved so much, the area in which I was born, was a landscape of vast steppes by the great salt lake of Dolon Nor, where tribes of Tibetan and Mongolian nomads have lived for generations. It was a spacious prairie whose inhabitants mirrored the open, forthright, hospitable qualities of the land itself. They were filled with reverence for the Three Jewels: Buddha, the enlightened being; Dharma, his teachings; and Sangha, the assembly of his enlightened followers. Their devotion to the Dalai Lama and the Panchen Lama was equally boundless.

During the 1940s, while he was visiting Kumbum Monastery, the Ninth Panchen Lama was invited to visit the Dolon Nor steppes. He was accompanied by Arjia Rinpoche and other important lamas. In this isolated region such a visit was rare, so the local people were filled with a special longing to receive teachings from the Panchen Lama. According to accounts of this historic visit, the site was packed with colorful Mongolian gers and Tibetan tents. Nomad drink and delicacies were plentiful. Because it was spring, people had set aside their homegrown sheepskin outerwear for traditional holiday attire stitched with brightly colored, store-bought thread and cloth. Mongolian women had decorated their dresses with turquoise and coral worked with silver, while Tibetan women wore hats trailing lengths of jewelry. The men competed in horse races and archery to welcome the Panchen Lama.

Although in those days Tibetans and Mongolians lived under very simple conditions—without even basic electrical appliances—they felt no lack of comfort. On the contrary, everybody could heartily enjoy a life that was free from the noise and worries of a busy, competitive society. The nomads of my country believed that the most precious things in life were a carefree state of mind and a friendship that was pure, and they passed their days in peaceful pursuit of these goals. My previous incarnation took such pleasure in the fertile beauty of the prairie, and in the enthusiasm and hospitality of its people, that he said, "If possible, my next life will begin there." And it had.

If a neighbor needed help on the steppe, everybody came to offer a hand, even if he or she was not a relative. Reliance on friends is an important aspect of nomadic life. The herding people of Dolon Nor moved three or four times a year, following the seasons in search of new grazing lands, where the grasses and water were fresh. For the most part nomads herded sheep. Having a flock of a hundred was common; a thousand sheep made a family wealthy.

Both Tibetan and Mongolian nomads settled our area, and you could tell the camps apart by their shelters. Whereas Tibetans lived in tents woven of yak hair, Mongolians lived in gers, or yurts—warm, domelike portable dwellings covered with felt. Each family built its own dwelling. Wooden parts were bought from a carpenter, but the nomads made the felt from their own wool using traditional methods and sewed the gers themselves. The felt was supported by wooden lattice walls, which could be collapsed like an accordion when it came time to move to a different site. From the top of the lattice rose thin, umbrella-like spokes, to a wheel-shaped hub at the pinnacle. The felt overlay was often decorated with appliqués of auspicious Buddhist symbols, with a curlicue design around the top of the tent. The inside walls were usually embellished with brocaded fabric if the family was sufficiently prosperous. When important people came to visit, more designs might be added to the walls.

In my childhood home the fireplace was located in the center of the ger. For fuel we used a mixture of dried yak and sheep dung, as the one burned hotter and the other burned slower. Surprisingly, there was no smell or smoke inside; it escaped through the center hole in the top of the ger. Opposite the entryway was our family shrine with its offering bowls, butter lamps, incense, and sacred objects such as statues of Buddhas. The seating area near the shrine was reserved for special guests. On the right side, as you entered, was the kitchen with its portable cupboards, pots, and other storage. Children and young couples slept on this side, while older children and parents slept on the left. Woven cloth and yak or sheep skins carpeted the floor for warmth.

Labor in our neighborhood gers was divided along traditional family roles. Men worked with the animals and sold them; with their older sons they would gather salt from salt flats to take to town for bartering. Women managed all

9

the domestic chores: looking after the children, cooking, and sewing. They wove yak-hair bags to store salt and other goods, and they were in charge of milking the animals. Social affairs, too, were in their hands: When visiting other families, the women arranged obligatory gifts of fabric, yogurt, or butter, as well as candy for the children. Management of a household was judged by how much fuel a woman had gathered for winter. Because Tibetan winters are extremely cold, having a big supply of dung and wood was crucial.

My family's ger was not big, but it was always well ordered, warm, and clean. Both of my nomad parents were hard workers, skillful herders, and very devout Buddhists. My father, Baldan, was tall and powerfully built. He was an honorable man of quiet strength, known for his fairness. A herdsman from boyhood, he was an expert at riding horses, tending cattle, shearing sheep, and moving tents as the family migrated from winter to summer pastures. No carts were used in the move; everything—including children—was fitted on the backs of yaks. Emptied water barrels were tied to the animals' sides and padded with soft sheepskin; very young children traveled inside the upright barrels, their little round faces shining out.

When my father was a young man, he often went to collect salt for bartering in the nearest market town, along with butter, meat, cheese, and wool. In exchange he got goods the family could not grow or make, such as cloth, noodles, flour, sugar, rice, and beans. When necessary, money was used to do business with itinerant traders or shopkeepers who sold needles, thread, lamp oil, or toys. Sometimes after a successful year, my family could even afford a special, treasured item like a watch or a telescope, which was useful when tending to our animals. When my father grew older, my eldest brother, Pema, took over the role of bartering at the markets while my father stayed home to handle the domestic responsibilities of our land and animals.

My mother, Tse Sang, was widely admired for her hospitality and for her ability to keep our ger clean and orderly—no small task when you consider that she had 11 children (I was the ninth). When nomads moved they traveled with horses and yaks across terrain where there was no road. At a new site (one with sufficient grass and water) the women immediately assembled the *tapka,* an oven made from three portable clay panels fitted together with arches at the bottom to allow for draft, and a tripod on which to rest the pot. When setting up camp, women demonstrated their homemaking skills by racing to be the first to get the fuel burning and hot tea made. My mother was always the winner.

She was also a good cook, providing our large family with healthy and tasty food. In the morning my mother mixed tsampa with butter and milk tea, adding sugar and bits of dried cheese. Sometimes we might have rice or homemade bread. For evening meals we ate *tukpa,* noodle soup with boiled lamb or yak meat; in winter our diet was augmented with potatoes or dried onions. Fruit was a very rare and special treat, which my father sometimes brought back from town along with noodles. When shopping, nomads always chose the highest-quality noodles they could find—and filled their sacks to the brim before returning home.

My mother enjoyed telling the story of how she met my father. It was love at first sight. He was tall, soft-spoken, and handsome, and he wore his hair in a single long braid, woven with dark silken strands, coiled about his head. In those days marriages were arranged, but my father's family was poor and the elders in my mother's family did not approve of the match. The one exception was my mother's grandmother, who was sympathetic to the young lovers. With her help as a secret go-between, my father stole my mother away from her family, and they eloped—the only way to marry based on love. Usually, with the help of a determined matchmaker and profuse apologies and pleas for forgiveness, such couples would be welcomed back into the family circle once the deed was done—which was the case with my parents.

My family home was warm and harmonious, perhaps because of my mother's kindness and hospitality and my father's integrity and honesty. Everyone in my family says I most resemble my mother and her brother, my uncle Gyayak Rinpoche. Like him I am very organized. If I used something that belonged to Gyayak Rinpoche, I always had to put it back exactly where I found it. When I opened a drawer to look in his desk, everything was always neatly arranged. It was my good karma that after I was discovered as Arjia Rinpoche, Gyayak Rinpoche became my spiritual friend and teacher. As a result, my life would become intimately entwined with his.

11

My uncle Gyayak Rinpoche was born in 1915, one of four children. Once he was recognized as the reincarnation of the Fourth Gyayak Rinpoche, he was invited to Kumbum Monastery to begin his life as a novice monk. From his earliest days he was praised as a serious and creative student, which enabled him to study and practice with many scholarly and eminent lamas.

He was also a model of simplicity. Although Gyayak Rinpoche was one of the most important rinpoches of the 30 or 40 living in Kumbum, his own quarters and lifestyle were always modest. Rinpoche was 10 years old when he received his first offering of money—copper coins threaded together with a leather thong through their centers. (In our tradition it is considered auspicious to bestow offerings on a monk or lama.) With this gift he bought materials for a traditional Tibetan painting, or *thangka,* of the Buddha. From then on he used his pocket money to mold statues of Buddha or to draw thangkas. He was not only a skillful artist, but he also embodied the practice of the six Buddhist virtues, or *paramitas*: generosity, morality, patience, effort, concentration, and wisdom. Gyayak Rinpoche was a very impressive man.

In the 1930s, the Ninth Panchen Lama (1883–1937) stayed in Kumbum Monastery for more than a year. Although quite young, Gyayak Rinpoche was the *khenpo,* or administrative abbot, of Kumbum Monastery, so he became very close to the Panchen Lama. According to the custom of Kumbum Monastery, when the Dalai Lama or the Panchen Lama visits, the khenpo offers his title to the honored guest as a sign of respect. The Panchen Lama happily accepted the honorary title, but as is also the custom, he returned the favor by deputizing Gyayak Rinpoche to act as khenpo during his stay. He also became the young abbot's teacher. A year later in 1937, the Ninth Panchen Lama left Kumbum Monastery to return to his home monastery, Tashi Lhunpo, in Shigatse, several hundred miles west of Lhasa. Sadly, at age 44, he passed away during the journey.

During his stay in Kumbum the Panchen Lama had often told Gyayak Rinpoche, "We will be together later," but Gyayak Rinpoche would not come to realize the meaning of these words for several years. When the search team for the reincarnation of the Ninth Panchen Lama recognized the Tenth

Panchen Lama, they placed the child in the care of Gyayak Rinpoche, who was eventually appointed his tutor. Only then did Gyayak Rinpoche understand the real meaning of the Ninth Panchen Lama's words: His former mentor had foreseen that their master-student relationship would continue through several lifetimes, only in this second lifetime their roles would be reversed.

I was not quite two years old when I went to live in Kumbum Monastery. In 1952 the monastery sent the Panchen Lama's big, Russian-built car to our small settlement to take my family and me to the city of Xining. (Once I was established in my new home, most of my family would move back to their Mongolian nomadic tribe.) The next morning we drove to Kumbum, stopping along the way at tents set up for us to take tea and to be welcomed by hundreds of enthusiastic monks and laypeople who had gathered from the countryside to greet the new Arjia Rinpoche. Smoke from burning incense, banners, chanting, and music preceded us to the next stop for more tea and greetings, where we were joined by hundreds more well-wishers. By the time we arrived at Kumbum Monastery, the procession had swollen to thousands of celebrants.

Of course I have no personal recollection of these events (I heard the stories later from my family), but a few days after my arrival, I was enthroned in a propitious and grand ceremony. The sounds of monks' chanting mixed with horns, drums, and trumpets filled the sacred space and must have startled me into silence, for there are no stories about my fussing. I was placed on the throne by my father, whose hands discreetly held me from behind and kept me from falling over or squirming away. This was the proudest moment of my mother's life. My parents stayed with me in the monastery for the next six months while I adjusted to my new environment. I can only imagine how painful it must have been for my parents when the time came to leave me at the monastery and return home. In our culture it is considered an extraordinary honor to have a son become a monk or a daughter a nun, much less a high-ranking incarnation, so their longing for me was eased by their devotion

13

to Buddhism and pride in their son. I was too young to recall more than a few fragmentary memories of that time, but I don't recall missing my family very much. I was too busy.

To ease whatever fears I might have had, my parents allowed my two older brothers, Nori and Chibo, to stay with me and serve as both parents and play-mates. They remained at Kumbum with me for six years, until I was eight. Also, my parents visited me at least twice a year during one or another of the four big religious festivals honoring the New Year or major events in the life of Buddha. Other family members also visited me from time to time, so I grew up with the feeling of having two families: my household in Kumbum Mon-astery, and the relatives who traveled there regularly to spend time with me.

When I was five years old the Dalai Lama and the Panchen Lama each passed through Kumbum, where the Panchen Lama gave a dharma teaching in the courtyard of our monastery. My parents, who were visiting at the time, held me in their arms while we all listened. I have no memory of the dharma teaching, but I do recall my first meeting with the young Dalai Lama who gave me a handful of crystal sugar. My hands were too small to hold it, and I spilled sugar everywhere, which was met with much laughter.

My early years at the monastery were spent getting used to my new life and learning prayers, rituals, and monastic customs. Nomad children enjoy what-ever games their imaginations can conjure up, but now, as a rinpoche and nominal abbot of Kumbum Monastery, I had real toys that visitors brought as offerings. I remember a toy airplane that I pulled to make the propeller spin; its wings were removable, so it could be put away in a box. When I was six, my older brother taught me how to make a telephone. We took apart two flashlights, leaving empty tubes. We stretched a very thin skin across the end of each tube and placed a string though a tiny hole in the skin, which we then strung from one receiver to the other. When the string was pulled taut, we could hear and speak to each other. Our telephone worked well in the mon-astery as long as we stayed within the limits of our connecting cord.

Part of my early education involved learning the stories of famous gurus and heroes from Tibetan and Mongolian mythology and history, which made a big impression on me. I also remember playing hide-and-seek and getting very angry when I was found too quickly. I broke out in wails of disappointment but stopped immediately when a playmate reminded me that heroes never cry.

Although I was only six, my uncle Gyayak Rinpoche took me and my childhood friend, Serdok Rinpoche, who was nine, to Labrang Monastery in what is now known as Gansu Province to listen to dharma teachings and to take my first religious vows. It was a trip full of new experiences: This was the first time that I had ever seen a bus, let alone ridden in one. Traveling with us were Serdok Rinpoche's tutor, our attendants, and a few young monks. We crossed the Yellow River and finally arrived at Labrang.

Serdok Rinpoche was born in 1947 as the Eighth Serdok Rinpoche. His previous incarnations made remarkable contributions to Kumbum Monastery. The Sixth, Lobsang Tsultrim Gyatso, a great practitioner and scholar whose books are still widely circulated and recited, was especially famous.

The Serdok Rinpoche of my generation was a boy open to everything: He was cordial, sincere, and spontaneous. He was especially fond of mechanical things, but what most people did not know was how seriously he took his devotion. Every day before dawn, while the rest of us were still asleep, he rose and circumambulated the temple, walking around it while reciting sutras and practicing dharma. We grew up together, and our shared experiences— including the hardships we later endured—made us the closest of friends. As we could see from the photographs on the walls of Kumbum Monastery, Gyayak Rinpoche, Serdok Rinpoche, and I had been the best of friends in our previous lives, and we were very close in this one.

Labrang Monastery, where we went to study and take our first vows, is located in the easternmost part of Amdo Province. Founded in 1709, Labrang is one of the six big monasteries of the Gelug sect, famous for the magnificence of its architecture, the quality of its university, and the precision of its practice. At the time of my visit, there were more than 4,000 monks in residence there.

Taking monastic vows is the most important ritual in a monk's life. Considering how little I understood at my age about what taking vows really meant, Gyayak Rinpoche thought that I should take only the most basic ones,

15

similar to lay vows that people take on festival days or on retreat. These include the five root vows: 1) not to kill sentient beings, 2) not to steal, 3) not to lie, 4) not to commit sexual misconduct (adultery), and 5) not to become intoxicated (drugs, alcohol). The lama delivering the vows was Aku Jigme Tsang, who was such a profound teacher that Gyayak Rinpoche felt his teachings would benefit me greatly even with my limited understanding of what such vows meant.

It was Aku Jigme Tsang who, after I took my vows, gave me my religious name: Arjia Lobsang Tubten Jigme Gyatso (which differs from my spiritual title, Arjia Rinpoche). Aku Jigme Tsang was more than 70 years old. He had snow-white hair and was very kind. We stayed at Labrang Monastery for his lectures and teachings, which lasted more than two months. The small dharma hall set aside for his talks was so crowded that "even water could not flow through the place," as we say. Rinpoches and eminent monks sitting in the front row took notes as they listened. For us children, these lectures were a chance to poke, pull, and tease each other, or to play with small toys hidden under our robes. Although these petty misdeeds made us very happy, excessive mischievousness would earn us scoldings from tutors and the older rinpoches.

At Labrang Monastery we stayed with a rinpoche who possessed many gadgets and strange things that we had never seen before. Every day, after listening to the teachings, Serdok Rinpoche and I looked for any opportunity to play. Sometimes we played house. Sometimes we dug up our host's carefully groomed courtyard to build roads so that we could run a small toy car back and forth, which always earned us a severe reprimand that we quickly forgot.

Our host was an amateur photographer, and one afternoon while we children were playing hide-and-seek, we found bottles of various sizes containing colored liquid. We were sweating from the heat, and our throats were dry enough to give off smoke. While there was no soda pop in Tibet, adults sometimes gave us sugar, which we put in water and drank. When we saw these colorful liquids, we thought they were sweet drinks and could not wait to sample them.

As we were pushing and shoving each other for the bottles, some liquid splashed onto one of our robes, instantly turning the material to ashes. At the same time, someone cried out, "It splashed onto my face and stings!" Someone else shouted, "Don't drink it! My puppy's pee smells like that!" The four of us were so frightened we immediately put the bottles back. Later we found out that these bottles contained developer and fixative used by Nyen Drak Rinpoche for his photos. It was my first—and by no means last—brush with danger, from which I was miraculously saved.

Serdok Rinpoche's tutor was outraged when he learned what we had done. He bowed respectfully to Serdok Rinpoche three times—then spanked him vigorously! Each of us in turn received our painful lessons. Later, after I returned to Kumbum Monastery and told my tutor this story, he said to me: "Do you know why you were not harmed? Because Gyayak Rinpoche taught you to pray to the Dharma Protectors daily. They turned a dangerous situation into an auspicious one, and kept you safe."

Since that day, I have prayed to the Three Jewels for blessings and have never stopped. The Dharma Protectors—the third Jewel—are emanations of a Buddha or a bodhisattva whose main functions are to neutralize obstacles that would keep practitioners from spiritual advancement. On many occasions in my life I have found that the more dangerous the situation, the more obvious the blessing of Dharma Protectors turns out to be.

After several months we returned to Kumbum Monastery. More than 3,000 monks from the monastery lined up in formal dress to welcome us. The monastery had been whitewashed and painted in our honor. Old monks held fresh flowers, incense, and khatas (long, white scarves) representing offerings to the senses (incense for smell, flowers for sight, khatas for touch). They were very serious and respectful—even the young monks restrained from naughtiness out of piety and reverence. This was because I was the "hereditary" abbot, the symbolic head of the monastery. (Many years would go by before I also became the administrative khenpo, or day-to-day head of the monastery.) Although I had been in ceremonies before, this was my first conscious experience of such a dignified, solemn, and respectful reception directed at me. I can still feel the overwhelming awe that filled me.

CHAPTER 2

RAISED BY A FAMILY OF 4,000 MONKS

One of the most powerful positions in the monastery is the estate and household manager, called a *changtso*. As hereditary abbot of Kumbum, I was the legal owner of all the property owned by the monastery, including lands and buildings as far away as Beijing. The changtso managed these on my behalf, in addition to running my household. Among other responsibilities, he has the authority to organize the group searching for a reincarnation, and the power to choose a tutor for the child. After our return to Kumbum, my changtso, Choe Gyong Jep, invited Tsultrim Lhaksem to be my tutor. My uncle Gyayak Rinpoche had recommended him. Of all my beloved teachers, Tsultrim Lhaksem would be with me for the longest time, and would have the greatest influence on me.

At that time, Tsultrim Lhaksem was already 60. Despite his eminence he always wore simple robes, without brocade or decoration of any kind. He was on familiar terms with my uncle Gyayak Rinpoche, and whenever they got together the two men were fond of teasing each other. Tsultrim Lhaksem had tutored the Fourteenth Dalai Lama's eldest brother, Tagtser Rinpoche, and had also taken care of His Holiness the Dalai Lama when he stayed in Kumbum Monastery just before taking office in Lhasa, Tibet's capital. Tsultrim Lhaksem often told me vivid stories about His Holiness as a child.

One day Tsultrim Lhaksem had noticed that the young Dalai Lama was playing with some insects. Knowing that squashing insects often amuses children, he hurried over to reprimand the child. When he got closer, he saw that His Holiness was carefully moving the bugs to a safer place off the path to keep them out of danger.

Another story was of the young Dalai Lama leaving Kumbum. His stay had been kept quiet because of political problems with a local warlord, so His Holiness was leaving without the fanfare that such a departure would normally require. But as it happened, a major renovation of a meditation hall on the outskirts of Kumbum had just been completed. The building was considered very sacred, so a big blessing ceremony was in progress—prayers were being recited and offerings of candy and dried figs were being thrown in the air. The celebration reached its height at the very moment the Dalai Lama passed—and so in the end, he received the auspicious public farewell that was his due.

When he first became my tutor, Tsultrim Lhaksem had about 80 students, but he gradually let the others go and moved into my residence. I lived across a sharp ravine from the main temples. When you enter the building, you pass through several courtyards, and in the final yard was my residence with rooms on all four sides: Buddha's shrine, a living room, and rooms for my tutors and me. The kitchen and storage rooms were in another courtyard. From the tiled roof of our building we could see the mountains that surrounded the monastery like leaves of a lotus flower.

When I was young, I was not as quick with my studies as the other monks and rinpoches. I was not good at reciting memorized texts, and to tell the truth, I didn't enjoy it much, either. In my recitations I would sometimes miss an important paragraph, which would make my teacher, Tsultrim Lhaksem, very unhappy.

I didn't do this to upset him, but I may not have been sufficiently remorseful, so Tsultrim Lhaksem found his own ways to tease me in response.

During the 1950s watches and clocks were still rare in Tibet, so we told time using a sundial in the courtyard. One day, while I was playing outside during recess, it grew cloudy, rendering the sundial useless. A few moments later,

Tsultrim Lhaksem told me to come inside for lessons. I knew that I'd only been playing for a few minutes, but I was afraid to contradict my teacher. Reluctantly, I went to class, although I frequently pretended I had to go to the toilet so I could check the sundial on my way across the courtyard. After doing this several times, I finally saw the sun come out, and as I had guessed, it was still far too early for class to begin. I immediately informed my tutor in an accusatory tone. He smiled innocently, as if completely unaware of what was going on. "Oh, have I made a mistake?" he asked.

Tsultrim Lhaksem owned a small, very sharp pocketknife, which I wanted very much to play with, but my teacher had forbidden me to do so. One day, after he left the residence, I found his knife in a drawer and took it out. He came home unexpectedly just as I was opening it. Too frightened to close the blade carefully, I snapped it shut on my finger, slicing my fingertip. I grabbed the injured finger and held it out of sight. When Tsultrim Lhaksem saw his pocketknife on the floor where I'd dropped it he was very unhappy that I had disobeyed him. In light of the fact that I had also not been studying very diligently, he decided to teach me a lesson, and this time he chose to forgo subtlety.

As I sat, head bowed, in front of him—still holding tightly to my finger—he whacked me across my shoulders with his back scratcher; the blow was too light to cause real pain, but at the same moment he shouted at me so loudly that I wet myself. He didn't see the growing wet spot on the carpet, so I continued to sit in the same position for the next few hours of my lessons to hide the stain—suffering a sore finger and an even worse loss of dignity. Although I never would have admitted it at the time, I was learning quite a bit about karma—cause and effect—in the process.

Because I was a high rinpoche, elaborate rituals were required for any visit I made. As a small child I was therefore instructed to refuse any invitation to another temple or organization, no matter what, so as to avoid those formalities. However, I could always secretly attend these events and observe from behind a screen or column. In 1957 this changed: I was old enough now, at age seven, to take on new responsibilities and training, so my tutor asked me to accept all invitations. This meant that the monastery had to arrange many formal welcoming ceremonies for me, which provided me with opportunities to gain experience in protocol and comportment.

On Losar, the Tibetan New Year, which falls in the first month of the lunar calendar, I was invited to attend the monastery's exhibition of remarkable butter sculptures, for which it is justly renowned. My parents had come all the way from Dolon Nor to join the festivities. I was placed in an ornate sedan chair covered in yellow fabric and carried on the shoulders of eight strong monks, preceded by other monks carrying lanterns, incense, umbrellas, and colored banners. The sound of beating drums, blowing horns, and playing pipes flowing together seemed, to my young ears, loud enough to reach the sky. It was a scene full of excitement. As people recognized me, they rushed forward, pressing against the sedan chair to receive the blessing that came from touching the Eighth Arjia Rinpoche.

The exquisite butter sculptures, meticulously designed and formed by the skilled hands of the monks, looked remarkably lifelike. Each of the colleges of the monastery competed to outdo the others and to be awarded the prize for best of show. They had worked for weeks in the winter cold with the hard butter, dipping their hands in warm water to bring feeling to their frozen fingers, then molding, coloring, and carving delicate shapes and intricate designs. Some depicted ancient legends and familiar stories, images celebrating bodhisattvas or famous kings and heroes; others were created for their sheer beauty. These used to be destroyed immediately, as an expression of impermanence, but today they are put in glass cases to be admired by the hundreds of visitors who pass through our halls during the year.

That same year I was considered old enough to attend all four of the monastery's great religious festivals for the first time. Three Tibetan calendar months after Losar comes a celebration of Buddha's birth and enlightenment, and that year in Kumbum 100 monks unfurled a huge embroidered portrait of Buddha, 90 feet long and 60 feet wide, on the cleared slope of the mountain behind the monastery. On the sixth lunar month, a celebration was held for the first teachings given by Buddha after his enlightenment. And the fourth great holiday, in the ninth month, celebrated the day Buddha returned to his followers to spread his teachings to the world. (Another great Gelug festival is the Lantern Festival, which celebrates the passing of Lama Tsong Khapa; for a few days butter lamps burn, and monks chanting prayers line the rooftops of newly whitewashed monasteries.)

The Tibetan tradition of reincarnation is intriguing and mysterious to most Westerners. Many of my Western friends have asked me, "Do you remember your previous lives?" I do not, but I do remember two anecdotes that might be related to my past incarnations.

As I have mentioned, when I was a boy, I was not fond of studying. Some sutras were easy to learn, but I didn't enjoy working on the difficult ones. Other young monks could memorize one or more pages a day, whereas I could hardly remember a single four-line verse. To be honest, I did everything possible to avoid the tedious work of memorization, which often made my tutor Tsultrim Lhaksem so angry he would smack me across the shoulders or bottom with his bamboo back scratcher.

When I was older, about 13, I continued having to recite and memorize sutras, of course, but with no greater fondness. One day, while my teacher was not around, I took the opportunity to entertain myself in other ways. I wandered through the library and came across a book on rhetoric. I don't know why I should have picked up this particular book, but when I did I was surprised to find, after reading only a few pages, that I immediately understood what the book was about. I had a strong feeling that I knew this book—that I had studied it before, although that was impossible. From that moment on, I found that I had an affinity for rhetoric, which later helped me with my monastic training. Could this incident be explained by my experiences in a previous lifetime? I can't be sure, but it's an appealing possibility.

Growing up in the monastery, I could have pretty much whatever I wanted. From an early age I enjoyed drawing, and I was encouraged by the positive reactions I received in response to my work. Because of my status as a rinpoche, people would take a piece of paper and say, "Please, please, draw something for me; make me a wind horse for good luck, like the ones on prayer flags." I drew on paper, but I drew even more on walls—usually horses, inspired by my earliest memories as a nomad child—and those pictures still cover the walls of my old residence in the monastery. During major teachings, which lasted three months or so, I would have to attend long readings every day. But because no memorization was required, I chose not to pay attention. Instead, I spent my time drawing. Where did this gift come from? I believe it came in answer to my predecessor's prayers.

Gyayak Rinpoche told me that when he was a young man he had been very artistic and enjoyed drawing, but his classmate, my previous incarnation Arjia Rinpoche, was not artistic at all. In fact, he always chided Gyayak Rinpoche for wasting his time drawing silly pictures; my predecessor was a serious man who thought that art was a childish distraction. Some years later, however, when the two friends graduated with their *Geshe* degrees (the equivalent of master's degrees), they volunteered to join a group of other graduates in making a sand mandala, a striking Buddhist image made with colored sand. This required taking notes and following instructions about how to design the mandala and the proper technique for laying the sand. The previous Arjia Rinpoche could make no artistic contribution at all, so he was stuck only taking notes. Having become aware that creating art could be a spiritual practice as important as memorizing sutras, he prayed that in his next life he would have artistic talent. Did I benefit in my lifetime from that prayer?

Laypeople who visit monasteries to observe a major holiday may assume that rinpoches are always flanked by dozens of attendants, that we always dress in formal robes and dine lavishly, and that like great feudal lords we enjoy all the trappings of wealth, respect, and public adulation. In truth, acquisitive monks and laypeople had higher living standards than most rinpoches. Our life was full of both joy and suffering, like that of anyone else. But I must admit that things were easier for me than for many in the village. Many did not have much to eat, especially during hard times, when most of them could not afford wheat flour or refined barley, and ate something called "black flour" made from highland barley, a rough, fibrous food. (Ironically, in Tibet today this unprocessed flour is considered healthier, and is therefore both harder to find and more expensive.)

23

It is true that at Kumbum I had many attendants, but our house manager, Choe Gyang Jep, the changtso, did not manage our affairs very well, despite having managed Kumbum's rather extensive properties. Being sent from his great responsibilities in Beijing to provincial Amdo in Tibet to manage a small household and a mischievous child was probably not what he had had in mind for his old age. He held himself aloof from other members of the household, and he had no friends.

The changtso, my teacher, and I ate separately from the other monks, and we ate quite well. One day, when the cook asked me if I was I still hungry, I said yes, although I had already eaten. He served me the only thing left in the kitchen, the food that the less fortunate monks were served: black flour mixed with water, potatoes, and leftovers. Because I had never eaten such things before, I asked many questions: "What's this? What's that?" My attendants had to lie to me, saying, "Oh, this is something new and special." They were afraid of getting into trouble for feeding the abbot of Kumbum Monastery such poor food.

In my room was a large, L-shaped sleeping platform that filled most of the space. Next to my bed was an old-fashioned cabinet, upon which sat a small shrine. In the cabinet drawers were my clothes, and in a drawer that was always kept locked lay a metal Chinese box that stored a variety of candies that had been sent to me. Each time my parents came to visit, my father was sure to open the cabinet and give me a treat. It was a moment I longed for: access to those delicacies stored so tantalizingly close but beyond my reach. I thought that only my father had the key to the cabinet, and that no one else could open it. Later I found out the house manager also had access to this key, but he had never offered me even a single treat.

When I was six my father decided to visit me and check on how I was being treated—specifically, how my diet compared with that in our nomad home. Although he (and, to a lesser extent, my mother) regularly made the long journey to visit, I don't think they ever suspected that my care was anything less than what they had been promised. Why he suddenly chose to investigate I have no idea, but he asked me how often my teacher and I drank milk. I told him very rarely. He continued to question me. "Do you often eat mutton and beef?" I replied that we rarely had much meat, except for a few slices of mutton in our noodle soup.

Then I told him that I had eaten food made from black flour. My father was not a man to lose his temper, so he quickly busied himself with the task of airing out my bedding in the sun. As he opened the coverlet, lice scurried everywhere. That was the final straw!

Later in the evening, my father invited the changtso and his two attendants to my room for a "family meeting." My teacher sat against a rolled-up quilt at the head of his mattress, and I sat next to him on mine. My father sat at the head of the room. He began the meeting in a quiet, controlled voice, but his anger was apparent. "My son has told me that he rarely has milk and meat. Of course, the house manager is doing his duty by being frugal, but my son is the child of a nomad family. Had he stayed home he would have been raised drinking plenty of milk and eating a lot of beef and mutton. I also heard that you sometimes feed him black flour. And today I saw lice crawling out of his comforter."

He paused. "I want to bring him home. Tsultrim Lhaksem can come with us so that my son will be able to keep up with his training, and when he is older, I will return him to the monastery."

Upon hearing my father's words, the house manager flushed violently, and sweat began to form on his brow. He sank visibly lower, actually sliding from the platform to the floor in shame, and started to mutter an explanation.

My father responded, "It's not necessary to give excuses. I'll relieve you of your burden by taking my son away." Then the house manager blurted out a torrent of apologies to my father. Tsultrim Lhaksem intervened, requesting that my father forgive the house manager; the two attendants begged my father not to take me away. My father gradually allowed himself to be persuaded, enabling my teacher to save face. I realize now that my father had not been serious about removing me from the monastery, but he knew how to get what he wanted. The next day the quality of our meals improved.

By nature, children love being playful. I was no exception, but I was not the rascal that some other young monks were. Some of their escapades were truly mischievous. For example, sometimes when a young monk dozed off in the meditation hall a young prankster would sew the robes of the unsuspecting sleeper to the rug. I'm not sure which gave us more amusement—anticipating what would happen, or the moment when the young monk awoke and tried to rise.

Sometimes, when all the monks were gathered for prayers in the dharma hall, a young monk would disrupt the proceedings by making a commotion. When the *gegue,* a sort of disciplinary dean who carried a big stick, came to punish the guilty one, he pretended that he had done nothing wrong, and often someone else was wrongly accused. I remember a situation in which the gegue was so upset by his inability to identify the culprit that he randomly picked someone to hit with his long stick. This poor young monk, who was totally innocent, protested vehemently, and from that moment on he was known by the nickname "Not Me."

When laypeople think about monks, they tend to view us as people who have renounced worldly life to devote themselves entirely to the dharma. This is true in some cases, but when you become part of monastic life, you realize that monks vary greatly. Some behave with strong moral principles and are deeply respected. Others have little moral concern themselves, or regard for others. In keeping with deep-seated Tibetan tradition, most families consider it an honor to have at least one son become a monk, but sometimes the reasons for sending sons to a monastery are purely financial or disciplinary.

Some young monks drink and behave in a very worldly way. Others, called *dopdo,* even form gangs. These gang members could be identified by the way they wore their robes, by their swagger, and often by a large, old-fashioned key hanging by a chain from their belts to use as a weapon in gang fights. About such monks we would say, "It is truly leaving home in appearance and staying home in substance."

Lobsang Tsultrim, the younger brother of my predecessor, the Seventh Arjia Rinpoche, was a well-known dopdo. His forehead bore a deep scar from a fight between two monastic gangs. In the 1940s the rules at Kumbum Monastery were often broken, until the Arjia Rinpoche who preceded me restored discipline, even to the point of expelling his younger brother. His brother then returned to life as a farmer, married, had children, and later traveled to Lhasa and India as a businessman. After his wife died, Lobsang Tsultrim lived with his son until he was 70 years old. In his old age, he once again became a renunciate, but this time he became a true monk, following the Buddha's six virtues—evidence that it is never too late to change.

In Tibet, choosing the life of a monk means taking on a serious, lifelong calling. Monks live a full life of practice and demonstrate their spiritual achievements even in death. My uncle Gyayak Rinpoche told me of a teacher named Dagpa Gyatso, whom everyone revered. As he departed from this world, Dagpa Gyatso used his death as a lesson to his students. In his final moments he told his disciples to touch his hands and feet so they could feel the heat of his life withdraw from his limbs. His mind remained crystal clear, and his students received a vivid demonstration of how consciousness leaves the body peacefully and continues into the next stages of life.

Tibetan Buddhists believe that our emotional state at the time of death is important to finding a good life in the next cycle; if we are not distracted by panic we are more likely to choose a better situation in which to reincarnate. This monk's life and his death were, in themselves, profound teachings. His story was often told in Kumbum Monastery to demonstrate how death is only a transition, and not to be feared.

When I was seven, my tutor arranged my first visit back home to see my family. I had been looking forward to this for a long time. For years my parents had been making the long journey to Kumbum Monastery to visit me, but now I was finally being given the opportunity to see all my brothers and sisters as well. My tutor, my housekeeper, my two elder brothers, and a handful of attendants accompanied me.

We started off on the long horseback journey from Kumbum with a formidable array of gear. As an important lama, I was expected to arrive bearing gifts to be generously distributed to my large family. The sorrel pony I rode was fitted with a special frame on the saddle to keep me from falling off. An attendant led the way on his own horse, holding the reins for

27

me, but I didn't like this and kept crying, "Give me my reins; I want to ride it myself, just like the others." He refused for the sake of my safety, much to my disappointment.

Normally it would take several days to travel by horseback from Kumbum Monastery to Dolon Nor, but in this case it took us much longer, as we frequently dismounted to rest along the way. Everybody seemed to be having a good time, and the sights were spectacular. At first I was intimidated by the vast spaciousness of the countryside, so different from the confines of the monastery. But soon I found myself enjoying the brightly colored fields of green grass and the thick blankets of yellow blossoms springing from the rich, brown soil. For the first time in my life I was seeing houses that were not huddled together but spread out—often at great distances—along winding country roads. I was overcome by two feelings I had rarely had an opportunity to savor: joy and wonder.

When we passed small villages and farms, peasants toiling on the land stopped their work to watch our entourage pass by. Children ran alongside our horses, calling out and laughing. From the long mountain road we could see beautiful valleys decorated everywhere with golden-green grasslands and emerald woods. The sounds of gurgling streams and singing birds darting here and there made me feel carefree and happy.

At one stop a local farmer gave me some green beans. I had never seen fresh beans before, so instead of chewing I sucked on them as if they were sticks of candy. Tsultrim Lhaksem teased me, "We give you sugar to suck and you bite into it; we give you beans to eat and you suck on them!" Everybody thought this was funny.

Even greater happiness awaited me at the summer encampment of my family's Mongolian tribe. Everyone in the community had gathered at my family's home to welcome me, the honored guest from a distant place. My parents were special people and very devout Buddhists, and my father, as the head of our family, was majestic in my eyes. Here in his domain I was awestruck by his natural dignity.

I had four sisters and six brothers. My sister Dolma was the eldest. Pema, my oldest brother, worked alongside my father; having a successor to run the

head housekeeper, assistant housekeeper, and several attendants came to my room and spoke with my tutor in hushed voices. It was clear they were discussing a very important matter. I was still unaware of how serious things had become, but the next day, October 15, 1958, I would see for myself.

That morning, during breakfast, Tsultrim Lhaksem said in a strange voice, "It is impossible to predict what will happen today. Don't believe everything you hear; don't go against your conscience; don't do anything you know is wrong. If you get into trouble, pray to the Three Jewels and the Protectors. You must learn to take care of yourself from now on, so try to be sensible."

After breakfast, we were summoned along with more than 3,000 other monks to gather at Yar Nang Choedra, Kumbum Monastery's great public courtyard where religious assemblies and festivals were held. For the first time I sat with my household, down on the ground, instead of up on a throne surrounded by other high lamas.

Dozens of well-armed soldiers from the People's Liberation Army were patrolling the main courtyard. Machine guns had been set up on the roofs, trained on the monks below. The platform normally used for religious assembly had been turned into a rostrum for Chinese officials, who looked down at us imperiously. Cruel-looking young monks with thick hemp cords and whips in their hands were pacing around the courtyard like fiends. It was eerily silent in the yard, and the tension was so thick that I found it hard to breathe. What happened next was the most sickening event in the 500-year history of our monastery.

A Chinese official broke the silence with a loud shout: "Reveal your suffering! If you have suffered, speak out; if you are oppressed, overthrow those who oppose revolution; uncover the lid of feudalism!" Every monk present was forced to echo these words.

To the shock and dismay of the crowd in the courtyard, positivist monks who had obviously been instructed ahead of time roughly pulled Raku Rinpoche out of the throng. Raku Rinpoche was about 50 years old, and he was one of the monks I liked best. Clever and deft, Raku Rinpoche loved repairing watches, and was also a good photographer. On holidays he would invite the rinpoches, including me, to dine at his residence, which was a perfect chance for me to play with his many wonderful toys. Once I started playing with them I hated to stop, and he was so kind that he had given many of them to me as presents.

None of us understood why Raku Rinpoche was the first to be dragged out. What crime could he have committed that would cause these people to be so rude to him? I was frightened and hid my face in my robe, but a cadre (the term for a soldier or representative working for the Chinese Communist government) tapped me on the shoulder and shook his head: I would have to watch. They dragged Raku Rinpoche up to the front of the platform, bound him tightly with rope, and began to beat him. Small and frail, Raku Rinpoche curled up under the blows, the sound of his pain coming from deep in his throat. When he pleaded to be released from his bonds, a positivist monk pulled them tighter. At that moment, as if they had simultaneously lost their senses, positivist monks, militiamen, and cadres began seizing hundreds of people in the courtyard. Panic broke out. Some tried to hide, but to no avail. One monk pretended to be one of the tormentors and began seizing others, but he was dragged out as well.

In that first wave of arrests, my entire household was taken from me, leaving me completely alone for the first time in my life. The seized monks were tied until their tormentors ran out of rope; then the monks' cloth belts were stripped from their robes and used as restraints. They were then forced to stand in front of the long bank of stairs that led to the platform, humiliated for all to see. Just in front of me stood my housekeeper, eyes on me, tears flowing.

I cannot describe my feelings beyond the horror of the moment and complete bewilderment. For three interminable hours, more and more people were bound, hauled to the platform, and denounced. Large empty spaces had now opened up in the courtyard, and those of us who remained were ordered to squeeze together. Then a new cycle of arrests began. In the second and third rounds, the cadres on the platform simply read off names of people, who were then handcuffed and marched out to waiting trucks. By three o'clock in the afternoon, my first meeting was over. I learned later that 500 people were arrested that day. One in every six monks at Kumbum Monastery was gone.

I don't remember how I got back to my rooms that day; I must have been in shock. By the time I got there, my living quarters had already been turned into a canteen for positivist monks. I had no idea where my teacher, Tsultrim Lhaksem, had been hauled off to, or my brothers Nori and Chibo, whom I usually saw as soon as I entered my house. My attendants were also nowhere to be found.

Until that moment, all of my daily needs had been taken care of by others. Now, at eight years old, standing alone in the only home I knew, I had no idea who was going to take care of me, or what I should do. The scenes of arrest and humiliation at the public accusation meeting kept replaying in my mind like a dreadful dream.

It grew dark as I wandered through the residence, longing for the familiar voice of my teacher and the company of my brothers. I was hungry and tired, but there was no one to bring me food. I started to weep, but no one paid any attention. Young positivist monks I had never seen before were busy settling in and arranging their belongings in rooms of my house around my court-yard, cigarettes dangling from their mouths. After a while, a man I had never seen before came over to me. His face was stern, but his voice was gentle. "Come, you should eat some food now."

Questions popped into my mind. Who was he? Was he going to be my new teacher? With no other choice, I followed him to his room, where he gave me something to eat. He said, "The head of our group has asked me to take care of you. My name is Chiangchub Gyatso. They call me Jamaga." (In Tibetan, *jamaga* means "good cook.") Jamaga was about 50 years old, and of average size. He had a small moustache, spoke little, and almost always had a serious look on his face. And so I began my life with a man who would become a dear friend and would serve as a model of integrity as I grew up. I soon found that even though he looked forbidding, Jamaga possessed true Buddhist compassion. Like a loving father, he patiently taught me an important new skill: independence. My life was caught in a new current.

Thereafter I attended many public accusation meetings, where "counter-revolutionaries" were publicly denounced. Sometimes these monks were beaten; sometimes their hair was pulled out; sometimes they were forced to drink urine from a bedpan, or burned with lit cigarettes. All this because they had not confessed to their "monstrous crimes." In the beginning we were horrified by these types of meetings, but after a time, something even worse happened: We got used to them.

Our Communist Chinese oppressors were not entirely mistaken when they accused Tibetan monks of corruption. Monastic discipline had indeed been loose, and more than a few monks were ignoring their vows. Instead of studying the sutras, some of these monks were engaged in trading goods from India and England. Some were even dealing in weapons and narcotics. As a result, a few monasteries had become barely distinguishable from outside society. However, these few cases were used by the Communist government as an excuse to persecute all monks, and to stamp out religion in the name of reform.

I was ordered to join a group of almost a hundred children who were either incarnations like me or novices training to be monks. Every day we studied Communist Chinese politics, attended meetings, and played in the courtyard. However, the main purpose of our classes was not dharma, or any other education, but to learn how to eavesdrop and report unsanctioned conversations to the authorities, and how to ferret out secret hiding places belonging to enemies of the state. (At that time, many monks hid their treasured sacred objects; uncovering them became a "glorious task" of the political movement.) In addition, we learned how to denounce counterrevolutionaries. For me this was like a great game of pretend. We practiced on our teacher, Comrade Shan Shui, by making him our object of humiliation.

The central government in Beijing was organized into two branches. One, the Communist Party, was responsible for policy, and the other was involved with governance. The United Front Work Department was a local branch of the Communist Party, and its director from Qinghai Province opened every public meeting with a harsh speech. Chief Director Du Hua Nan was a short man with a cruel gaze. When he took to the podium, none of the monks dared look at him.

On this day I had to denounce someone for the very first time. My "enemy" was the great disciplinarian Gegue Gendan Sopa. I stepped up to the podium dutifully and recited such slogans as "Leniency to those who confess their crimes, and severity to those who refuse." In my ignorance, I spat on him.

That evening when I returned home, I was surprised to see my brother Nori, whom I had not seen in several weeks. After the first public accusation meeting, my brother Chibo had been sent home, and my brother Nori had been put in another group on the other side of the monastery. Now he told me how ashamed he was to see me denounce someone. "The Communists consider all of us class enemies, including the great master Gendan Sopa. What right do you have to denounce him and spit on him?" I tried to explain that Comrade Shan Shui had taught me to do this. I knew that Nori understood, but he admonished me to remember my place and to pay attention to the words of Jamaga, my newly appointed guardian.

That night Jamaga told me that a person should never act contrary to his own conscience. He himself was morally compromised, he said, because he had decided that in order to help others, like me, he would cooperate with the Communists who were now running Kumbum.

Jamaga then recounted a story about the principle of karmic justice. He said that one of the monastery's monks, a man named Pema Tashi, was favored by the Chinese for his vicious denunciations and beatings of monks, rinpoches, and masters. He was a tall, rough-looking man who dressed in a blue Mao suit, as did all the Chinese cadres, but his face still betrayed his Tibetan heritage. He carried a pistol on his right hip, displayed for all to see.

One day Pema Tashi killed three or four dogs by using them for target practice. That night the Chinese authorities called a reeducation meeting for children and provided meat soup for the event. After the meal, many children got sick, and some of them developed swollen stomachs the next day. The meat was from the dogs killed by Pema Tashi, who knew that it is taboo for Tibetans and Mongolians to eat dog meat.

Due to his evil reputation, Pema Tashi was promoted to leader of a large local district. Before his transfer took effect, he celebrated by drinking too much alcohol and raping a hotel maid. The next morning he was placed in jail for having shamed the Party.

Thirty-nine years later, I would come across Pema Tashi again. He was in

37

his seventies, living a pitiful life in a small, remote temple, with no one to care for him. Jamaga had been right: Pema Tashi's life was a shining example of karmic justice.

By the end of 1958, the Three Red Flags symbolizing the Great Leap Forward, socialism, and people's communes were flying above Kumbum. Monks had been forced into the fields, where they labored long after sunset. Electricity was installed in a small tent on the mountainside above the monastery, where the Chinese hooked up loudspeakers to broadcast propaganda and motivational music all day long and through the night.

Female high school students had been brought to live in the monastery for the purpose of encouraging the monks to marry, rather than lead a celibate life. Those monks who married were supposed to abandon their vows and become laypeople, although some monks brought their brides to live in the monastery. The Communists loved to talk about how decadent monasteries had been in the past, but this went far beyond anything Kumbum had ever seen.

One night, the cooks in our kitchen were making flour twists and buns. I begged them to let me help make buns too, and finally one of the cooks relented. He said, "Hurry up. If anyone sees this we will all be in trouble." Just as I was getting the hang of it, the canteen supervisor discovered me and launched into a furious tirade: "You and your capitalist bloodsuckers. You don't appreciate the efforts of the laboring masses, and you waste food like dirt." But I hadn't wasted any food! From that time on, I stayed out of the kitchen.

By now the fervor of the Communist Religious Reform Movement had led to the total suppression of all religion. Kumbum had been closed as a working monastery for several months, and monks were no longer allowed to wear robes. Classified by the Communist Chinese as members of the exploiting class, they were forced to perform slave labor. Because I could no longer continue my Buddhist studies, my maroon robe was cut up, dyed black, and used to make a small suit. Soon after, eight young monks from Kumbum, including Serdok Rinpoche and me, were sent to the county public school not far from Kumbum.

When the eight of us entered the classroom for the first time with our black suits and shaved heads, the teachers and students, mostly Chinese, were surprised and curious. They asked us many questions, and in the beginning we felt embarrassed. Everything was so strange. Instead of just reading and reciting sutras with a private tutor, as I had in the monastery, I sat in a classroom with first through fifth graders on benches behind long tables. Students were arranged according to size—smaller students in front. We newcomers were placed together in the first row, even though most of us were larger than our tablemates. Although this was intended as a welcoming gesture, it made us feel awkward.

For the first time I encountered educational disciplines other than Buddhism, including arithmetic and Chinese. At one point we even learned some Russian. We soon got used to school, and before long we started to like it; I especially enjoyed drawing. Like all students I wore a red scarf, and was very proud when I became a captain in the Young Pioneers, a patriotic youth group, and was given a badge with two stripes. Altogether I had four years of secular schooling, from first grade through fourth grade.

Those years that I went to school left a deep impression. Even now I can vividly recall my teachers and classmates. My first-grade teacher, Miss Xu, was young and shy. She often had tears in her eyes because she could not gain control over her unruly students. By contrast, the severity of our male teachers kept us in fear of them; when we misbehaved, we were often made to stand bent over with our heads under our desks for up to half an hour. For a time we also had a pretty, young female teacher named Miss Zhang. She was serious but friendly, and all of the children liked and obeyed her.

I remember some of my Chinese classmates, too. I shared a table with Li Yin, who was a very serious student. If she did not get a good grade, she wept. Another student, He Hai, was one of my best friends. His father was the county's Communist Party secretary. Because of this, He Hai was very familiar with the county courthouse. One day, he and I were sent to the courthouse to get water, which we carried in buckets hanging from a pole balanced across our shoulders. On the way back, He Hai showed me a long tunnel under the building, part of the heating system that ran from the boiler room to a tall smokestack. We decided to explore it together. The tunnel was filled with soot and grime, so we came out of it filthy but very proud of our adventure!

39

In general we children had a great time playing together, although during these early years of Chinese Communist oppression food shortages began to color every aspect of our lives. We didn't know it at the time, but the Communist government's push for industrialization came at the expense of the farmer, which inevitably led to less food. For the first time in my life, I experienced hunger. At school, whoever found the biggest "pig's ear" (a wild edible plant) for the teachers' lunch was praised. In the meantime, every student was responsible for exterminating the "four pests" (sparrows, rats, flies, and mosquitoes) in order to protect our shrinking food supply. If a student killed a sparrow or a rat, which "stole food from our mouths," or displayed a collection of flies he had killed, he was highly praised.

After school we often went to the fields on the mountainside and played in the dark while the monks worked until almost midnight, when they were finally allowed to return to the monastery. Sometimes we children would reenact the marriage of Tsoichen Gyatso and Han Yinhua (a monk and one of the young women now living at the monastery). Theirs was the first wedding ceremony we had ever seen, and probably the first one ever in Kumbum Monastery. After seeing the Communist propaganda film *The People's Liberation Army Attacking Their Enemy,* we also acted that out, taking turns playing the different characters from the movie.

After the communal system was imposed on Kumbum, monks were not allowed to live separately. Many young monks were now wearing fashionable clothing and getting drunk. Smoking was also a favorite activity. These secularized young monks thought such a lifestyle was good, but their elders remained faithful to the monastic way of life, even though they could not wear robes and were forced to let their hair grow long. Seeing the behavior of some young monks, they sighed and prayed in secret to the Three Jewels, hoping to purify themselves of the sins taking place all around them. They longed for the old ways to return.

I found myself somewhere in between the young monks and the old: I was shocked by the behavior of the young monks and very aware of Jamaga's disapproval, but sometimes their cavalier attitude appealed to me; I thought it was cool.

Many of Kumbum's young monks were recruited as miners for the Datong coal mines near Xining. Some were accepted as students in nearby colleges. Others gave up their robes to return home as laypeople. The monastery's population was much reduced and, as a result, a great deal of reorganization occurred in Kumbum. The remaining monks were sorted into three big groups. I belonged to the one commonly known as the First Canteen. Others belonged to the Second or Third Canteen.

For the time being, my physical needs were being taken care of as before, but in all the turbulence around me I had lost track of my family. I had no idea what was happening to my father, my mother, or my siblings. Jamaga was my sole tether to a life that had disappeared. Around me was a new world, a world as foreign to me as the monastery would be to a modern youth. Everything felt tenuous, and in this alien landscape I could take only one careful step at a time, hardly daring to understand what lay around me. Soon, however, the most immediate threat would become very obvious: hunger.

In the fall of 1959 I noticed that instead of three daily meals in the monastery I was being fed only twice. Then the size of our steamed buns became smaller, and our soup no longer had noodles. Within a few months it consisted of just a few vegetables with a sprinkling of flour on top. But this was better than what lay ahead. Messages were coming in from neighboring villages that people had begun to die of starvation.

As the year drew to an end, our soup became thinner and thinner. Now it consisted of wild vegetation, a few potatoes, and almost no flour. All of us had terrible diarrhea, and some of the monks' faces had turned a sickly green. Other monks were becoming too weak to walk. To keep up my spirits, Jamaga reminded me how Milarepa, the famous poet, yogi, and meditator, had survived as a hermit living in a cave by eating nettles that turned his skin green, too.

After 1958 it was rare to see nomads at Kumbum, so when one day Serdok Rinpoche and I noticed a family of nomads we went over to see them. We saw they had some meat, so we stood and looked at it longingly, our mouths

41

watering. A man came over to us and asked roughly what we wanted, thinking we were Chinese. To the man's surprise we answered in perfect Tibetan. He said, "Who are you? Are you monks?" We said, "Yes, we are rinpoches."

The man bowed to us, and called his friends over to share his good fortune. Making the most of this chance to gain merit, the nomads gave us some precious raw meat, wrapped in newspaper. I hid the meat under my jacket and Serdok Rinpoche and I ran back to the monastery with it. The monks were still working in the fields, so we lit a fire in the fireplace, boiled some water, shredded the meat, and cooked it in four tin cups, along with some dried turnips we had been saving. Oh, the smell was so good! We dipped into our cups with chopsticks, thinking we would just have one taste, but after a few bites we completely lost control and wolfed down the few handfuls of food remaining.

We had set two cups of food aside for Jamaga and my brother Tenba Gyatso, but we couldn't keep from dipping our chopsticks into their share, too—for just a few bites. Suddenly we realized it was getting late and the room was still redolent with the smell of our dinner, so we burned cedar chips to hide the smell. When Jamaga and Tenba Gyatso came in with the others, very late, we pulled them into the room I shared with Jamaga and closed the door. We showed them the cups of food we had prepared. "Where did you get this?" Jamaga wanted to know, his eyes opening wide. We told them what had happened while they ate with their eyes closed, savoring every bite.

The food situation got worse. The harvest on the mountains was very poor, due to both government mismanagement and an ongoing drought. The monastery was now like the rest of the country: Most of the food stored in the canteen was gone.

One day, on our way back from school, we saw an extraordinary sight: A huge group of nomads, several hundred of them, had gathered at the entrance to the monastery. Men, women, and children were dressed in rags, looking pale and weak. I learned that they were from the Jigu area in the south, where the Tibetans had been fiercest in their resistance to the Communist Chinese invasion. Jamaga told me these nomads had been falsely accused by the local Communist Party of being conspirators; they were arrested and sent to labor camps. Now, several years later, these innocent people had been released, but without any means of returning home.

Because their home villages were remote and the nomads had learned that there was widespread famine along the way, they had decided to come to Kumbum for refuge. They started going from house to house in the monastery, begging for scraps and garbage, and we gave them what we had to spare, but there was little we could do to ease their suffering. We had barely enough to feed ourselves.

The nomads took shelter in resident halls abandoned by departed monks. At first, the nomad infants and small children grew weak and despondent, and then, as the weeks passed, they died. After that, their parents began to lie down more and more frequently. After a year only a few would be left.

In the face of growing famine, the central government started another campaign to achieve its ambitious industrial goals, called "The Great Steel Making." The Chinese Communists chose a place called Round Rock Mountain, some 10 kilometers from the monastery, to be the new site for a mine. Monks were sent there to work, but once word got out about the desperate conditions in the mines, everyone secretly prayed not to be sent to Round Rock Mountain.

In spite of widespread hunger, the tempo of the great steel movement did not slow down. According to Communist Party leadership, no one was dying from hunger or overwork, but we knew better. At school, children had not been receiving lunch for a while now, but compared with the students from the farming villages we youngsters from the monastery were very lucky. Our soup was thin, but it was better than nothing at all. Publicly we dared not complain, but privately we dreamed about the meals we had taken for granted in the days before Communism. How we longed for those days to return!

One weekend afternoon I was walking home when I saw a crowd gathered by the side of the road. One man declared, "Yes, it is edible, it's edible." Another said, "How can you eat that? These are roots of plants that even animals avoid. You'll get sick, or die." A county official announced, "According to a new government proclamation grasses and roots are not to be eaten," but a few people laughed scornfully. We had been eating them for many months now. What else did we have?

During these years of famine there was a young man in our town who

43

pretended to be Serdok Rinpoche in order to receive food offerings. After his actions had been made public, everyone took to calling him "fake Serdok Rinpoche." Ironically, at one point both the real Serdok Rinpoche and the fake Serdok Rinpoche were rounded up and put in a detention room for 10 days to receive indoctrination. During this time together they became fast friends!

In the evenings, when everyone else had gone to meetings, I overcame my fears and began to sneak back into the kitchen. When it was very cold on those winter nights, the cooks sat me on the earthen stove to keep me warm. When it got late and I had fallen asleep, they would gently carry me back to my own bed. They were like mothers to me. Although so many people were hungry at the time, the cooks included, they continued to slip me a little food when they could.

By 1961, many of the empty houses on the grounds of Kumbum Monastery were collapsing in ruins. (By this time, instead of housing 4,000 monks, the monastery was home to just hundreds.) One day a group of strangers moved into the vacant residences that were still standing. Rumor had it that these were the high lamas, intellectuals, and former officials who were too important to be arrested but still needed to be detained. A few days later, the new arrivals all went down to work in the fields. I knew then that they had come to what the cadres called our "socialist academy." Sometimes they did participate in sessions on Marxism and Leninism, but the only academy graduation I ever saw was death from starvation. Eventually the task of disposing of the dead became so overwhelming that their bodies were thrown into ditches on the temple grounds. On our way to and from school, we children learned to avert our eyes from this terrible sight, and to hurry past.

Then, for some unexplained reason, more food started to gradually appear in the marketplace. The famine was lessening. Jamaga said that we must thank Chairman Liu Shaoqi, whose new policies, such as encouraging people to grow food in private gardens, had saved our lives. But even after the arrival of more food, people still died. We were told that if a person had been eating grass for a long time, a sudden switch to grain and wheat could puncture the stomach, so we ate carefully to keep from getting sick, or worse.

CHAPTER 4

FOLLOWING A TIBETAN HERO

When I finally received news of my family, it was not good. In fact, it was terrible. During the Religious Reform of 1958, Soviet engineers had chosen Dolon Nor as an ideal place for developing Chinese nuclear power. As a result, residents were forced to relocate. Cadres divided them into three different groups. Those who were considered lower class, the poorest nomads, were allowed to stay nearby. The middle class (small landowners) was forced to move farther away. Those people classified as ruling class were imprisoned or forced to relocate to uninhabitable areas.

My father, brother-in-law, uncles, and other relatives were classified as ruling class. They were not allowed to take their belongings with them, or even eat a meal before they were dragged out of their homes and forced to walk for more than 10 days without adequate food. Fortunately, it did not snow heavily during the long trek. They were finally resettled at a place called Toli, but were given nothing to eat. They scavenged for cans discarded by the Chinese military, which littered the ground. They were forced to sleep in the open for lack of tents. When word of these terrible events reached me, I wept with helplessness and sorrow.

One day during the late winter of 1961, a Communist committee came to our public school to speak specifically to me. "You must wear your robes tomorrow to meet with a well-known person. Never mind who that person is. For now, that is confidential." This brusqueness was typical, so it didn't surprise me. At age 11 I understood how things worked. "Yes, yes," I said, but I was thinking that I no longer even owned robes. Except for a schoolbag, my school uniforms, and a few articles for sleeping, I owned nothing. I spoke carefully to the leader, not wanting to offend him.

"I don't have robes. Where can I find some?"

"We have prepared some clothing and some living room furniture for you. Jamaga will tell you more about it."

When I returned home from school that day, I discovered that the reception room of our residence had changed completely. Brand-new carpets had been put down, and our few shabby pieces of furniture had been replaced. There were even ceremonial dharma objects on display, such as bells and drums. Jamaga explained, "These things come from the Bureau of Confiscation. Several people came over and worked here for a whole day to make it look presentable. However, I have no idea why they are doing this."

Early the next morning, Jamaga helped me into my robes and fussed over how I looked. Several people then came and took me to the formal reception area of the monastery, where a small group was already gathering. Serdok Rinpoche was among them. Everyone wore robes and looked solemn. I whispered to Serdok Rinpoche: "Who is coming?" Looking puzzled, he shook his head.

Just then we were startled by the sound of a car horn. A short while later, an old man with white hair and great energy strode in, accompanied by several policemen and officials. Someone introduced him to us.

"This is the chairman of the Buddhist Association of China, Geshe Lharampa Sherab Gyatso. This is Arjia Rinpoche, the abbot of Kumbum Monastery, and this is Serdok Rinpoche. They are good children who go to school every day, and wear red scarves!"

Geshe Sherab Gyatso was born in Amdo Province in 1884. When he was five, he was sent to Guru Monastery to study the sutras. Soon he was able to bless laypeople and lead chants. At age 14, he went to Labrang Monastery to further his studies. Within five years he had completed courses that ordinarily require 12 years of study. Because of his brilliant academic record, he was sent to Lhasa for advanced studies at Drepung Monastery, where he delved deeply into Buddhist sutras, commentaries, and other classics. He obtained the highest degree in Buddhist studies, *Geshe Lharampa* (equivalent to a doctoral degree), and was invited by the Thirteenth Dalai Lama to organize and edit the Kangyur, the complete works of Buddha. According to rumor, he overstepped his bounds in editing so he was sent back to Labrang.

Geshe Sherab Gyatso was no monastic recluse. Throughout his career, he had also been involved in politics. Although he was a supporter of the Chinese government, he, like the Panchen Lama, devoted his life to maintaining the autonomy of Tibetan culture and making life better for the Tibetan people. During the upcoming Cultural Revolution, he would be tortured for criticizing the Communist Party, and he would die in house arrest. But on this day, he was still an eminent figure, bringing us a taste of things as they had been before the purge and before the famine.

After we all sat down, tea was served. Geshe Sherab Gyatso asked, "Do you wear your robes every day?"

"Um . . . " I was unsure how to answer, so someone spoke for me: "Of course they wear robes daily. Everyone is free to believe in religion. How great is our party's policy on religious freedom!"

Geshe Sherab Gyatso nodded dutifully, and then asked: "Do you two boys know how to say your prayers and chant sutras?"

Fearing that if we answered "yes" he might test us and we would be embarrassed, we replied in unison, "No. No. We have forgotten how."

"As rinpoches, how could you not know how to chant sutra?" Geshe Sherab Gyatso scolded us. "Come and repeat after me:

I bow my head to the chief of the Sakyas,
Whose body was formed by 10 million perfect virtues,
Whose speech fulfills the hopes of limitless beings,
Whose mind sees precisely all objects of knowledge.

I bow down to Ajita and to Manjushri,
The supreme heirs of the unequaled teacher.

Having assumed the burden of all the Conqueror's deeds,
They emanate in innumerable buddha-realms.

As we repeated each phrase, Geshe Sherab Gyatso laughed and said: "How could you say that you did not know how to chant? This is chanting." He also taught Serdok Rinpoche another four lines:

I bow to the feet of Nagarjuna and Asanga,
Thoroughly renowned throughout the three levels,
Ornaments of Jambudvipa who wrote exact commentaries on the intent
Of the Mother of Conquerors, so difficult to fathom.[1]

"Good! Good! Boys need contemporary knowledge but they must not forget the sutras."

"Indeed, indeed," the people accompanying us answered in unison.

We ate with Geshe Sherab Gyatso that day. It was the first time since the famine had begun that we had tasted a real meal. The dishes, although probably ordinary, tasted heavenly to us. Serdok Rinpoche and I stuffed ourselves until we could not manage another bite. And then Geshe Sherab Gyatso left. The memory of that delicious meal lives within me to this day.

Not long after Geshe Sherab Gyatso's visit, we were urgently called to a meeting announcing that the Panchen Lama was coming to visit Kumbum Monastery. We felt an immediate sense of urgency to get our public halls ready. They were in a disgraceful state. However, in a remarkably short time everything was put right again. The four-year accumulation of dust and cobwebs that covered the dharma throne in the main assembly hall was scrubbed away. Sacred scriptures that had been scattered about were organized, and sacred ritual objects were set in their proper places on the shrine. Then we caught the smell of rice being cooked in the monastery kitchen. It permeated the air, and the nearly forgotten aroma reminded everyone of how delicious a real meal could be.

---

1 *The Great Treatise on the Stages of the Path to Enlightenment,* by Tsong Khapa, translated by the Lam Rim Chenmo Translation Committee

When a message arrived that the Panchen Lama had postponed his visit for a day, hungry monks, never short of ingenuity, took the opportunity to devour the tasty rice, which had already been set out. Before officials could remove the meal to save it for the next day, there was almost nothing left. With an unaccustomed sense of joy, the monks in the kitchen started to make their preparations all over again.

The Panchen Lama arrived the next day. There is a special protocol for receiving high-ranking religious leaders such as the Dalai Lama or the Panchen Lama. First in line are dignitaries of the monastery, followed by a procession of musicians and honor guards. The other monks (and laypeople) stand on both sides of the visitors' path, carrying flowers, khatas, and incense, chanting mantras in greeting. As the Panchen Lama walked through the crowd to the hall, a golden carpet decorated with auspicious symbols was rolled out for him. Because the carpet was not long enough for the considerable distance involved, monks unrolled one length of the carpet for him as he marched forward, while others curled up the lengths behind him. Then they ran ahead so these could be laid out again, ensuring that the Panchen Lama's feet would never touch the bare ground.

Standing on both sides of the path, monks held poles displaying decorated banners. A monk followed the Panchen Lama, holding a yellow parasol over his head. He was accompanied by the sounds of horns, trumpets, flutes, and drums. Finally he walked through the ornate doors of the Serdung Chenmo, the Great Hall of Golden Tiles, built to honor Lama Tsong Khapa.

Having no memory of the Panchen Lama from the time I had seen him from my mother's arms, I was astounded by his stature and the power of his person. He stood a full head above the old monks crowded around him, touching him. Tears filled their eyes, and some even started complaining about the horrors of the past few years. In a clear voice, firm but serene in the turmoil, he said, "Please calm yourselves. We will meet tomorrow to discuss whatever issues you wish to raise. We will talk then."

The Panchen Lama's reception was the grandest event we had organized in years, but despite the general enthusiasm, some monks restrained themselves out of fear that afterward there might be a settling of accounts. Indeed, everything

49

we were doing to celebrate the Panchen Lama's arrival belonged to what the Communist Party called "superstition," and as such had been strictly forbidden for nearly three years.

I was doubly delighted because Gyayak Rinpoche, my beloved uncle, was traveling with the Panchen Lama. I knew he had been released from prison because he had come back to Kumbum for a short time a few years earlier, but he had not stayed long before he was sent to Beijing to study "socialist principles" as part of his rehabilitation. I suspect the Panchen Lama may have arranged for Gyayak Rinpoche's transfer, knowing that life would be easier for him in the capital under the Panchen Lama's protection. But now my beloved uncle was finally home.

I had been warned by Jamaga not to prostrate or show any signs of reverence, but I had difficulty restraining myself. My uncle gave me a warning look, and signaled that I should sit quietly beside him. A little of what had been taken away from me—my sense that I had a place in this world, and that I would be cared for—had been returned by the mere presence of my old teacher.

The next day was a fever of activity. Most of the few hundred monks who had survived the Religious Reform Movement gathered in the main prayer hall. The Panchen Lama, sitting on a high throne, was served tea and food while receiving the faithful who came to pay their respects. Thousands of people, lay and religious, gathered to prostrate and receive his blessings. The area outside the main hall was packed.

After the ceremonies, the Panchen Lama called for people to come to Labrangze, also known as the Auspicious Palace, to attend what became an unforgettable meeting. Each member of the audience had to be approved by the government, and many didn't even ask to attend because they were afraid of repercussions. Those who did fell into roughly three groups: high lamas who were attacked during the Religious Reform Movement but had since been forgiven; people who were sentenced to "reform through labor" but were later released; and the "revolutionary heroes" of those days, which was code for monks who had aided and conspired with the Communists.

At Kumbum the chairman of the administrative committee was still the infamous Ngawang Jimba, considered a "revolutionary hero" by the Chinese government. The former monk was, by this time, married to Yang Jinhua, who became equally notorious by joining him in the violent beatings of people at our *thamzigs,* public accusation meetings. Because he was the monastery's highest authority, people called him "Chief Director." On the day of the Panchen Lama's visit, the chief director was dressed in a monk's robes, clothing he had, in all ways, cast off years before. His hair was plastered down so that it didn't look much different from the cropped hair of other monks.

The Panchen Lama was only 24, but he was already an imposing figure, and in complete control. As he was on a politically sensitive mission, he spoke in a frank, firm, modulated voice, choosing his words with care. "Today, at the request of the Central Committee, I have invited every one of you to attend this meeting. You all know that the Party's religious policies are very correct. However, during the Religious Reform Movement, in certain areas there were mistakes of extreme leftism. Some monasteries were unnecessarily destroyed. Many good people were either arrested or sent to labor camps. Statues were destroyed, scriptures were burnt, and many people starved to death.

"Since these things are already past, we will not try to assign blame. But in order to prevent such mistakes from happening again, we must carry out investigations as to what occurred, and report our findings to the Central Committee. Therefore, I'd like every one of you not to worry about telling us what you think; tell us the truth. We have a comrade from the department of the United Front of the Central Committee here today, as well as leaders of the province."

This was the beginning of what became known as the 70,000 Character Petition, a devastating account of the atrocities of the Great Leap Forward, which the Panchen Lama would eventually present to the Chinese Communist Party leadership.

He finished his peroration with "Now I'm not going to talk more. Today I am here to listen."

At that point someone started babbling about things being very good, but His Holiness interrupted him. "I realize that some of you still have worries that this may be a trick to uncover discontents. So let me start things off for you. Comrade Director Ngawang Jimba, let me ask you a question. Since you are already married, why are you wearing a monk's robes today? You have taken vows, so you know that our religion clearly prohibits laypeople from wearing robes; if you wear robes, you are not a layperson. Which are you? Choosing not to be a monk is your right. But at the same time you cannot break the rules of our religion by pretending to be what you are not!"

Ngawang Jimba said nothing, but he looked extremely uncomfortable.

Then an outspoken and respected old monk, Zon Dri Gyatso, shouted: "Your Holiness, today is the day that we long expected. We can speak freely now. Since the beginning of the reform, hundreds of monks have been arrested. We have been sent to labor camps and denied the freedom to read scriptures. We were made to raise chickens and pigs in the monasteries, and were forced to eat at canteens, and some of us even starved to death . . . " He broke into sobs, and could no longer speak.

By then, people began to vie with each other to present their stories. As I listened, I wondered how all the injustices since the beginning of the reform could be resolved by a single meeting. How could the famine of four years be sufficiently expressed in just a few sentences?

The discussion continued for hours. At one point I was surprised to hear my name mentioned. Someone had suggested to the Panchen Lama that Serdok Rinpoche and I be sent to Tashi Lhunpo to live and to resume our studies of the dharma. The Panchen Lama said, "This is a good idea. We must train the next generation of teachers. We are suffering from a terrible lack of young scholars." Both Serdok Rinpoche and I were delighted by this decision, although in truth we were more excited by the opportunity of seeing new places than we were by the prospect of renewing our spiritual studies. As a child I had always wished to travel far and wide. To get a chance to go to Lhasa and Shigatse in central Tibet was a dream come true.

The Panchen Lama's visit to our monastery was a turning point. From then on monks enjoyed a bit more freedom, and were allowed to wear robes. Authorities took the surprising step of holding a monthlong conference to officially honor minority cultures in the northwest region of Tibet and China.

At that point, many monasteries instituted a "semi-opening," easing the required physical labor to half a day, and allowing academic study of dharma during the other half. Although I still attended public school with other young monks, I was sometimes allowed to return to the monastery to attend religious studies. The bad news was that by this time I had forgotten almost everything I had learned when I was younger, so I felt very put upon by having to memorize scripture while also managing my regular schoolwork.

After the restrictions on religious activities began to relax, Kumbum's handful of surviving rinpoches, about 10 of us, gathered together to form a Rinpoche Group. This included my uncle Gyayak Rinpoche, who was nearing 50; Tashi Rinpoche, a gentle person whose glasses gave him a scholarly look; and Shagre Rinpoche, known for his thick, black eyebrows and penetrating eyes, who had been a fierce positivist monk active during the Religious Reform Movement. Monks were quite afraid of him. Serdok Rinpoche and I were the youngest members of the group.

Once the Communist Party announced a new tolerance of religion, the number of people who came to Kumbum on pilgrimages increased. Living arrangements were reorganized, and my older brother Nori moved into our group. I had not seen him for a long time, and was not even certain he was still at Kumbum. It is impossible for anyone not living in our circumstances to understand how our lives could be so regimented and restricted by the cadres that I could be completely unaware of his presence, but that was exactly what had happened. No doubt Nori was also fearful that any indiscretion on his part might have jeopardized us both. Fear and paranoia infected the authorities and their victims equally. I had often been annoyed by Nori's bossiness when we played together as children, but now he was a welcome piece of my life being returned to me.

Jamaga was still the person I felt closest to, and to whom I gave my absolute faith and trust. While my official manager was in prison, Jamaga had become the acting changtso, my estate manager for those properties that had been returned to us by the Confiscation Bureau, and he had gained new status and respect for his fair and competent management. There were three categories of confiscated objects. First, all gold, silver, and precious objects were absorbed

53

by the Chinese government. Second, monks' robes, ritual objects, and furniture were all put into secondhand store stalls that lined the streets. Such a stall was called a "Store to Get Rid of Things." The items were sold very cheaply, and because virtually no one bought any of them, they remained there for many years. Often as my friends and I were walking home from school, we would wander into the stalls and check the status of my belongings. The third group consisted of items that were reclaimed by the government and eventually returned to me. Jamaga kept careful account of all these items.

Not only was a greater variety of goods now appearing in the market, but they were beginning to sell at normal prices. For example, a piece of candy that had sold for ¥12 ($1.50) on the black market now sold for ¥1.2 (15¢), and a small box of matches went from ¥15 ($1.88) to 2¢. Regular food items replaced "ration foods," a term used by the authorities for the wild plants, grass roots, and questionable vegetation that we had been eating. People's complexions slowly returned to a healthy color.

After the Panchen Lama left for Beijing to report on his findings, Serdok Rinpoche and I began eagerly anticipating the day we could set off for Lhasa. We were excited by the Panchen Lama's promise that he would come back for us and take us to Tashi Lhunpo. Every day we looked for his arrival, just as we did the rising of the stars and the moon. However, spring followed winter and still there was no sign of him. It is hard to describe the mix of excitement and fear of disappointment that filled us.

Finally, in June 1962, Gyayak Rinpoche returned from Beijing and explained that the Panchen Lama had had many meetings to attend, including one with Mao Zedong himself. Mao had publicly praised the courage and work that was done by the Panchen Lama in compiling and presenting the 70,000 Character Petition, which listed the many terrible events of recent years. (However, the unofficial word was that Mao was privately furious with the report.) At their meeting, Chairman Mao had requested that the Panchen Lama carry out further investigations, a request that would eventually have dire consequences for us all. For now, none of that mattered to Serdok Rinpoche and me: The Panchen Lama was on his way back to Kumbum! In fact, he was already in Xining, not 20 miles away, and we were to depart for Lhasa the next day.

And so I bade a tearful farewell to Jamaga and to Kumbum and departed for Xining Airport. Many monks came with us to the airport to see us off, including my brother Nori. The Panchen Lama spoke briefly to the assembled crowd. "I apologize to you all for not having a chance to visit the monastery this time, but I want you to know that you can safely put your young rinpoches in my care. Please do not worry; I will take good care of them."

We boarded an old-fashioned military aircraft, and I watched out the window as three men scrambled to spin the propellers and get the engines started. Instead of seats we sat on metal benches that ran the length of the plane. The roar of the engines was deafening. Baggage shifted dangerously in the space in front of us. But none of that mattered; we were aware only of being on an airplane for the first time and heading to a new life.

The flight took three hours. As we made our descent, I thought what I saw outside was the white snow of Lhasa; instead it was a salt flat in Golmud, a thousand kilometers of tortuous road north of Lhasa. Severe weather over the high mountains had changed our pilot's flight plan. We would have to drive the rest of the way.

Our entourage of nearly 100 people got into some 10 or 15 cars, accompanied by several trucks carrying our luggage, supplies, and gifts on a rough dirt road that would take us over an 18,000-foot mountain pass. Our group included the Panchen Lama, his mother, father, and teacher Gyayak Rinpoche as well as another teacher, Gnuchoe Rinpoche. We could see that the Panchen Lama took after his father, a tall man with a frank manner. His mother was simple, unpretentious, and kind. She went about taking care of us all like a true Tibetan woman.

Also along on the journey was the infamous Ngapo Ngawang Jigme, one of the four powerful members of the Tibetan ministerial cabinet, the Kashag. Ngapo Ngawang Jigme had played an influential part in the early events of the Chinese occupation, negotiating the "Seventeen Point Agreement," which essentially doomed Tibetan independence. He was now the most important Tibetan policy maker in the government. A tall, lean man, he was constantly at the Panchen Lama's side now that the Panchen Lama's standing with Mao seemed to have risen. With Ngapo Ngawang Jigme was his wife, a pretentious and affected woman from a noble family who was dressed loudly in the latest fashions.

Along the road we saw soaring mountains in dramatic, jagged shapes in a barren landscape with no trees and no brush, only green bogs—so different from the rolling hills and green meadows of Amdo. We saw winding rivers and lots of wildlife, including wolves, wild asses, and antelope. Except for the army camps and dusty administrative settlements where we spent nights, there was virtually no sign of humanity in the region.

It took five days to reach Lhasa. Then suddenly the famous Potala Palace stood before us, its gleaming red and white walls capped by blazing golden roofs. The sky above the random puffs of white clouds framing the imposing monument was blue-black.

We made our home near the Potala Palace at Shukling Dorje Podrang, the residential palace of the Panchen Lama, whom we saw every day. His teacher, Gnuchoe Rinpoche, gave him teachings and sometimes taught us as well. Many monks and lay officials served under the Panchen Lama, and they performed their duties in an administrative area called the Panchen Nang Makhang, the Panchen Lama's Directors' Conference Hall. Unlike much of Tibet reorganized by the Chinese Communists, the hall was strictly maintained in a traditional Tibetan manner.

The Panchen Lama had started a special school here, the School of Mechanical Engineering, attended by 100 students from all five regions of Tibet. Here, in addition to Buddhist scripture and Tibetan and Chinese literature, they could receive an education on a variety of academic subjects and practical skills. Also, in keeping with the interests of the Panchen Lama, the school offered courses in horseback riding, shooting, and modern subjects such as repairing and maintaining electric appliances and motor vehicles. Given free rein, the Panchen Lama's innovations were flourishing.

Little did we know that none of this would last very long. In two years, the Panchen Lama would be labeled a counterrevolutionary who was following a revisionist path. Disastrous times were coming.

PART II

UNDER THE
DRAGON'S CLAW

When I see, hear, or think of those
Who struck, beat or maligned me,
May I be without anger, speak of their virtues,
And meditate upon patience.

—*Lama Tsong Khapa*

"COMETS IN THE SKY, CHAOS ON EARTH"

My long-held dream of visiting Lhasa and the spectacular Jokhang Temple had come true! By dawn on the day Serdok Rinpoche and I arrived in June 1962, hundreds of pilgrims had already formed a long line at the temple's entrance, their eyes closed and their palms together, waiting patiently to enter the massive, four-story, gold-topped temple that has long been the ultimate destination for Tibetan pilgrims. Excitedly, Serdok Rinpoche and I joined them in the familiar Buddhist prayer that all sentient beings, including the two of us, could leave suffering behind and find a happy life.

Many reverent Buddhists were performing full prostrations: they stretched out flat on the ground with arms outstretched in front of them, touching their foreheads to the pavement; then they stood back up, stepped forward to the spots where their foreheads had touched the ground, and began the next prostrations. In this way they slowly traveled the considerable distance around Jokhang Temple. It was a very powerful expression of the depth of Tibetan devotion. Gyayak Rinpoche had already directed us to prostrate in front of the Jokhang Temple to show our devotion. I was only 12 years old, but I knew to do so without his cue.

The Jokhang Temple was built in the seventh century, during the reign of Songtsen Gampo. For 1,300 years monks have stood on the roofs and poured new coatings of thin white plaster down the temple's sides, leaving the rain and wind to carve grooves on the ever-thickening walls—a silent testimony to the enduring spiritual traditions of my country. The golden tiles on the pagoda-shaped roof are protected by fierce gargoyles, and countless prayer flags flap festively in the wind.

After we finished the prayers and prostrations, Serdok Rinpoche and I went into the temple from a side entrance. Inside, a strong feeling of reverence welled up inside me. Flanked by statues of protective deities, we entered the Dharma Hall, with its rows of platforms polished to a high shine by centuries of praying monks. My eyes rested on an ornamental bronze mirror with Sanskrit letters of blessing—*om mani padme hum*—inscribed in pure gold on a maroon wall. The soft glow of countless butter lamps cast flickering light on thangkas and statues around the room. Surrounded by dramatic images of bodhisattvas (saints) and dharma protectors, a gold statue of Sakyamuni Buddha dominated the room, conveying a feeling of compassion and peace.

My uncle Gyayak Rinpoche had asked us to look for a large slab of stone at the threshold of the second gate. Tradition has it that if you stand on this stone and pray for a particular attainment in this life or the next, that wish will be fulfilled. I found the stone. Standing upon it, I recited a prayer for my mother's health, for the happiness of my good friend Jamaga, and for the Panchen Lama, wishing for him the fulfillment of our spiritual accomplishments. I was elated, floating on a tremendous surge of joy.

After that, whenever the opportunity arose, we visited Jokhang Temple. We often went to other, smaller temples, too, especially Ramoche Temple, also called the small Jokhang. One thing I regretted was being unable to make a pilgrimage to the awe-inspiring Potala Palace, whose white and red walls tower 1,000 feet above the Lhasa valley, or to the three large monastic universities in Lhasa. Gyayak Rinpoche did not want us to go to the Potala Palace alone; he wanted us to wait for the Panchen Lama to be there, which would make our pilgrimage more meaningful.

Because the road between Lhasa and Shigatse was still under construction, we could not travel to the Panchen Lama's home monastery, so we stayed in Lhasa for almost two months. After spending some time each day studying,

Serdok Rinpoche and I wandered the streets of the city and played by several small lakes in the hills nearby.

One day we were playing at a lake when we found a raft used by local people to float out to a small island and gather duck eggs. Serdok Rinpoche and I were eager to try the raft ourselves, but we hesitated, worried about our fancy boots, decorated with silk, which all young rinpoches wear. Then we gleefully climbed onto the raft, pushed off, and began poling out to the island. After we explored it thoroughly, we went back to the raft only to find it stuck in the mud. For a few minutes we were afraid we couldn't get it free, even after we got out and pushed. Finally it began to move, and we jumped back on.

By the time we got back to the temple our trousers were soaked and our boots were covered with mud. When Uncle Lobsang Donyol asked us what we had been doing, we tried to distract him by talking about how much we had enjoyed the sights of Lhasa, but he was not to be deterred. He became very angry, and, picking up a stick, demanded to know exactly where we had been. We told him the truth.

Uncle Lobsang was one of the younger brothers of Gyayak Rinpoche. He was a short person, always smiling and laughing, except at moments like this. During the Great Leap Forward he was imprisoned and forced into a hard labor camp, but somehow he had retained his sense of humor. He was especially good at arranging schedules and making the lives of rinpoches easier. Gyayak Rinpoche had decided that he should watch over us, and he took this duty more seriously than we would have liked. We were lucky to escape with no worse punishment than a good tongue-lashing.

In our quest for adventure during the breaks between classes Serdok Rinpoche and I often ventured into the garage where the Panchen Lama's vehicles were maintained. We did so with impunity, knowing that we'd have plenty of warning if the Panchen Lama were approaching, since he always traveled with a sizable retinue. On this particular day we were exploring the crowded shelves in the garage when we heard a flurry of activity. Suddenly the Panchen Lama's jeep came skidding around the corner and spun full circle before it came to a stop and the Panchen Lama stepped out, calmly adjusting the fedora that he wore. Serdok Rinpoche and I stepped out of the door as quietly as we could, hoping our presence would not be noticed. Our good luck held.

The Panchen Lama loved to drive anything with wheels and an engine. He had a Russian motorcycle with a sidecar that we envied as teenagers, but his mechanic was the only person other than him allowed to touch it. One day, to our amazement and delight, he invited Serdok Rinpoche and me to join him for a ride. The two of us squeezed into the sidecar while the Panchen Lama pulled down his goggles. He gunned the engine and took off down the palace's long drive, the wind bringing tears to our eyes. For a moment we hoped he'd take us into the countryside, but he took a long loop inside the gates and returned to the garage, smiling at us as we piled out of the sidecar, thrilled by our adventure.

The Panchen Lama also enjoyed all types of guns—rifles, and handguns, too. He loved teaching his students how to shoot. One day he organized an excursion and invited all the young students to join him. Along with his retinue, we numbered about 100 people in all. Our long caravan of cars, trucks, and jeeps headed to a remote area in the towering mountains some distance from Lhasa. When we arrived, young students distributed rifles, boxes of ammunition, and paper targets, which they set up on pulleys. Spotters shouted back with the results of the shooting. The Panchen Lama was a superb marksman who fired very quickly at multiple targets and hit them with great accuracy. At first we boys were a bit frightened, but soon we came to enjoy ourselves.

The Panchen Lama had invited an army commander of the Mongolian cavalry to train with his horses and his men, and once we were invited to attend a demonstration of their skills. We watched as the young men shot their guns while mounted on horseback and swung their wicked-looking swords at straw targets. The nomad horses were superbly trained, and would even lie down on the ground to provide cover for riders who fired machine guns over their necks. It looked like real military training (perhaps because it was), which was very exciting to us boys. It made me especially proud to be a nomad, just like the Panchen Lama.

Young people came to the Panchen Lama's special schools in Lhasa and Shigatse to study Tibetan and Chinese. More than 100 young students from all over Tibet also came to attend a mechanical engineering school the Panchen Lama had started. They studied Buddhist philosophy as monks and also trained as soldiers, learning military skills. Exactly why he wanted to train them this way, I don't know. Perhaps he simply enjoyed these things, or perhaps he had goals that he did not share.

A few years later, during the Cultural Revolution, the Panchen Lama was denounced for these schools, which were considered evidence of his antirevolutionary crimes. I suspect the Chinese officials did not like the Panchen Lama providing what looked like military training to his young supporters.

After several months in Lhasa, we undertook the second leg of our journey. Finally Serdok Rinpoche, his attendant, and I arrived in Shigatse. We were brought to the Panchen Lama's large new palace, Dechen Podrang, where we were put up in a spacious room. The next morning, we were taken to see the Panchen Lama, and in the daylight we marveled at the palace with its red gate and yellow walls.

Dechen Podrang was traditional and beautiful—a classic example of Tibetan architecture. Inside, sunlight shone through skylights, and massive ceiling beams stretched across the open, two-story structure. After we met with the Panchen Lama, an attendant gave us a tour. He pointed to the building across from the palace and said, "That is Tashi Lhunpo Monastery. At the Panchen Lama's request, the monastery has arranged for your lodging. Tomorrow you will go there."

The First Dalai Lama founded Tashi Lhunpo Monastery in 1447. Since the time of the Fourth Panchen Lama, all Panchen Lamas have resided there. In the foreground of the mountain range behind Tashi Lhunpo sits Mount Drolma, its iron-rich rock lending the mountain an oxidized bronze glow. Shaped like a sitting Green Tara (the female Buddha of Compassion), Mount Drolma holds Tashi Lhunpo in her lap.

The architecture and golden roofs of Tashi Lhunpo attest to the monastery's long, rich history, and to the accumulation of merit by the monks who have lived and prayed there for generations. I felt as if the breezes moving the colorful prayer flags and golden prayer wheels were beckoning us.

Serdok Rinpoche and I couldn't hide our excitement—we were going to receive traditional instruction in the dharma and the five branches of Tibetan Buddhist studies at the famous monastic university at Tashi Lhumpo. We would each have our own room, our own books, and a place to pray. Upon our successful completion of the curricula and exams, degrees would be conferred, depending on the number of years we had devoted to the program. In our case, we would surely live here perhaps 20 or 30 years, and become geshes. Many monks who went to study at large monastic universities like this never returned to their homes. Thinking of this provoked a sudden wave of homesickness for Kumbum and my family.

The next day, someone took us to Shartse Dratsang, one of Tashi Lhumpo's colleges for the study of the five classes of Buddhist philosophy. Our living quarters were at the very top of the six-floor building, where we had our own bedrooms and shared a kitchen. Uncle Lobsang took charge of our daily needs and looked after me as well as Serdok Rinpoche. We felt privileged to have such wonderful living arrangements, especially as it was the Panchen Lama himself who had chosen them for us.

When we studied the dharma, Serdok Rinpoche and I had always had our own private tutors, but here at Tashi Lhunpo we were going to be educated just like everyone else, which pleased me greatly. We were fortunate to become students of Karlchen Dawa La, the khenpo, or dean, of our college. He was a renowned scholar who had come from a poor family. When he was studying for his geshe degree he had had to get up very early in the morning to gather dung for the family fire, and then make the long trek from his village to the monastery. By the time he got home each night it was dark, and because his family had no money to buy oil for lamps, he studied by the glow of incense sticks, pointing the tips downward to illuminate the page. Many of his personal sutras were marked by small burn marks.

On a day off from our studies, two friends from Amdo invited Serdok Rinpoche, Uncle Lobsang, and me to bring food and set up a tent by a small stream, where we sat and enjoyed the spectacular view. Nearby, other monks were enjoying the day just as we were. Some were playing popular games, such as Wheel of Life, an ancient board game. Others were simply resting, or scrubbing laundry on rocks in the river and then spreading it out on the green carpets of grass; young novices scampered among them, playing.

The high altitude and desert conditions at Tashi Lhunpo were not as hospitable as our greener home region of Kumbum. However, thanks to the efforts of Uncle Lobsang, Serdok Rinpoche and I were very well cared for. Sometimes, when Lobsang went out to run errands, we got into mischief—stealing his food, scaring our teacher's puppy, or boxing with each other. One bright moonlit night, after Lobsang fell asleep, we put on our New Year's robes, a forbidden act, and pretended we were celebrating the New Year. Another time we scaled the high wall around the roof, 100 feet above the valley, and had a walking competition. This was very dangerous, for a fall would have meant certain death, but of course this was precisely what made it so appealing.

On another night, a monk named Tenzin visited us. He was a humorous fellow, and we always enjoyed listening to his stories. On this particular visit he told us about a ghost that lived in the room next to ours. A few hours later we suddenly heard the teacher's puppy barking fiercely, as if a stranger were approaching. We found the puppy backing away from a wall, growling as if it were going to bite someone's leg, but no one was there. It looked very much like the puppy was seeing something we could not. We were so afraid we had goose bumps! As the evening came to an end, Lobsang asked Serdok Rinpoche to see Tenzin on his way, and to lock up the house. While he did this, I hid in a dark corner. When Serdok Rinpoche came back inside, I stepped out in front of him from the shadows, loudly clapping my hands. He was terrified, and ran to Lobsang. I must admit I felt guilty when I saw how well my plan had worked. Once they realized what had happened, they both yelled at me.

Life at Tashi Lhunpo was certainly not all play. Right after breakfast in the early morning, students would join the rest of the monks in the Buddha Hall for the daily recital of mantras and sutras. Sometimes we chanted in unison, and at other times we created a cacophony of voices, which we children considered more fun. Young novices, between 6 and 10 years of age, usually studied sutras at their teachers' houses in the morning, took classes at the debating hall in the afternoon, and spent every spare moment memorizing sutras in preparation for exams. Those who passed the exams, usually taken after a year of study, were admitted to the college's formal monastic education.

In the evening all the students would go to the roof of the building where they were living and recite prayers aloud under the canopy of stars. During ceremonies and special occasions, such as Buddha's Day or Lama Tsong Khapa's Day, more than 1,000 monks would gather in the main hall to chant prayers. Their voices flowed together like the wave of a great ocean.

Fluent recitation of sutras in class often elicited praise from our teacher, but memorizing and copying sutras was a daunting task; failure resulted in public scolding. Fortunately, in our three years at Tashi Lhunpo, Serdok Rinpoche and I advanced greatly. We studied grammar and calligraphy and memorized many sutras; I had outgrown my earlier difficulty remembering them. We also learned Buddhist philosophy and mastered debating skills. It seemed we were finally on our way to receiving the education we needed to fulfill our life's work.

In the late summer of 1964, when I was 14 years old, rumors began to circulate that a new wave of political reeducation was coming. The monks of Tashi Lhunpo didn't react much to the rumors. Political campaigns there had not been as oppressive as they had been in other regions; the Panchen Lama had provided some protection. When Lobsang Donyol confirmed the rumors, monks and novices like Serdok Rinpoche and me, who had come from other monasteries, felt a terrible jolt of panic: memories of the torture, humiliation, and imprisonment of beloved friends and teachers were still all too fresh in our minds.

Not long afterward, several hundred cadres in green uniforms came into Tashi Lhunpo and took up residence. Because the monastery is built on the slope of a mountain and the cadres stayed in the courtyard below, we could easily keep an eye on them. We observed them drying their comforters in the sun, oiling their guns, and reading books and documents. We weren't sure what they were up to, and our curiosity was undeniably tinged with fear.

Then we were all called in for a motivational meeting. With sinking hearts we learned that we were about to begin a "Campaign of Three Educations." In Marxist Internationalism and Marxist Patriotism meetings, we would all wave little flags in support of Cuba, although we novices didn't even know what Cuba was. In Marxist Socialism meetings we learned about the internal struggles between rightist and leftist factions in China, and we were told which ones to support. In every meeting, cadres took turns reading documents in Chinese, which were then translated word for word into Tibetan. Those of us unfortunate enough to understand both Tibetan and Chinese got a double dose of reeducation.

At the beginning of this campaign, the Chinese soldiers spent a lot of time explaining to us the utopia of Communism and the superiority of socialism. After enough repetition, the message started to have an effect: Some monks began to think that what was being promised was better than the Buddhist image of the Pure Land, and started to speak out in favor of Communism. The longer the political campaign continued, the more monks were won over. Because the more highly educated monks—the rinpoches, geshes, and teachers—were considered enemies of the proletarian class (and were less susceptible to brainwashing), the cadres and newly won-over monks often criticized us.

Six or seven months passed, and things went from bad to worse. We were forced to give up our robes, and we young teenagers had to join the older monks in hard labor. Monks of higher rank were assigned the worst jobs of all. The most disgusting work was digging out the latrine. In our building the latrine was on the third floor, where the waste dropped three stories into a deep pit at the bottom of the building. Once a year a great quantity of soil was added to the pit, which was then cleaned out in a process known as accumulating fertilizer. Previously, farmers had been hired to haul dirt up to the toilet on the third floor, dump the soil down into the pit, and then clear out the barely processed fertilizer. Now I stood barefoot with other lamas in the wretched, stinking muck in the basement, digging it out with shovels and hoes.

When I first started to work in the pit I became light-headed from breathing in the foul air all day, but when I recalled what my teacher taught me, I felt better able to abide the stench. "Human waste is like morning dew. It comes from the earth's produce, is transformed in the human body, and finally evacuates the human body to return to the earth." He also reminded us that our greatest enemy was always our best teacher, and that the filthiest and hardest work is the best way to cleanse ourselves of our karmic misdeeds.

We also performed hard labor outside Tashi Lhunpo: We plowed fields, constructed irrigation projects, cut thorny shrubs for kindling, and cleared brush. Of all these tasks, building the Unity Canal was the biggest project. Everyone who lived in the Shigatse area, including monks, was pressed into service for this task.

To build the Unity Canal, we were required to dig a 37-mile trench between the towns of Gyantse and Shigatse. Serdok Rinpoche and I worked with a group of 300 monks, carrying our gear on our backs. We stayed in tents every night. At dawn, on hearing the first whistle, we rose quickly; by the second whistle, everyone had to assemble; at the third whistle, we walked in a line to the construction site.

The engineer on our site was a college student from China, Comrade Yang. He did not understand Tibetan, and the monks did not speak Chinese, so I became his translator. At first he didn't trust me, and felt that I was too young for the job. But over time his attitude toward me changed, and I remember him as a decent man.

One night, several positivist monks ordered our team to attend a meeting, even though it was very late. When our group of five or six entered the leader's tent, we saw a draped object on the floor that looked like a low couch. Tired after the long workday, I joined others resting against it. Then the positivist leader said, "Changchup from your home region has died. This is his corpse," pointing to what we'd thought was a couch. I leaped up, horrified. Changchup was a good monk who had become ill and had asked for sick leave, but the positivist monks had accused him of feigning sickness. Death had finally settled the issue.

The leader declared that there was no time to cremate the body because everyone had to work day and night on the canal. We could not bury the body, as the ground was frozen. He pointed to the wrapped object on the floor and said, "We will use the Yarlong Tsangpo River to give him a water burial.

"There are a couple of holes already cut in the ice, but they are upstream from here. If we place the body in one of them, we will not be able to collect drinking water until the current has carried the body past us. But after two or three days the water will be clean."

So we found a hole in the ice upstream and placed the body in it. After a few days, we thought that the body must have made its way downstream, so we began drinking water from the river. Some time later, a worker went upriver and saw the body still floating in the same ice hole where we'd placed it. I was very upset by the realization that I had been drinking "meat soup" from our friend's body for several days.

In this same winter of 1964, I was sent with 60 or 70 other monks to cut and gather black thistles in the remote, semidesert area of Chushar, about 50 kilometers from Tashi Lhunpo. It was a hard trek, but I enjoyed it, knowing it meant I could avoid the hateful political campaign meetings. The black thistle plant is made up of very strong stems reaching about six feet in height. It serves as a good fuel for cooking and heating, but the thistles are very sharp, so we wore protective pants and leather shoes, along with thick leather gloves. Some monks stayed in the mountains for months, cutting and baling the thistles, while others hauled the square bales of thistle on their backs all the way from the mountains to Tashi Lhunpo.

As one approaches Tashi Lhunpo there is what looks like a little fort off to the left. It measures about 200 feet square and is more than two stories high. As you draw closer, however, it becomes obvious that the walls are made of black thistle. New bales of thistle are carried up stepladders, and monks with pitchforks place them neatly on top of the existing walls, in a process that has been ongoing for centuries. As I set my bale of thistles into the wall, stepped down, and looked back, the contribution from my bale that had felt so huge and heavy during my long journey back from the mountains looked insignificant.

69

Among those of us gathering thistles in Chushar, there were some positivist monks. They pushed us to have occasional meetings, but these meetings were not nearly as horrendous as those at Tashi Lhunpo. And although the workload was heavy, I found opportunities to take breaks with friends and to fool around when we were out of view of the group leader. I was far happier harvesting the thorny black thistles in the open air of the country than digging out the latrine; there was no doubt about that.

One night, just before dawn, the leading positivist monk woke us in our tents with a shattering blast from his whistle. We awoke to see a glittering white light streaking through the sky: a comet! The next day we whispered about what it meant. The positivist monk fretted, because Tibetans and Chinese have the same saying: "Comets in the sky, chaos on earth." Not long after returning to Tashi Lhunpo, we realized that the comet had indeed been a harbinger of dark times ahead.

After returning to the monastery from Chushar, we were ordered to attend a "class struggle" session and were herded into the meeting area. At first, the meeting seemed routine, except I noticed cadres wearing their pistols on the outsides of their coats, which was odd. Then I grew fearful when I saw that many positivist monks such as group leaders Dorji Shara, Kampa Basang Norbu, and others, were standing rather than taking their seats—another bad sign that reminded me of the worst days at Kumbum.

A cadre opened the meeting with a speech:

Our campaign has made great achievements: We have raised our consciousness on the class struggle. Our class enemies who have ridden on our necks for thousands of years cannot hide themselves anymore. The wolf is showing his tail under his sheepskin. Now let us relentlessly expose him, denounce him, and firmly knock him down . . . .

Before he had even finished his speech, cadres began wildly yelling out slogans. "Down with the antirevolutionary Panchen! Expose the scandal of his 70,000 Character Petition!" Other positivists joined in, "Down with antirevolutionaries!" All the monks were forced to shout the same slogans for 10 minutes. Then the positivist monks took turns on the stage speaking out against the Panchen Lama, while the rest of us bent our heads in silent sorrow.

It became clear to us that our "political study" was actually part of an orchestrated plot by Mao's henchmen in Beijing to bring down the Panchen Lama. As the speeches went on I began to wonder if the soldiers were planning to bring the Panchen Lama here to publicly humiliate him. The thought of this proud man with his hands and legs cuffed and cadres forcing him to bow his head was almost unbearable. As it turned out, the Panchen Lama did not appear. Instead, positivist monks read for hours from prepared lists of the Panchen Lama's alleged transgressions.

Just like the religious reforms of 1958, cadres were mobilizing positivist monks and using them to force all the rest of us to participate. At first the monks in our team refused to speak, but under relentless pressure from the cadres, one monk after another bent to the cadres' demands, and I was no exception. What made this especially humiliating was that the first teaching of Tibetan Buddhism is to respect your teacher. The dharma, or philosophy of Buddha, is centered on compassion and wisdom, the basic foundations for how a practitioner of Buddhism should treat all sentient beings. To learn how to advance in his practice, the practitioner must rely on his teacher, for only our teachers can guide us to the Buddha's ultimate teachings. As a practitioner, I was obligated to never betray my teacher in speech or action. The slightest disrespect would harm my practice and sow the seeds of negative karma, guaranteeing me a future rebirth in a lower realm.

The political campaigns of the 1960s were not created by cadres and positivists, but rather by their leaders. Our tormentors at Tashi Lhunpo were just loyally implementing the plans and commands of their superiors. But what a horrendous crime we were forced to commit! Every day we had to criticize and denounce the Panchen Lama, our teacher, in violation of everything we stood for. I felt debased by this, but in my fear I also felt I had no choice. Monks who refused to go along were tortured, sent to prison camps, and even

71

killed. We didn't dare to discuss our feelings amongst ourselves, for betrayal was all too common. Day after day, our torment grew. I felt the weight of negative karma pushing me deeper and deeper into a dark hole far worse than the latrine, for this time I could find no comfort in a beautiful teaching.

The Chinese government now formally took the position that the Panchen Lama's 70,000 Character Petition was an antirevolutionary act that undermined socialism and the Communist Party. His possession of arms and vehicles and his apolitical education of young Tibetans at the School of Mechanical Engineering were cited as proof of his support for Tibetan independence. Even the spare tank of gas in his jeep was seen as evidence of his intention to flee to India.

As if this weren't enough, the Panchen Lama was also accused of sexual misconduct: his sister-in-law was alleged to be his mistress. Upon hearing the trumped-up evidence offered by the cadres, most monks refused to believe any of it. The cadres responded by saying that if we did not believe it, they would call a special meeting and invite Pema Yangchen, the Panchen Lama's sister-in-law, to come and tell everyone the sordid details of the Panchen Lama's sexual transgressions. To avoid such terrible blasphemy, we pretended to believe the accusations. We were aghast at the thought that she might actually come in person to denounce the Panchen Lama. In fact, she never did show up, and the cadres gave the excuse that she was too embarrassed to expose herself to the monks in person. However, we knew that it was all just part of the charade and had nothing to do with the truth.

One day at a meeting, a cadre forced us to listen to a recording of the Panchen Lama's sister-in-law. Over the loudspeakers used for large political meetings we heard a woman's voice say, "On such and such a day he insulted me; at another time, he raped me." She was very specific about the accusations, and when they had allegedly occurred. The voice over the loudspeaker sounded like Pema Yangchen's voice, but I could not tell for sure. A monk named Tsendor secretly shared with us another rumor that the cadres were circulating amongst themselves—that Serdok Rinpoche and I were the illegitimate sons of the Panchen Lama. Hearing this, I was not upset, knowing it was just propaganda, and the absurdity of the charge helped me to realize that the voice of Pema Yangchen was a fake.

This second political campaign lasted 16 months, after which time most of the cadres left the monastery. Only a few stayed on to guarantee the transformation of those of us who were considered parasitic members of the exploiting class. The last steps of this transformation into true members of a socialist society would be accomplished through farmwork. Tashi Lhunpo already had a few farms, but a Communist Chinese official (nicknamed "Black-Nose Xu" by the monks because he had a large mole on his nose) ordered us to start a new farm called Khampo Gyamda.

It's not easy to describe the foolishness of some of these official Communist Chinese mandates. In the meeting in Beijing where they were conceived they must have sounded totally plausible: "Ah, we need more food; let's dam this river and use its water to irrigate the land over there. What a great plan! And let's send the monks over there to provide the necessary labor." But here in Tibet things looked very different. In this case the future farm was located in the desert, and there was no water nearby.

Meanwhile Serdok Rinpoche and I were both feeling very homesick. We had recently requested leaves of absence to return to Kumbum, and Black-Nose Xu had approved our requests in private. Now we saw that the cadres had put our names on the list of monks to be sent to build the new farm. Everything was up in the air again. Would we ever be allowed to return home?

CHAPTER 6

ENTER THE CULTURAL REVOLUTION

One morning a positivist monk came to Serdok Rinpoche and me to inform us that we could return to Kumbum Monastery. In fact, we were to leave that day. He further informed us that according to new directives, we were not to bring sutras or sacred images with us, only our clothes. Trembling with fear, our attendant handed him a document that the Panchen Lama's office had given us, declaring that everything we owned was ours to keep. (It was written in anticipation of just such a moment as this.) The monk took the letter, tore it to pieces, threw the scraps to the floor, and stomped on them, yelling, "The Panchen is not in charge. That day will never return! We proletarian monks are now the masters!"

We set out for Lhasa in the back of a big, open truck. As it drove away from the fallen splendor of Tashi Lhunpo, Serdok Rinpoche and I looked back on the monastery and couldn't help but notice how different it seemed from that day when we had first arrived filled with joy and optimism that our monastic lives were back on track. Then the monastery had seemed so vibrant and full of life. Now so many buildings stood empty. We noted the stark contrast between the sad monks we were leaving behind and the excited cadres driving our truck, looking forward to a trip to the city. As I thought about what our lives might have been like at Tashi Lhunpo if the Chinese Communists had never arrived, tears ran down my cheeks.

Two days later we arrived in Lhasa, cold and tired. Serdok Rinpoche and I looked at each other and laughed, barely able to recognize each other under the layers of road dust and dirt. After four years, Lhasa looked unchanged, but appearances proved to be deceiving. The gates of Jokhang Temple, Ramoche Temple, and other holy sites were locked tight; no crowds of people prostrated or circumambulated the abandoned buildings. Where Barkhor street had been alive with vendors and throngs of Tibetan shoppers drifting from stall to stall, loudly bargaining for *dorjes,* bells, and other religious souvenirs, now it was deserted. The heart of Lhasa had been ripped out.

We checked into a guesthouse, where the front desk clerk scrutinized our documents. For days we eagerly waited for bus tickets to continue our journey. Finally a cadre from the United Front of the Tibet Autonomous Region (TAR) turned us over to a group of cadres heading to their hometowns in Tibet and China. We rode with them in a large bus for the weeklong drive to Xining, and then on to Kumbum.

It had been eight years since that terrible day in 1958 when I last saw my teacher, Tsultrim Lhaksem, being forced into a bus on his way to prison. But now, as we entered Kumbum, here he was, smiling warmly at me. With great joy I discreetly prostrated to him, as he warned me with raised eyebrows not to let other people catch me doing this; it would bring trouble down on my head and his. Tsultrim Lhaksem, now 70, looked much older to me; his years in prison had taken their toll. I also saw my beloved Jamaga, as well as my second brother, Tenba Gyatso, my brother Nori, and Drashi Gyaltsen, who would later play an important part in my life. Despite the suffering etched in their faces, I was thrilled to be in their presence once again. Even in sorrow, there can be joy.

At Kumbum we were put to work in the fields. The team leader assigned me to lead oxen for plowing, drive horse carts, pull weeds, harvest grain, and perform other farm tasks that I gradually learned to do very well. Like regular farmers, we peasant monks did not work the land in the winter, so in the winter after our return to Kumbum, Serdok Rinpoche, Nori, and I took a walk on the streets of Xining. We were surprised to see factory and office

75

workers debating the correct interpretation of the words of Chairman Mao, discussing the meaning of such phrases as "protector of the ruling class," and "guarding the socialists." We listened to the arguments with curiosity but did not understand their significance. It turned out this was the beginning of the infamous Great Cultural Revolution of the Proletariat, launched by Mao Zedong to erase the history of Eastern Asia going back thousands of years. The year was 1966; I was 16.

During the Cultural Revolution, Chairman Mao claimed that liberal, bourgeois elements were taking over the Communist Party and needed to be purged from their positions of power through a postrevolutionary class struggle. One key element in this struggle was China's youth, which he mobilized in the form of the Red Guard. From my perspective as a Tibetan novice, this campaign differed from its predecessors by being less brutal but better organized—our daily routine felt much more like being in prison. As monks we were not permitted to live a normal life, let alone practice the Buddha's teachings. We were closely watched; we had to ask permission to leave the house; we had to report what we did every day.

At my first class-struggle meeting, I saw that some monks were being forced to wear paper hats that marked them as traitorous counterrevolutionaries. This hat was an invention of Mao Zedong, and wearing one was a form of punishment for people whose crimes weren't serious enough to warrant imprisonment, but who required correction in the form of public humiliation. The shape and size of these paper hats differed somewhat, although most were at least two feet tall and were painted with terms like "Antirevolutionary" or "Evil Element." They looked like dunce caps. Sometimes this accusation was also printed on a placard, which was worn around a person's neck whenever the offender was in public. Later the use of physical paper hats was discontinued, but the stigma survived in the form of a notation on a person's identification papers: *dai maozi*—wearing hat.

Once you were given a paper hat, you were singled out for ongoing special attention. "Paper hats" no longer had the right to speak and could no longer celebrate holidays. They had to engage in the harshest physical labor, or serve the cadres without receiving the minimal pay others sometimes earned. Any proletarian at all had the right to supervise and discipline these poor monks. Gyayak Rinpoche was among the first at Kumbum Monastery to be forced to put on a paper hat, and he was subjected to relentless denunciations for more than six months.

Although the fanatical flames of the Cultural Revolution burned brightly around me, thanks to my teachers I never lost my devotion to the Three Jewels. One day after I had been working in the fields, Gyayak Rinpoche asked me what I had studied at Tashi Lhunpo, so I showed him some of my writings. After that, each time we met he would inquire a little more deeply into my studies. With the encouragement of Gyayak Rinpoche and Tsultrim Lhaksem, I was able to continue learning the dharma in secret. Eventually, under the guise of teaching us Chinese, Gyayak Rinpoche taught Serdok Rinpoche and me Tibetan grammar and Buddhist sutras. Because Tsultrim Lhaksem and I shared the same house, I was able to benefit from his secret teachings of the dharma every day.

Whenever he was put on stage to be denounced, Gyayak Rinpoche appeared calm, confident, and fearless. He indeed practiced a bodhisattva's great patience and endurance in the face of suffering, embodying the fulfillment of his bodhisattva vows. He repeatedly cautioned Serdok Rinpoche and me not to waste our youthful years but to master Buddha's teachings, poetry, and history, and, if we had time, to learn Chinese and other foreign languages as well. (Previously we had only pretended to study Chinese to hide the fact that we were studying Buddhist texts, but now we studied it in earnest.)

In the winter it was often too cold to work outside, so we had a lot of free time to study. In addition to Buddhist texts, I read Chinese classics such as *The Romance of the Three Kingdoms, Investiture of Gods, Dream of the Red Chamber, Heroes of the Marshes, A History of Confucian Scholars,* and other works. Serdok Rinpoche and I were incredibly fortunate to have Gyayak Rinpoche as our mentor during these terrifying times.

By late 1966, the Cultural Revolution had swept through all of China. In the past, lamas, landowners, and businessmen had been cast as villains, making it easy to know who to denounce, but this time the wrongdoers were more difficult to identify. One group of cadres would be pitted against another, each claiming to be of a lower class, more proletarian, with a greater understanding of Chairman Mao. One thing remained constant: Serdok Rinpoche, Gyayak Rinpoche, and I, being the only reincarnated lamas left at the monastery, were regularly denounced as bourgeois antirevolutionaries. When the next winter came around and there was little work to do on the farm, Serdok Rinpoche, my brother Nori, and I, without much hope, requested leaves of absence to visit our families. To our surprise, the team leader approved our requests.

We set out from Xining by bus. After traveling several hundred kilometers, we finally arrived at Za Marki (red rock), a town at the foot of Ahrik Mountain. In the 1960s, travel was difficult; there were no good roads and no buses at all, so Serdok Rinpoche, Nori, and I had to walk from Ahrik to Toli, the remote town where my family had been forcibly relocated.

For three days we walked from dawn to dusk, carrying our meager belongings and a little food. However, we were warmly received by the locals, who provided us with meals and showed us great respect. This surprised us, as we no longer wore robes; nor, as members of the "exploiting class," had we expected such good treatment. To our surprise, people kept asking us, "Have you met Chairman Mao?" When we told them we had not, they didn't seem to believe us, and finally one of them remarked, "You are very humble. This is a noble quality of the Red Guards; you are truly worthy of being role models for us." We assured them that we were not Red Guards, which only increased their admiration. But at least we finally understood the reason for our warm reception.

We had been mistaken for Red Guards because at the beginning of the Cultural Revolution many students stopped going to school and traveled throughout Tibet and China spreading the teachings of Chairman Mao from his *Red Book*. "Red Guard" was the name given to these young students, no matter their nationality. They also visited each other to share their revolutionary experiences. Since the Red Guard were all that most country folk in remote areas knew of the Cultural Revolution, any traveling students (or those who looked like them) were welcomed, either out of fear or genuine warmth.

Our first stop was Serdok Rinpoche's home in Toli. His mother was so overcome with joy to see him after all these years that she burst into tears and could not speak. When she recovered, she imparted the family news, none of it good. Serdok Rinpoche's brother, who had been a monk at Kumbum Monastery, had returned to secular life. The families of Serdok Rinpoche and Gyayak Rinpoche had stayed in Toli, but my family had been moved to another place, even more isolated. Although we were now in a nomadic area far from any cities, the power of the Cultural Revolution was still very much in evidence. Two of my maternal uncles had been forced to wear paper hats. Every day they had to "petition at dawn and report at dusk" to the proletarian peasants in charge of the area. Serdok Rinpoche's family was being so closely monitored that we moved on after three days, fearful that our presence would make things even worse for them.

We set out for Dolun, the area where my family now lived. After several more days of walking across the silent grasslands, we finally saw a ger. Unfortunately, it was the home of Yuto, the team leader responsible for monitoring my family. His wife was home. With some trepidation she asked politely, "Where did you come from? Are you Red Guards? Are you cadres from the county?"

When she learned who we really were, her attitude changed completely. She demanded to see our identification documents. When we showed her the travel permit issued by our work team leader at Kumbum, she rotated the letter in several directions, trying to figure out what was written on it. Like most nomadic women, she was illiterate, so she told us, "The letter is stamped, so it must be official. You may go on now. When you arrive at his home, send the antirevolutionary Pema over here to report to us."

We walked on, speaking in hushed tones. It was clearly a bad time for a visit. What awaited me was an excruciating scene: On our ger hung many posters denouncing my family; inside, my mother was mending a torn poster of criticism, her face a study in sorrow; my younger sister and brother stared at us without saying a word. They were very formal and tentative. Cowed by fear, none of them recognized us.

Finally my sister-in-law showed a flash of recognition. "Are you Nori?"

she asked my brother. "Who are these two young men with you?" It turned out that just before our arrival, several Red Guards had searched the ger, making chaos of everything, and had taken my oldest brother, Pema, away for a class-struggle meeting. My family had assumed that we were a second gang of Red Guards.

Nori said to them, "This is Surku and Bakshi." These were our pet names; my mother had used them when we were children. Pema's wife began to sob with relief. My mother looked shocked, as if she could not believe her eyes. Overcome by emotions of loss and discovery, she said nothing. After a long silence, she began to weep loudly. My younger brother and sister, who still did not recognize us, continued staring.

That night, Pema returned home from the class-struggle meeting after having been denounced all day, his face gray and drawn. He recognized us immediately, but there was no smile of welcome. Instead, he expressed concern that our coming might cause the family greater trouble. Pema sat down, lit his pipe, and puffed thoughtfully, gazing at us. Usually at night in the gers family members would catch up on the day's events. But out of respect for what Pema had just been through, we sat silently. As the night went on, however, we began to speak, quietly sharing accounts of the hardships we had experienced in the years since we were last together. As we sat around the *tapka,* the tears of my mother and sister-in-law punctuated our stories. Listening to my family, I felt that by comparison my struggles in the monasteries were nothing. My father and more than 10 people from my family had been imprisoned. A kind man from Dolon Nor who was also arrested in 1959 had brought a letter to our family describing a deceased prisoner who matched my father's description, but we never knew for certain. To this day, I still do not know the circumstances of his death.

That night was cold. People in other gers had already retired, but in ours no one slept, even after the fire died into embers. The denunciation posters flapped outside in the brisk wind. They, too, seemed to be sighing sadly for the suffering we had endured. If the posters were damaged by the wind, we would have to repair them in the morning before the Communists accused us of intentionally ripping them.

We decided it would be prudent to cut our visit short and stay only a day or two more. This brief family reunion did not afford us nearly enough time to express our affection for each other after such a long separation, but the Red Guard could descend on the gers at any time. Fear forced us to leave our loved ones too soon, but at least we had reconnected, and had wept together.

At four o'clock on the morning of our last day, after my mother comforted us with reminders about the laws of cause and effect, and of dependent arising, she sent us off, smiling through her tears. We followed my brother through the dark to Yuto's place to report our departure. Tsultrim called out to Yuto from outside his ger, and after a few minutes, we could hear someone talking inside. Finally someone called out, "Are the relatives of the antirevolutionary Pema leaving now?" "Yes," said my brother, the moonlight revealing the resignation on his face. I knew how much he hated his forced submission to Yuto. When Yuto eventually emerged, he and his wife came out. While both of them carefully examined our luggage with their flashlights, I made a point of taking a good look at their faces. They looked nothing like the heroic comrades in Chinese movies; instead, looking at their small, closely set eyes, I saw rodents. It was only through great force of will that, in keeping with my Buddhist training, I was able to feel compassion for them.

On the trip back to Kumbum Monastery, we saw many Red Guards brandishing red flags and beating drums and gongs as they marched through towns. We also saw a profusion of banners hung across streets with slogans such as "Revolution Is Not a Crime," "Rebellion Has Reasons," "Tear Down Traditions and Build a New Society," "Down with the Ruling Class," and "Defend Chairman Mao."

When we returned we saw that in the short time we had been away the internal divisions caused by the Cultural Revolution had now fully invaded our monastery. Ngawang Jimba, who had been administrator of religious reform at the monastery since 1958, led one group of positivist monks. Lobsang Rabgyal headed up another, claiming that Ngawang Jimba, having been longtime director of the Democratic Management Committee of Kumbum

81

Monastery, was part of the ruling class. Uneasy about the accusation, Ngawang Jimba directed his followers to burn sutras and smash Buddha statues in an attempt to demonstrate his loyalty to the revolution.

One night, as I was sound asleep, the clanging of gongs awoke me. By the time I sat up, Ngawang Jimba and his followers had already crowded into our courtyard. I ran over to Tsultrim Lhaksem's room. One of the positivists, who had once been a student of Tsultrim Lhaksem, was asking my teacher to surrender his robes to be burned in the yard.

My teacher had worn his robes for nearly 60 years. During the religious reform of the 1950s he hid them in a vase, and he was delighted to find them still there four years later. But today his former student wanted to burn those robes, and there was no escaping the edict. This broke his heart. How could robes offend anybody? What "interests of the people" could these pieces of ordinary cloth oppose? I had known Tsultrim Lhaksem all my life, and this was the only time I ever saw him cry.

One cloudy autumn day, while we were harvesting green peas in the field, we heard a voice come over the loudspeaker demanding that we attend a meeting. We sensed that something terrible was about to happen. When we arrived at the courtyard, we saw that a crowd had gathered, including hundreds of college students; where they had come from, we did not know. They began a political study session, but the meeting was chaotic, and they began to argue among themselves.

Suddenly, several college students started fighting at the front gate of the Great Hall of Golden Tiles. They looked crazed. From their shouting I realized that some wanted to destroy everything in the hall, but a woman student wearing a Red Guard armband opposed them, advocating protection of the ancient objects. Unfortunately, she had few supporters. When the majority of the Red Guards moved to enter the hall, the gatekeeper, a monk named Tsering, locked the gate. Some Red Guards went to the leader of the government work team stationed in the monastery, who ordered Tsering to open the gate. Tsering had no choice but to surrender the key.

The Red Guards swarmed into Maitreya Hall next door and began to toss bundles of ancient sutras into the courtyard from the second floor of the

Buddha Hall. They lit a fire, and soon the monastery was filled with the thick smoke of burning books. Some monks lost control and began to wail. Others stood motionless. Still others joined in the destruction of the sutras, spurring on the students. Panic and rage were everywhere, like demons unleashed. I watched in helpless horror as the Red Guards burned the sutras in Gyayak Rinpoche's personal shrine. After a few hours, a cadre halted the Red Guard's atrocities because he suspected they were stealing valuable works of art. Many students left, disappointed that their plan for total destruction had failed.

After this incident, monk positivists and Red Guards destroyed many more statues and sutras on their own. According to Chinese history, the first emperor of China burned books and killed scholars more than 2,000 years ago. It was considered his great achievement. True to this ignoble tradition, burning sutras and smashing Buddhas were great achievements of the Cultural Revolution in Tibet.

One day a cadre from a government work team ordered monks to move all the printing blocks from which we printed our sacred texts out of the printing house into the street and to burn them. More than 300 years old, these price-less printing blocks were one of the great treasures of Kumbum Monastery. Destroying printed pages was one thing; destroying the original blocks was another. They included the works of Lama Tsong Khapa's three original dis-ciples, four large volumes of Tibetan medicine, and the works of the previous reincarnation of Serdok Rinpoche. Quickly a huge stack of printing blocks was piled up in the street.

Just as the fire was about to be lit, a clever monk remarked, "These blocks are made of fine wood. It's wasteful to burn them. Why don't we make them into useful tools for working in the fields, which will support the revolution?" Quite a few other monks joined in, saying, "Good idea, good idea! It's wasteful to burn them." The blocks were not burned that day, and several days later, the monks were ordered to move them back into the printing house, where they were hastily stacked and stored away. And so these trea-sures of our monastery were miraculously preserved.

The fierce struggle between opposing groups of positivist monks in Kumbum ended with the triumph of Lobsang Rabgyal over Ngawang Jimba, 83

84   a victory of youth over age, despite the fact that Ngawang Jimba had done such an outstanding job of torturing, insulting, and denouncing monks. Now Ngawang Jimba himself had been deemed an antirevolutionary. If he ever considered what his teacher had taught him about the retribution of karma, he would have seen that he was providing a powerful example of karma at work in this lifetime.

The triumphant Lobsang Rabgyal had also been a youth positivist in 1958, but he had not had many opportunities to demonstrate his abilities. As the Cultural Revolution began he had seen an opportunity to redeem himself. However, only a few days after he deposed Ngawang Jimba and took the position of director of the Democratic Management Committee of the monastery, a directive came down from Beijing stating that all monks belonged to the exploiting class and therefore were not qualified to become Red Guards. As a former monk, Lobsang Rabgyal's political ambition was foiled at the very moment when he seemed to have achieved his goal.

During the Cultural Revolution, dictates from on high never ceased. One day we were called to a meeting where a cadre said: "You all need to go up mountains and descend to villages." We did not understand what he meant, so he explained. "'Go up mountains and descend to villages' means to return to wherever you came from. Did some of you come from nomadic regions? If so, 'go up mountains' means returning to your home areas. Did some of you come from farming areas? 'Descend to villages' means going back to where you came from. Anyway, 'go up mountains and descend to villages' means go home. Monasteries are homes to the exploiting class. You must go back to farming and herding to reform yourselves. Leaving today is better than leaving tomorrow! Leaving in the morning is better than leaving in the afternoon! Sign up if you want to leave now."

He demanded that most of us leave, although some monks were assigned to maintain the monastery as a museum, showcasing the workings of the exploiting class for the revolutionary education of the masses. The cadre began to call out monks' names; those who were not called would have to leave. Gyayak Rinpoche, Serdok Rinpoche, and I were not called. We were to "go up mountains and descend to villages." I was devastated by this development, knowing that my return would only make a terrible situation for my family even worse.

Back in my room after the meeting, I broke the bad news to Tsultrim Lhaksem. "From now on, please take care of yourself, beloved teacher. I will no longer have the good fortune to serve you." I broke down in tears. My teacher comforted me, saying, "There is always a mouthful of grass waiting in front of every sheep. I think our lives will be connected ultimately." Incredibly, the following day a cadre informed Gyayak Rinpoche, Serdok Rinpoche, and me that there had been a change in plans. We would stay at the monastery. In all, about 100 monks were asked to remain.

Those who stayed were forced to attend many political study sessions and receive a great deal of education from proletarian peasants. In these sessions, Gyayak Rinpoche, Serdok Rinpoche, and I were always singled out for special humiliations. Even though I should have been inured to this brutality by now, the endless hatred still pained me. Nevertheless, I knew from my teachers that terrible experiences were the best opportunities for practitioners. My own experience supported this, too, having taught me valuable lessons on the workings of karma, impermanence, ignorance, and discontent.

Looking back on the Cultural Revolution, I am struck by the absurdity and waste of it all. During this time Chairman Mao's *Red Book* of quotations was the only book people were allowed read; all others were illegal. His statue was the only statue that people could worship (and by this time, nearly all Buddhist statues had been destroyed). Everyone had to "support what our enemies are against and rebel against what our enemies support; if you don't knock them down, the antirevolutionaries won't fall by themselves." These were the slogans of Chairman Mao that we had to recite every single day.

Before setting out to work in the fields, all monks had to gather in front of the barn that served as the office of the monastery production team. One morning a bizarre event occurred. Team leader Lobsang Rabgyal called everyone to the front of his house and requested that we straighten our wrinkled clothes. He led us inside to a picture of Chairman Mao on the wall of his room and reverently bowed to it three times. After that, he demanded that every morning we report to "Chairman Mao" to explain what we expected to accomplish for the day. He himself did it this way:

> Our beloved Chairman Mao, how are you? On behalf of all commune members of the first production team of Rusar People's Commune, I report to you. We will accomplish all spring farming tasks under the correct leadership of the people's commune and the work team. We promise to diligently study your quotation book and always remember the sweetness of the new society and the bitterness of the old one. We promise to continue your revolution and increase our production under the principle of class struggle. We entreat you to trust our promise . . .

These words shocked everyone. We wanted to laugh, but dared not do so aloud. Chairman Mao was a living human being who did not believe in gods and spirits, and yet we were expected to speak to him through his statue. How absurd! But similar worship was taking place all over Tibet and China, twice a day, as the day began and as it ended. Our obeisance to Mao, known as the "petition at dawn and report at dusk," continued for years.

One day our production team pulled us from the fields and sent us to work on a dam. At the construction site we saw hundreds of workers transporting materials like a busy colony of ants, pulling carts filled with materials that weighed half a ton or more. Over the din of sledgehammers and shovels, loudspeakers blasted revolutionary news and played songs like "The East Is Red" and "Sailing in the Ocean Depends on the Captain." They also broadcast constant praise for the Communist leadership, such as "Long live Chairman Mao" and "Good health to Lin Biao," who was Mao's second in command.

We worked at least 10 hours nonstop every day, for which we were paid little, usually in food. Technically, however, we were not slaves. Mao was trying to build a new, egalitarian society, and in order to join it, former rulers—such as high-ranking monks—had to pay a price.

At the dam, monks were only a tiny part of the workforce. Thousands of local laborers hauled carts and wheelbarrows full of dirt, alongside donkeys, mules, and horses. A vast sea of tents housed these workers. Electrical wires and tools were scattered everywhere. Incredibly, everyone seemed to be working with enthusiasm, which I could not fathom. Did they all regard themselves as the materials of socialist construction? Were they naïve? Were they afraid?

We went on to build many dams, including Huangshu Wan Dam, Lijiashan Dam, and Mayi Gou Dam. At first we followed the same basic construction methods. Gradually, however, changes occurred. For example, when we were building Mayi Gou Dam, we began to use small tractors as well as horse-drawn carts, reducing the number of laborers needed. Later, while we were building Gyarts-ang Dam, cadres started demanding bribes and gifts, such as cigarettes, liquor, and even cash, in exchange for lighter work assignments. Corruption, which at first had played no part in Chinese Communism, was becoming rampant. Some monks were quick to learn this new system of raising money and paying bribes to get what they wanted.

Laborers also learned the benefits of bribery, because not only did it lead to the best job assignments, but it could also provide a chance to steal construction materials or to falsify production records so as to claim more pay. When I looked at these often drunken engineers and cadres, and then over to those who were doubled over, pulling heavy carts, working themselves to death with necks straining and sweat dripping off their faces, I felt an overwhelming sense of futility. This was egalitarianism?

There are too many unfair things in this world. I found some comfort in remembering what Gyayak Rinpoche had so often told me: "Some people are consuming the karmas of their past, while others are making karmas of their future. We must have compassion for them, and, in the meantime, be careful of what we say and do."

CHAPTER 7

REMOVING
PAPER HATS

In our sadness lay one major hope for change: We waited for Chairman Mao to die. As the madness of the Cultural Revolution stormed around us, we dreamed that once Chairman Mao passed away, Buddhism would revive and Tibet would be free. Sadly, my teacher and mentor Tsultrim Lhaksem was not able to wait that long. On February 11, 1973, he passed away at the age of 84. I had studied dharma with him on and off for more than 20 years, during which time he had lived through terrible privation. Before 1958 he was an ordinary, albeit brilliant, monk. But because he had been selected for the honor of teaching the older brother of the Dalai Lama, two Arjia Rinpoches, and other famous khenpos of Kumbum Monastery, he was made to suffer in prison for years.

Tsultrim Lhaksem was the first monk to whom I personally attended as he prepared for death. His passing brought home just how different a monk's attitude toward dying is from that of a layperson. It also made me reflect on the nature of impermanence: He passed away after being sick for only three days.

On the second day after Tsultrim Lhaksem was incapacitated by a cold, he called Gyayak Rinpoche and me to his bedside and told us that he had been a monk for more than 70 years, and that looking back he had no regrets. The only thought that saddened him was that he would not be able to see the day of Buddhism's revival with his own eyes. Tsultrim Lhaksem told us that he knew that his energy for this lifetime was coming to an end, he expressed his deepest thanks for the care Gyayak Rinpoche had given him, and he praised me for my loyalty. He told us not to recite prayers for him, because he wanted us to avoid trouble with the cadres.

My teacher had cared for me just as my own father would have done. And now he was leaving us. I felt lost, alone, and a familiar sense of helplessness. Besides the warm tears of my heart, what else could I offer him?

I went into the small kitchen and prepared food for Tsultrim Lhaksem, including the small, soft, fresh dumplings that he liked so much. After dinner, as I helped him wash up, he smiled his thanks and whispered to me, "You will see a better life in the future."

After Tsultrim Lhaksem bade us farewell, Gyayak Rinpoche told me what to do for my teacher's passing. He reminded me that when a layperson is dying, many rituals must be performed to benefit the departed, including the reading of *The Tibetan Book of the Dead* to guide the person's life thread through the *bardo* (the stages between this life and rebirth). However, when a monk is passing away after years of Buddhist practice, he does not need much help; a few whispered reminders will do.

Usually, as the moment of his death nears, the Buddhist practitioner, especially a monk, likes to do familiar things. For example, most dying monks like wearing their robes, touching ritual objects, and looking at photos of their teachers. So Gyayak Rinpoche told me to prepare my teacher's special set of ceremonial yellow robes, which had been given to him secretly by a disciple after Tsultrim Lhaksem's other robes had been burned. I also located his *dorje* (the small scepter held in the right hand by Tibetan lamas during religious ceremonies) and bell. Gyayak Rinpoche also asked me to recite the Guru Mantra, a Sanskrit prayer: *"Namo Gurube, Namo Buddhaya, Namo Dharmaya, Namo Sanghaya,"* which means "Take refuge in the teacher, the Buddha, the Dharma, and the Sangha." My recitation of it would be Tsultrim Lhaksem's cue that it was time to pass into nirvana. Although it was dangerous for us in this political climate to follow these Buddhist rituals, not reciting the mantra would be damaging to the departed.

On the third day, when Tsultrim Lhaksem's disciple Lobsang Gyatso came

89

to see him, I had everything prepared according to Gyayak Rinpoche's instructions. My teacher had not opened his eyes for hours now. After Lobsang Gyatso prostrated to our teacher, he quietly said to me, "This is the time to put on his robes." Along with his ritual objects, dorje and bell, I had kept the robes safe for him. Only Lobsang Gyatso and I knew where these items, which had helped to heal the sadness in Tsultrim Lhaksem's heart, had been hidden. We then dressed him in his robes, and Lobsang Gyatso went out to get Gyayak Rinpoche, who joined us right away.

As soon as I had the dorje and bell in my hands and began reciting the Guru Mantra, Tsultrim Lhaksem started to slip away. His breathing became shallow and irregular, as if it might stop at any moment. I recited "Namo Gurube, Namo Buddhaya, Namo Dharmaya, and Namo Sanghaya" in time with the rhythm of the bell. Tsultrim Lhaksem's eyes half-opened for a moment, and he stared at the ceiling, as if the sound of the bell had stirred him from the state of calm abiding. He nodded gently and exhaled. I waited to see him inhale, but the moment never came. He had passed away.

Lobsang Gyatso and I stepped out of the room. When we returned I looked at Tsultrim Lhaksem again, hoping he was still with us, wanting to hear him draw breath one more time. His face looked peaceful, as if he had fallen asleep and would get up as usual the next day.

Under the direction of Gyayak Rinpoche, Lobsang Gyatso, and Jamaga, we secretly performed the seven-day ritual to complete Tsultrim Lhaksem's peaceful passing. Although the seven days seemed interminable because of the danger of being discovered, nobody found out what we were doing. After the ritual was complete, we followed Gyayak Rinpoche's instructions to move my teacher's body to an open area on a mountain about eight hours away for a sky burial. In Tibet, a sky burial is the traditional way to dispose of the earthly body. The deceased is brought up to a mountain, where the body is cut into pieces and left for the vultures. This is the final act of generosity, offering the body that is no longer needed to sustain the lives of other creatures.

Unfortunately, because of increasing human activity, vultures had become rare in these mountains, so we stayed with the body and waited. Gyayak Rinpoche had told us that if sky burial was not possible, we should cremate the body. We decided to perform the cremation the next evening, after we prepared the site.

That night a strange thing happened. Sometime after midnight, Lobsang Gyatso woke us up, pulling us out of our tents. Pointing to my teacher's body he said, "Look at the fire, the fire!" We all clearly saw flames dancing above Tsultrim Lhaksem's body. We wanted to get closer, but Lobsang Gyatso held us back. The flames formed an orange fireball that lasted three hours, but the next day, when we checked my teacher's body, we found no charring, no sign at all of what had happened the previous night. Filled with awe, we recited prayers and sutras as we cremated Tsultrim Lhaksem's body in a hollow we had dug into the side of the mountain. In this way my first mentor departed from me.

When we returned to the monastery and reported the strange flames to Gyayak Rinpoche, he said calmly, "It was not fire, but rays of emanations leaving his body." From that day on, I no longer felt uneasy about death.

Not long after this, my closest and dearest friend, Jamaga, who had cared for me since 1958, suffered a severe stroke. He could no longer speak, although he was aware of everything around him. I took care of him at his bedside and secretly recited the Heart Sutra to him every day. Often I felt sleepy because I had worked hard during the day, so recitation and short naps alternated with each other. Sometimes when I awoke from my nap, I found him staring at me, as if reproaching me for not being more attentive.

For nine days, Jamaga grew weaker and weaker. However, on the 10th day, he was wide awake and alert. He gestured to me, but I could not understand what he wanted. I got closer to him and touched his face and hands. When I touched his head, he closed his eyes tightly and I began to recite prayers. Tears streamed down his face, and after a few minutes he lay still. He was not a high lama, just a simple monk who peacefully departed this world listening to the words of the Heart Sutra, the Mother of All Conquerors, the Prayer of Enlightened Beings, and the Wisdom Sutra.

When I discussed Jamaga's death with Gyayak Rinpoche, he told me, "Any person who is kind and compassionate will die in peace and without worry about the next life. But if he thinks only about making a profit, and treats Buddha's teachings as a means of making money, and does not practice the

91

dharma, he will die miserably and be reborn in the realm of misery. So no matter how many sutras we have studied, we must understand their true meaning, which is to have compassion for all sentient beings. In these days we are not allowed to learn the dharma, but we do have opportunities to practice on our own. Grasp those precious moments."

Gyayak Rinpoche's teaching was simple and clear. It is always with me, and I have seen the truth of his teaching in the lives of others. A monk we knew had spent his life charging people for performing rituals for the dead, motivated by personal gain. Although he had devoted much time to reciting mantras and to transferring the souls of the dead to other worlds, when illness began to torment him in his old age he could not control his fear and anger. When his friends reminded him to recite mantras for himself, he became so distraught that he could not remember a single prayer. At the time of his death, he was bewildered and panicky.

Another monk we knew did not learn many sutras. He hadn't had the opportunity due to religious reform, but he was kind and considerate to people around him. During the Cultural Revolution, he often said to me, "I have not been able to do much for people, yet I've never hurt anybody." The day he was to depart from this world he was chatting with his friends, who had come to visit. He said he could not sit, and wanted to lie down instead. He requested that his friends not leave him. He wanted them to talk about virtuous topics from the dharma. While everyone shared their joy with him, he passed away with the most peaceful smile on his face. Like Jamaga, he lived the teachings; they provided him with a good death and most likely a higher reincarnation in the life to come.

Fortunately, the basic architecture of Kumbum Monastery survived the damage wrought by positivist monks and Red Guards during the Cultural Revolution. After the wave of destruction to temples and historic treasures receded in the mid-'70s, we received a placard from the Beijing government. It read: "State-Protected Unit of Cultural Relics." Kumbum was to serve the same function as the handful of other surviving monasteries: provide a model of demonic traditions, a negative example from which young Red Guards could learn about exploitation in Tibet's feudal past. Monks were to become displays in a living museum.

Carried on a wave of leftist enthusiasm, thousands of people, mainly soldiers, farmers, and factory workers, visited our monastery-museum. Every year we received a sizable budget for maintenance of the main buildings. Of course the government sent a work team to manage the renovation projects, but in relative terms we had to consider ourselves lucky.

During the Cultural Revolution, thousands of monasteries, churches, mosques, and Taoist temples were shut down or destroyed. In a monastery there had been three kinds of property: public space (the temples), areas that were both public and private, and private homes owned by the monks. Although many temples had been saved, these homes became the focus of reformists, who tore them down so the land could be assigned to farmers living in the vicinity.

I was there when the work team sent laborers to the monastery to tear down houses that had belonged to monks and to sell the furniture and wooden structures. I saw hundreds of local people flocking into the monastery with their horses, donkeys, carts, and small tractors. The monastery was packed, and the sounds of shovels and hammers were deafening. Soon the houses were reduced to rubble. By afternoon, vehicles transporting logs and boards were leaving the monastery in a long, undulating dragon's tail. It was a clear day, so we could see the first truck reach the county seat, two kilometers away, just as the last one began its journey from the monastery.

The destruction lasted a month. All income from the sale of logs, boards, and other materials went to the government treasury. Finally, a report was issued that stated, "Under the directives of Premier Zhou [Enlai], your monastery has been preserved without any damage!" I could only wonder: How did the Communists define "damage"?

Fortunately, there was construction as well. In the summer of 1973 the head of Kumbum's production team of monks ordered some of us to take part in repainting damaged artworks. I took this opportunity to use my artistic and building skills, and there was much to do. Although some of it had been

93

destroyed, and the number of monks it housed had shrunk from more than 7,000 to 60, Kumbum Monastery was still very large.

Later that year our work team was assigned to renovate part of the main meditation hall, with its combination of Tibetan and Chinese architecture. Traditional Tibetan architecture required special wall decorations made from whip jute, which comes from a shrub. Ten young monks, including me, were sent out to collect whip jute and transport it back to the monastery on horse-drawn carts. We were all strong young men. Although it was a physically demanding task, we were excited about the opportunity to be on our own once again in the open country, away from the tightly controlled monastery.

We walked for two days to get to Changya Forest, a beautiful, dense woodland. It was a peaceful place, far from the nearest town. After we located the keeper of the forest and handed him our official assignment papers, he directed us to a place to pitch our tents. By working hard for several days, we collected a great mass of whip jute and took turns transporting it back to the monastery. After the first cartload left the forest, the nearest townspeople learned that *tulkus,* or reincarnated lamas, were cutting jute nearby, so they came to our campsite with food and tools to cut the jute for us, saying that monks don't know how to do such work. We knew that in their hearts they were doing this to help us; they just had to be careful about what they said.

Serdok Rinpoche and I were assigned to the second team among the eight monks. We had four horse-drawn carts, so we divided into two groups of four and took turns driving the carts. Before we set out on our return run, Oser, our team leader, told us to let the horses rest and feed on the new green grass poking up through the snow for a day. The following morning, as we prepared to leave the forest, it began to snow heavily. Oser told us to wait for one more day. However, when we emerged from our tents on the third morning, thick snow completely blanketed the ground, and tree branches were bending under the heavy, snowy canopies, like old men rising from heavy blankets.

We decided to set out anyway, but because of the snow, the carts became very heavy. The roads were muddy and icy, too, which made maneuvering the carts more difficult. When we finally approached the top of a mountain pass, the horses were straining at their traces but the heavy carts barely moved.

The threat of a cart slipping off the road and over the mountainside was constant. It was six in the evening before we finally stopped for what we cheerfully called breakfast.

While we filled ourselves with food, our hungry horses ate jute from the carts, which turned out to have such an intoxicating effect that they fell down. We thought they might be suffering from altitude sickness, so we tried to blow cigarette smoke up their nostrils—a local remedy. Unfortunately, it did not work. We had to find a local veterinarian. When we did, he told us our horses had been poisoned by the jute, and injected them with an antidote. They recovered, but the trip to the town of Chungja took us three days instead of the usual two. Horses and drivers alike were exhausted and suffering from snow blindness. Along the last leg of our journey, nomads and farmers who had heard that two tulkus were bringing whip jute back from the forest kindly brought us yogurt and bread.

Back at Kumbum, someone had reported our contact with various locals to the police. Our trip became a new example of exploiting the working class, for which we were denounced during the following 10 days of political meetings.

One gloomy day in September 1976, as I worked on a construction project outside the monastery, I suddenly heard funeral music blaring from the loudspeakers. After the somber dirge ended, a newscaster from the Central Chinese Radio announced, "The great leader, the revolutionary teacher, the founder of Chinese Marxism and Leninism, our beloved Chairman Mao Zedong has passed away."

We looked at each other, speechless. Then Lobsang Gelek, one of the monks, began to sing with elation. We silenced him immediately before he got into trouble. That same afternoon, cadres of the work team called together the monastery's monks for a meeting. They announced an urgent directive from the Beijing government regarding the imminent threat from the Soviet Union and possible domestic disturbances. Fear permeated the meeting. The next day, on the order of the cadres, we had to gather at the Huangzhong County conference hall, wear a white dahlia and a black armband, and keep our heads bent, to demonstrate the depth of our mourning for Mao.

People from all over the county arrived, wailing, sobbing, and sighing, although much of it struck me as theatrical rather than heartfelt. I looked inside myself for compassion for Mao, and I found it. Gyayak Rinpoche and Tsultrim Lhaksem had often said to me, "Life is impermanent; black and white karma follow us." Now it was Chairman Mao's turn to fear what was coming to him in his next life.

During his long rule, Chairman Mao had loved to torment his enemies. The most powerful dictator on earth had used his position to treat the 1 billion people of Tibet and China like hapless insects. What Mao hated most was religion and tradition, and he tried his best to erase all of China's culture, as well as that of Tibet and Inner Mongolia. His enemies were landowners and intellectuals. He humiliated his own loyal ministers, such as Zhu De, Liu Shaoqi, Peng Dehuai, and Deng Xiaoping, and some he put to death. Now he was facing his own passage through the bardo of death, where his authority would be useless. Death does not spare anyone; it treats the king and his subjects with total equality. Because Mao lacked compassion and had accumulated so much negative karma during his life, he could not help himself at this time, nor could others.

All of the monks at the county conference hall were having this same thought, I'm sure, but who would express it in public? Obeying an order, we lined up and bowed in front of Mao's death shrine. Once I had finished my part in this absurd spectacle, I returned to the monastery.

A few days later, the county government called for a huge memorial to honor Chairman Mao. Director Zhang of the county Revolutionary Committee told us that the entire country would be hearing the Beijing ceremony broadcast over the radio at the same time. The atmosphere of the gathering was tense: Soldiers and militiamen were heavily armed and on highest alert. Then the voice of Wang Hongwen, the vice chairman of China (and a member of Mao's notorious junta later known as the Gang of Four), came through the loudspeakers. He was followed by Hua Guofeng, the immediate successor of Chairman Mao, who praised Mao's accomplishments and began to wail with grief. Upon hearing this, Commissar Zhang signaled the cadres of Huangzhong County to commence with their keening. All the rest of us then copied the behavior of the cadres, screwing up our faces in pretended grief, knowing that if we did otherwise, we would be accused of antirevolutionary sentiments.

In the immediate aftermath of Mao Zedong's death, there were no political changes. At Kumbum we followed our usual routines in the fields, including sometimes pretending to be sick or just quietly taking off for a jaunt on our bicycles. One day, Serdok Rinpoche and I rode to Xining. We were young and loved riding bikes, watching movies, and bathing at the public baths—in other words, doing all the things we were not allowed to do. Sometimes we got caught and were denounced, but recently we had become less fearful of the cadres, sensing some uncertainty in their behavior.

On this day, the streets of Xining also seemed different. Instead of working, people were milling around, talking. We saw many big posters that said, "Down with Jiang, Wang, Zhang, Yao." Many people were looking at these posters and discussing what they meant. Some said, "Jiang refers to Jiang Qing, Mao's wife. This means the end of the dynasty of Mao Zedong." We were surprised and happy to hear this, and relayed the good news to Gyayak Rinpoche when we returned home.

Gyayak Rinpoche's reaction was cautious. "Nobody can predict what will happen, but one thing is for certain, this is a coup d'état. We'll have to be careful." In fact, the leadership of China did undergo great changes. First the Gang of Four was overthrown and jailed, then Chairman Hua Guofeng stepped down, and finally, Deng Xiaoping became the new ruler of China, beginning a new era.

During the Cultural Revolution, a management team consisting of seven or eight cadres had been stationed in the monastery to oversee our cultural relics. Fortunately for us they were honest, for we had heard many accounts of such teams in other monasteries selling off religious objects and pocketing the proceeds. One day, this team, which was still in place, assigned Gyayak Rinpoche, me, and another monk to take inventory of the monastery's sutras, which badly needed reorganization. During Mao's era, Gyayak Rinpoche and I could only dream of studying sutras, but now we were being asked to handle them!

Among Kumbum's most priceless treasures was a set of 111 volumes of the Kangyur, the Tibetan Buddhist canon, which had been copied by hand by Buton Rinpoche (1290–1364), one of our greatest scholars. He was especially

97

famous for respecting and honoring all the traditions of Tibetan Buddhism. His was the best preserved of all the sutras. It is said that Buton Rinpoche hand-copied only seven sets in his lifetime, and ours was one of the seven. There were also printed versions of the Kangyur at Nartang Monastery (built in 1153) near Shigatse. Although Nartang was not as large and spectacular as Tashi Lhunpo Monastery, it had a longer history. Forty or 50 volumes of their sets were missing, however, presumably burned by Red Guards along with the printing houses of Nartang Monastery. Our first priority was to replace the missing volumes with copies from a complete set. We wrote to the authorities explaining our mission, and we were allowed to proceed. The project lasted two years and included a complete reorganization of our library. What joy I felt at the chance to help restore some of the Buddhist canon, and to handle these rare, sacred volumes!

When Deng Xiaoping became leader, the Chinese government formally admitted that the Cultural Revolution and the Gang of Four were wrong. This announcement was followed by rumors that antirevolutionaries would be rehabilitated to normal life and political prisoners released. For more than 20 years we'd prayed daily for this day of change, and now that it had arrived, we could only wonder what future awaited us. Were we to be considered rehabilitated? After everything that had occurred during the Communist Chinese occupation, what would "normal" mean now? We were in a state of disbelief, relief, and uncertainty.

For many years Gyayak Rinpoche had suffered the relentless humiliation of being considered an antirevolutionary element. After the Cultural Revolution came to an end, three local police officials came to Gyayak Rinpoche's door and told him they were clearing his name of all crimes. (Of course, everyone knew that he and others like him were not guilty of the accusations leveled at them.) The police chiefs visiting with Gyayak Rinpoche looked sheepish, and probably felt guilty, too, because they had vehemently denounced and tormented him in the past. Now Gyayak Rinpoche would be their equal, and might even be appointed to an official position senior to theirs. If they had known this day was coming, they probably would have checked their revolutionary fervor. But it was too late for second thoughts.

The police chiefs felt awkward and uncomfortable, not even knowing how to address Gyayak Rinpoche. In the past they hadn't used his name or title, but had called him an "antirevolutionary element"; they could no longer do that. No official edict had been issued to allow them to call him "rinpoche." "Comrade" wouldn't work; that title was reserved for Communist Party members. Finally one of them came up with "elder." The other called him *shifu* (master), a title used by factory apprentices for their instructors.

After forcing Gyayak Rinpoche to "wear the hat," now they not only wanted him to forget the past, but to praise the Communist Party. Soon a big poster was hung on the front wall of Gyayak Rinpoche's house, stating his innocence while at the same time praising the Communist Party for its generosity. Not long afterward, Gyayak Rinpoche's innocence was publicly announced. We were relieved for our teacher, but Gyayak Rinpoche greeted this change with his usual equanimity.

Other good news also poured in. There were all sorts of people in my large clan, some wealthy, some poor, but all of them had suffered during the Cultural Revolution. Gyayak Rinpoche, my brother Pema, sister Dolma, Uncle Lobsang, Uncle Gheypa, and others had been made to wear hats, and my mother was humiliated along with them. Pema and Dolma had been forced to become servants of cadres, production teams, and positivists. My father, my brother-in-law, Uncle Chungchu Yengdan, Uncle Chungchu Oser, and Uncle Tsetar had all been sent to prison labor camps. My teacher, my house manager, and others also had been imprisoned. Some of them had disappeared, some had committed suicide, and others had died under murky circumstances. This nightmare had lasted more than 22 years. Those of us who had survived were indeed fortunate, and now were being freed to pursue their lives in a normal way. Some of my family members became monks, some started small businesses, some were recognized as tulkus, and some became chiefs of their tribes.

One day I heard that all remaining political prisoners were going to be released. I had never been so joyful. At long last, sanity seemed to be returning to my beloved Tibet. The role of Kumbum Monastery as a museum did not change, but it did expand. In addition to tourists, busloads of released prisoners were now being sent to Kumbum. This was how the government apologized to its former prisoners: They were given a small amount of money, an apology, and a tour of Kumbum.

When they arrived at the monastery, every one of these former enemies of the state held a bouquet of plastic flowers. Many of them had mixed feelings of grief and joy, but none could control the excitement that bubbled up from within. A distant relative we knew as Big Lobsang broke down in tears when he saw me. He and Uncle Oser had been imprisoned in the same cell, but although Big Lobsang had been released, my uncle was still in prison. Big Lobsang said, "For these many years, your uncle and I have worked together in the labor camp. I had to leave him behind, and my heart is aching even more than when I was forced to leave my parents and family a long time ago. Now he's working alone like an orphan, a helpless calf without its mother. Every day to him is as long as a year. Now is the time to visit him, if you can possibly do so."

I took his words to heart. The next day, Gyayak Rinpoche encouraged me in my decision to set out for the labor camp to visit Uncle Oser. "Be sure to comfort him and assure him that we will find a way to secure his release." Everyone knew the labor camps scattered all over Tibet and China were merciless hells. I often heard stories of the prison farms in my area: Kamdo, Serke, Wayu Shingka, Tsatsa Shingka, Delinkha, Nomenhon, Golmud, Homen, Guinan, Shandy, Nantan Prison, and others. Each prison had hundreds of work teams. Every county police bureau was in charge of a detention center, a prison, some labor camps, and reeducation centers. Some prison labor camps were, in themselves, as large as small counties.

Who were the prisoners, and how did they end up there? Some, of course, were there for being members of the exploiting class. Others had been incarcerated to settle private quarrels; their enemies had managed to convince the authorities that they were antirevolutionaries who needed to be locked up. Still others, like the nomads who were arrested to fill government quotas, were simply in the wrong place at the wrong time. And of course, there were a few criminals who had committed homicides and other serious crimes.

After prisoners were arrested, they were subjected to lengthy interrogations and then either locked up in cells or sent to prison labor camps. Sentences varied from 3 years to 10 or more. Some prisoners were granted a "rebirth," and although they had served their sentences they continued to live in the prison camp, receiving wages for their farm work. Now they could get married, have children, and live in the part of the prison camp set aside for married people, but they had no other personal freedoms.

Armed with an address provided in Uncle Chungchu Oser's last letter, I took a 24-hour bus ride and finally arrived at the command center of Delinkha Prison Farm. The next day I hitched a ride on a horse cart to my uncle's production team, where I found his friend, Old Wang. Old Wang was from Shanghai and had been in the prison labor camp for 20 years. He had been free for the last 10 years and had married a woman from Shanghai. He made noodle soup as a special treat for me and arranged for me to sleep in his dormitory.

With help from Old Wang, I finally found Uncle Oser on the third day of my search. He and his friend Old Zhu from Zhejiang Province were out herding horses. They were camping in a lone tent on top of a hill, far away from the farm. Uncle Oser looked careworn, but he had lost none of his wit and good humor. That night we stayed up until sunrise, regaling each other with stories and catching up on family news.

Uncle Chungchu Oser had been the previous Serdok Rinpoche's house manager, and in that role he had traveled to India and Beijing. After he had seen "Land Reform" coming to China, he realized it was only a matter of time before the government started taking land away from the monasteries. He had planned on taking the present Serdok Rinpoche to India, but nobody had supported his idea, and when someone reported his scheme to the Communist Chinese authorities, he was thrown in prison. Those prisoners who had been charged with being antirevolutionaries had been released by now, but because Uncle Oser's record contained the additional arbitrary charge of profiteering, he had not been allowed to go home.

While I was with him and Old Zhu, I asked why the prisoners didn't find ways to escape. Old Zhu told me that the police force and the army were so numerous that most attempted escapes had failed. One former nationalist military intelligence officer hid beneath a truck and successfully escaped to Hong Kong, but he was unusually lucky.

101

After a few days, when Uncle Oser learned that I was preparing to leave, he sat me down. "Now that I have seen you, I find it impossible to continue my life here. I must return to my family. Can you help me?"

"I will do everything I can once I return to Kumbum."

"I fear that I may not live that long. I will tell the warden I need to see a doctor, and perhaps he will grant me permission to leave with you."

Old Zhu broke in. "The warden will never agree to that. Do not anger him by trying."

Uncle Oser then decided to tell the labor camp authorities that his mother was on the verge of dying. We went along with him to the camp office to support his claim.

Supervisor Zhao was polite to me but treated my uncle rudely, speaking to him condescendingly, saying, "Chungchu, you have behaved well, but you're not eligible for release at this time. You have sufficient reason to visit your mother, but you must have official letters from her hospital and her commune. Once you obtain these documents, the prison will consider your request."

My uncle bent his head and cried. After we walked out of Zhao's office, I said to my uncle, "I promise to get these documents ready, and to mail them to Zhao so that you can return home. Please, just hang on until then." As I left the camp I looked back through the bus window and saw him standing there looking dejected, a solitary, hunched figure in a vast landscape. The moment I returned to the monastery, I made haste to secure these documents; we were elated when he soon returned home to Kumbum.

The release with rehabilitation of Uncle Oser and older prisoners like him was largely due to the heroic efforts of Tashi Wangshuk, the Communist revolutionary who had walked with Mao on the Long March but who had also always remained loyal to his Tibetan brothers. In the late 1950s, when many Tibetans rose up against the harsh policies of the Communists, the government cracked down on these rebels, and many were killed or imprisoned. In the 1980s, when Deng Xiaoping came to power, he proclaimed that the government had to right all wrongs. He ordered freedom and rehabilitation for all who, like him, had been imprisoned during the Cultural Revolution. But a solitary voice rose in protest. Tashi Wangshuk insisted that freedom and apologies and recompense should also be given to those who had been imprisoned during the Religious Reform Movement of the 1950s. His demands were met with opposition by the government officials in Qinghai—those who had been responsible for the injustices—and a fierce struggle ensued.

Tashi Wangshuk met privately with Deng Xiaoping, reminding him that they had been comrades during the early days of Mao's rise to power and making his case for those Tibetans who had been persecuted in the 1950s. Deng Xiaoping finally agreed, but on the condition that Tashi Wangshuk find evidence of injustice.

A team was formed to assist Tashi Wangshuk in his mission. One person in the team, Ma Yu Li, Tashi Wangshuk's secretary, described a frightening moment in the investigation. The group was working in the government offices of Qinghai Province when the building was surrounded by local soldiers. The task force locked the doors, fearing for their lives. They realized that they were investigating the very officials who were now in power, but they courageously opened the files from the 1950s of those Tibetans from the Amdo area who had been killed and imprisoned. Then they presented their findings to Deng Xiaoping.

I asked Ma Yu Li how many Tibetans had actually been killed. He said he couldn't tell me because it was "top secret." But as a result of the investigation, the provincial government had to publicly admit its mistake, and offered freedom along with apologies and compensation to those Tibetans who had managed to survive the injustices of the 1950s. I was pleased that Uncle Oser had benefited from the heroic efforts of Tashi Wangshuk and his staff. I only wished that my father had lived to enjoy this moment.

In the new environment following Mao's death and the end of the Cultural Revolution, the Communist Chinese government of Qinghai Province organized a meeting for religious personnel and local religious leaders, including lamas and rinpoches, imams, priests, scholars, and some local celebrities. Most of those attending had just been released from prison labor camps. Even before the cadres began to speak, we knew that Communist Chinese state policy would be changing to allow religious activities. The Party had already made its decisions in private: 30-plus years of experience with the Chinese State told us that much.

In this new climate, many people spoke up at this meeting, saying, "We need faith; we need religion." A small number disagreed, and spoke ingratiatingly about the need to maintain the current state without religion. Choesang Rinpoche was 70 years old, and had spent the last 20 years in prison. During the Cultural Revolution he was imprisoned with Kuomintang nationalist army generals and had won their respect because of his firm Buddhist faith and practice. He told us an interesting story.

During the Cultural Revolution, two opposing factions of the Red Guard, the "conservatists" and the "rebels," fought fierce battles to demonstrate their revolutionary spirit. When the conservatists won out, they sent the rebels to prison, where the guards treated them very harshly. However, just a month later the political atmosphere changed completely when Chairman Mao decided to rehabilitate the rebels. Upon hearing of their imminent release, the rebels in prison swore to settle their old score with the conservatists, and to kill those policemen and guards who had brutalized them.

When the prison guards caught wind of this plan, they quietly unlocked the prison cells at midnight and slipped away from their posts. The next morning, when the rebels were formally granted amnesty, they rushed out of their cells looking for the guards and policemen, chanting the slogan "Long live Chairman Mao." But they found no one; the guards were long gone. That night the rebel inmates returned to their own cells and went to bed, since they had made no travel arrangements and had nowhere else to sleep. When they awoke the next morning, they found their cells locked again, and the harsh voices of the guards and policemen ringing in the hallway. Mao had changed his mind yet again as to who the enemies of the state were.

Choesang Rinpoche also told everyone the story of a prisoner who found two glass IV bottles and cut them open by taking a string dipped in lamp oil and wrapping it around the top of the bottle in a ring, which he then set on fire. While the glass was still hot, he poured cold water on it, cracking the glass neatly where the string had been. The prisoner used paints left over from making propaganda signs to embellish the insides of the bottles with exquisite renderings of flowers and birds, and displayed the painted bottles in his cell.

A guard saw the painted bottles and asked the prisoner where he had gotten them. Upon hearing that the prisoner had painted them himself, the guard scolded him and confiscated the bottles. Later, when the supervisor of the prison saw the bottles, he was equally impressed with their beauty and claimed them for himself. The bottles continued to be passed in this way up the chain of command until they reached the chief warden of the prison. He was so taken with the prisoner's craftsmanship that he decided the bottles would make good gifts. He sought out other prison artists and established a "Prison Leaders Gift Factory." Choesang Rinpoche was among the artists. This factory lasted two years, during which prisoners painted countless IV bottles.

Choeshi Rinpoche, another released prisoner, spoke up as well. He told us that prisoners often had to wash the feet of their guards. If they were good at it, some of them were promoted to "nurse" in the prison hospital. While working as a nurse, Sonam Tsemo Rinpoche learned how to perform catheterizations. Often he was called to treat patients in their cells under the supervision of a guard. He was so gentle and became so skilled that his patients rarely felt any pain.

One of Sonam Tsemo Rinpoche's experiences with catheterization was a source of much inmate humor. The prison supervisor's wife suffered from a urinary tract infection. The supervisor asked Sonam Tsemo Rinpoche to catheterize her, but he had only ever worked with male patients. To make matters worse, if he made a mistake with the supervisor's wife, there would be terrible consequences.

The supervisor's wife removed her pants and climbed onto the clinic table, in great pain, while the supervisor stood next to her. Sonam Tsemo Rinpoche had no experience with female anatomy, so he wasn't even sure if the tubes designed for men would work on a female patient. He picked out a tube that he hoped would be appropriate and inserted it into her vagina, paying close attention to her facial expressions.

She frowned, lips pursed, indicating pain. The supervisor cautioned him, "Be gentle, be gentle." Sonam Tsemo Rinpoche carefully poked her with the tube for a few moments, but nothing happened. He wanted to ask the supervisor a few questions, but wasn't sure how to phrase them. He began muttering to himself. The supervisor said, "Don't mumble. You must accomplish this task!"

Sonam Tsemo Rinpoche then picked up a flashlight and began to look closely at his patient's private parts. This time he discovered something significant, so he asked the supervisor, "Do you think there are two holes here, one above the other?" The supervisor was abrupt: "Of course!" So Sonam Tsemo Rinpoche inserted the tube correctly, and a flood of urine poured out on the table, much to the relief of the supervisor's wife and to that of Sonam Tsemo Rinpoche. When the supervisor turned to express his gratitude, Rinpoche had already ducked out quickly.

At this meeting there was a spontaneous outpouring of stories, most of them remarkable for their absurdity, reflecting the happiness of those who had recently been set free. According to some cadres, this time release was not merely amnesty with rehabilitation; it was "release with leniency," which seemed to mean that due to the mercy of the government, everyone was being fully pardoned for their "crimes."

Throughout the meeting I heard people prefacing their stories by saying, "Now that life will return to normal." Normal? What was normal? What, after all these years, could the word possibly mean?

I was now 26. For the past 18 years—since I was 8 years old—my normal life had included living in the empty shell of what had once been a great monastery. I had survived the first famine ever experienced in Tibet, induced by Mao's Great Leap Forward. I had rubbed shoulders with death with an awful and numbing frequency. Years of forced hard labor and public denunciation had reduced my self-image to that of a leper. If not for the secret, steady guidance of my teachers and protectors—Jamaga, Tsultrim Lhaksem, and Gyayak Rinpoche—how could I have stayed in touch with my own humanity? It was the seed of dharma that sustained me, soothed me, and, eventually, I hoped, would give me the strength to somehow escape the dragon's lair.

The horror of my story was not just what had happened to so many Tibetans, Mongolians, and Chinese—that was normal in Tibet throughout the 1960s and again in the 1980s. No, the true horror resided in the possibility that those terrible experiences might divert our Tibetan people's karma away from the blessings of future happiness.

PART III

ON THE POLITICAL STAGE

Seeing all living beings to be my mothers most kind,
bless me that I, recalling the sufferings of the weak,
turn from practice born of self-interest
toward an effortless love and compassion.

—Lama Tsong Khapa

CHAPTER 8

A COMMUNIST MATCHMAKER MEETS THE PANCHEN LAMA

One day in 1978, Gyayak Rinpoche called me into his rooms at Kumbum. He was seated, as usual, on his sleeping platform, leaning against a rolled-up quilt, with a small table in front of him. He asked me to stir up the hot coals in a small brass brazier, and as the unburned straw flared up, I took the pot and poured us both some tea.

We were alone in the room. Quietly, he turned to me and said, "I have some disturbing news. Our Panchen Lama may get married soon. I want you to go to Beijing as a secret emissary on my behalf. No one must know of your mission. When you arrive, please give my letter directly to the Panchen Lama. He'll understand the situation. His parents are living with him in his home in the Eastern District of Beijing. Apah and Amah (this was how we addressed the Panchen Lama's parents) will be absolutely opposed to the idea of marriage. I want to reassure and comfort them, and at the same time instruct the Panchen Lama on the correct way to release himself from his vows, should he choose to do so. After you hand him my letter, tell him that if he can get permission from the government, I will travel there in person."

I was surprised at Gyayak Rinpoche's words, wondering how he had received this startling information and feeling a mixture of joy and sadness. I was happy because I was going to see the Panchen Lama after more than

15 years. I must also confess that I was thrilled about going to Beijing for the first time. But I was very upset by the idea that he was about to marry; I could not understand how he could give up his life as a monk and return to lay life now that the bad times seemed to lie behind us.

I had to be careful on this mission not to draw unwanted attention to myself. Fortunately, I had invited my mother to live with me and help manage things some five years earlier, after Tsultrim Lhaksem passed away in 1973, so it seemed perfectly natural to invite her and another monk, my friend Bhadi, to travel with me to Beijing for some sightseeing. After two days and nights, our train pulled into Beijing station at five in the morning. I stood in line at a small window to register, as was required of all visitors to the city, and then deposited my mother and Bhadi at a friend's house, where we would spend the night. Then I set off in search of 57 Eastern Headquarter Lane, the address Gyayak Rinpoche had given me.

When I eventually found the place, its massive iron gate was locked. Through a crack in the gate I could see soldiers guarding the grounds. The Cultural Revolution had conditioned me to be nervous whenever I saw policemen, militiamen, or government officials, so I was afraid to knock or call attention to myself. Fortunately, I had exchanged my Tibetan *chuba* for an ordinary Mao suit, and like so many Chinese I was wearing a medical mask for protection against the freezing air of Beijing, which helped to hide my uneasiness. Praying that the Panchen Lama's parents would come through the gate before too long, I ducked in and out of a small candy shop across the street for warmth until the shopkeeper began to peer at me suspiciously.

After half an hour, my prayers were answered. A little side gate opened and Amah emerged on her way to market. Although I had not seen her for more than 10 years, I recognized her immediately. However, when I rushed to greet her, she did not recognize me and was frightened. Delighted once she realized who I was, she took me to a small restaurant and began plying me with questions, having been so long out of touch with the land of her birth and the people she knew. When she inquired about Gyayak Rinpoche, the Panchen Lama's lifelong spiritual teacher, she broke down in tears. After a few minutes, she went back to the house and returned with Apah.

Both of them were overcome with emotion. Tears streaming down their cheeks, they repeated again and again, "We haven't seen anyone from home for so many years. . . ." They described the hardships they had suffered during the Cultural Revolution and bemoaned the Panchen Lama's decision to marry. "No previous Panchen Lama has ever married. If he gets married, he will have to renounce his vows; his reputation will be ruined. If we ever are able to return home to Tibet someday, how will we explain this?"

Finally, they calmed down enough to ask why I had come to Beijing. After I told them I had a letter from Gyayak Rinpoche for the Panchen Lama, they invited me for a visit to their home the next day and asked that I bring my mother and Bhadi along.

The following morning I called to arrange our meeting. Apah answered, and, to my surprise, he said we should come over immediately. When we arrived at the house, Apah was waiting at the gate. He tried to explain who we were to the gatekeeper in broken Chinese: "Relatives, relatives . . . home-town, hometown . . . ." Finally the guard made a note of our names and let us pass. Inside the gate I realized that 57 Eastern Headquarter Lane was a mansion, built in the Russian-inspired socialist style reserved for government officials. Apah told me that Shi Liang, a woman cadre member close to Mao's inner circle, also lived on the estate.

The house was heated to feel like summer—something we were not used to. Amah greeted us, and we followed her through the silent splendor of the house, hearing only the echoing sounds of our own footsteps. Suddenly I felt as if I was in a sacred place, far from the noisy world of modern China. In my imagination I could hear His Holiness the Dalai Lama walking the halls of the Potala Palace and the Panchen Lama strolling through in his quarters at Tashi Lhunpo.

We entered the Panchen Lama's study, which was furnished as a small sitting room. Everything was neatly arranged and very simple compared to the elegance of his former quarters at Tashi Lhunpo. We waited a few minutes for the Panchen Lama to join us, and when he walked in I was struck once again by his height, his remarkable charisma, and his good spirits, all the more remarkable after the many years he had spent in prison. He greeted us in the Amdo dialect. My mother was so moved by his presence that she started sobbing as we prostrated and offered him a khata. I handed him Gyayak Rinpoche's letter, which he lifted above his head as a gesture of respect for his teacher. As he opened it and began to read, he grew excited, and I knew that he was drinking in every word—an expression of the deep bond between teacher and disciple.

The Panchen Lama invited us to dine with him in his formal dining room. Besides the Panchen Lama, his parents, and the three of us, only two other people were present. One of them was the previous Panchen Lama's *má chin-mo,* or chef, a highly respected man who was also close to this Panchen Lama. When I had first met him many years earlier, he had been a robust man with a heavy beard and thick black eyebrows. Now, in his seventies, he was thin and his hair, gray.

The other guest was Shadrong Karpu, a high-ranking rinpoche from Amdo who had been sent by the government to persuade the Panchen Lama to get married. I had met him many years before when he was a deputy director of the Qinghai Provincial People's Congress. About 50 years old now, he looked like a scholar, but many suspected that he was secretly a member of the Communist Party. I later learned that the first person the government had asked to persuade the Panchen Lama to get married—and to mediate with his father (who they knew would be opposed to the idea)—was Tashi Wangshuk, one of the first Tibetans to become a Communist revolutionary. However, when Tashi Wangshuk refused, Shadrong Karpu enthusiastically accepted the task. Perhaps he had wanted to validate his own lifestyle: He himself had given up his vows in order to get married.

Dinner was a precious opportunity to spend time with the Panchen Lama, but I remember it as a gloomy affair. Everyone was weighed down by thoughts of the Panchen Lama's upcoming marriage. I left with a feeling of uncertainty as to whether arrangements could be made for a visit by Gyayak Rinpoche, but at least the arrival of his letter had somewhat lifted the family's spirits.

Because Communist China was moving away from the repressive authoritarianism of the recent past, people in Beijing were happy, and the city was lively. I took my mother to visit the Forbidden City, the Summer Palace, and the Heavenly Platform at the foot of Tiananmen Square. As we walked through the city, we were regarded curiously because my mother wore traditional Tibetan dress with the identifying striped apron, and Bhadi and I clearly looked Tibetan. Local people and foreign tourists alike took great interest in us, and snapped photos.

Soon after we returned home to Kumbum from our mission, Gyayak Rinpoche, as he had hoped, was contacted by the central and provincial United Fronts, requesting that he meet with the Panchen Lama. He did so, and stayed for several months. After he returned from Beijing, he told us all about his visit.

The Panchen Lama had told him that soon after he was released from prison, Yang Jingren, a Muslim radical leftist and director of the central United Front, met with him, encouraging him to forget the hardship of the past years and to support the political liberalization of Deng Xiaoping. Also, as one minority member to another, Yang encouraged the Panchen Lama to get married as an expression of his loyalty to the government and as a way to help make things better for the Tibetan people. According to Yang's argument, if the Panchen Lama were to marry, the government would be reassured of his undivided loyalties and thereby be more inclined to put into effect any plans he might have for the future. The Panchen Lama agreed to consider Yang's suggestion.

Right after this meeting, Yang began to spread the rumor that Tibet's "Living Buddha," the Panchen Lama, *wanted* to get married. When Dong Qiwu, an 80-year-old former general of the nationalist government and a mahjong partner of Yang, brought this news home to his family, his daughter perked up with interest. She had two daughters herself. Li Jie, the younger one, was a smart, pretty college student, so her parents were not concerned about her future. However, the elder daughter, although attractive, was in her thirties; time was passing, and the family felt a certain urgency to get her wed. What a relief they would feel if the Panchen Lama would marry her.

They met with Yang, asking him to be the go-between, to which Yang happily agreed. He made arrangements for Dong Qiwu's daughter to bring her older daughter to visit the Panchen Lama. Li Jie, however, insisted on tagging along: She wanted to have a look at this famous Tibetan leader. Surprising everyone, the Panchen Lama did not want to marry the older sister,

113

but he took a lively interest in Li Jie. It was truly the case that "The flowers carefully planted do not blossom, while unattended willow shoots grow into shade trees."

Yang insisted that the Panchen Lama send an application to the central government, petitioning them to grant his wish to marry. The Panchen Lama did as Yang suggested, no doubt expecting that such a request would take months, or even years, to be answered. To everyone's surprise, he received a response the same afternoon. Obviously the marriage had support at the highest levels.

Some supporters of the Panchen Lama claim that the Chinese must have had a metaphorical gun pointed at his head to force him to disavow his religious commitments—that he would do so only under heavy coercion. Others are convinced that he had fallen in love and wanted to leave monastic life in order to marry. My personal view is that the event has to be considered in the context of the time. Living through the years between 1958 and 1978, whether in or out of prison, left a peculiar stamp on all Tibetans, and perhaps all Chinese as well. Unless one has grown up in a situation in which everything is torn away and replaced by regimentation and slogans and fear, it's impossible to comprehend the profound effects of such conditioning.

During that time our perceptions were shaped by trauma in a way that made us see and think in peculiar ways. The entire population had been held hostage, so perhaps all of us were suffering from a sort of mass Stockholm syndrome. When Comrade Yang said that by marrying, the Panchen Lama would be helping the Tibetan people, he spoke the truth as he saw it. Party faithful viewed a Muslim who tended pigs, in violation of his faith, as a more reliable Communist, and therefore as a more loyal and trustworthy person. In much the same way, a former monk who had married was considered to be truer to Communist ideology and therefore deserving of greater reward. I know that the Panchen Lama would not seek reward for himself, but that he would make any sacrifice necessary for the Tibetan people. Yang's clever manipulation preyed on perceptions left over from the Cultural Revolution.

Nevertheless, times were changing. It wasn't long before the central government—in fact, Deng Xiaoping himself—realized that to let the Panchen Lama marry would be a grave political mistake. Even the *appearance* that the Chinese were forcing him to renounce his religious vows would cause an international scandal. Unfortunately, this realization came too late: The couple had already married. The government's solution to this dilemma was to forbid the Panchen Lama's marriage to be publicized. His wife was never allowed to attend religious or public events with him.

The softening of policies made possible by Deng Xiaoping's reforms began in December of 1978 and would last for more than a decade, until the tragedy of Tiananmen Square in 1989. In this new climate of liberalization the Communist Chinese gave more authority to local government and greater opportunities to individuals. More importantly for me and those around me was the fact that monks now had growing freedom to practice and reestablish monasteries. I felt a deep sense of relief, and excitement at the possibility that now I could resume my education. As a boy I had chafed at my studies, but now, in my late twenties, I knew that only with proper spiritual training could I fulfill my destiny as a rinpoche—and I had a lot of catching up to do.

In 1978, along with a young Tibetan man named Tsering, who shared my ambitions, I tried to apply to Qinghai University for Nationalities. The two of us spent several months running about the county gathering the necessary documents, signatures, and stamps. We rode our bikes to the university in Xining to apply, only to be told that the university didn't give out applications; they could only be obtained from our local administrator. For several more weeks we were passed from office to office, from those who didn't have jurisdiction to those who were out of applications. At last, Tsering managed to contact a relative in the bureaucracy, who reluctantly parted with two tattered applications buried in his desk. He handed them to us with disdain, as if to say that a farmer and a monk had no business in a university. We didn't care—we had the applications. We excitedly filled them out and went in search of the town mayor to get his signature. After several months of being told that he was either busy or not in, the application deadline passed. Liberalization had not yet reached us. That was the old way.

A year later, Serdok Rinpoche and I were approached and asked if we would like to enter the newly formed Department of Tibetan Studies at Qinghai University for Nationalities. Students were needed. We applied without approvals, signatures, or seals, and were promptly accepted. This was the new way.

Gyayak Rinpoche held a special gathering at Kumbum—a sort of farewell party with family and friends—to celebrate the resumption of our formal education. Upon arriving at the school, Serdok Rinpoche and I entered the new graduate-level program. No matter how reluctant I once had been as a student (and Serdok Rinpoche had felt the same way), our second chance was a dream come true.

The program began with seven students—six Tibetan and one Chinese Buddhist. We all spoke fluent Tibetan as well as Chinese. Most of us were not monks; instead, we came from many different professional backgrounds. Some of us were teachers, some bureaucrats, one was even a Party cadre—but all of our colleagues had solid educations and had performed a great deal better at their studies than Serdok Rinpoche and I had. We had to work very hard to keep up, because while we had been working in the fields for the past 15 years we had been forbidden to read books, and our secret studying had been intermittent at best. Although our Tibetan classmates showed us respect as rinpoches, our skills and familiarity with academic subjects lagged far behind theirs.

Shar Dong Rinpoche, a very knowledgeable and exceedingly virtuous man, taught our core classes. He had been born to a poor family and had practiced and studied Buddhism at Cha Chung Monastery. At a young age, Shar Dong Rinpoche had already become quite learned. During the religious reformation, he was labeled a counterrevolutionary. Despite the hardships he suffered, Shar Dong Rinpoche treated those chaotic years as an opportunity to practice forbearance, and he maintained strict religious discipline. Such virtuous behavior led people to respect him deeply in later days. After years as a laborer on a communal farm near his village, he was appointed to a teaching position when the university reopened in 1978. Shar Dong Rinpoche was one of my Buddhist masters who inspired me, and to whom I can never express enough gratitude.

English was one subject in particular that I had always wanted to study.

What a happy surprise it was when I arrived at Qinghai University for Nationalities and found that English would be offered as a subject. I registered immediately. The English teacher, Mr. Zhuang, was a former officer of the nationalist army of Chang Kai-shek who had been in jail for more than 20 years. He had studied law prior to being an instructor in English. Although he claimed that he had forgotten all the English he had once learned, the other teachers still appreciated his language skills—at least his pronunciation—since it sounded to their ears just like what they heard on our English-language recordings.

However, a year later, my accomplishments, or lack thereof, in the study of English were confirmed when I tried to communicate with a visiting English speaker. I could not understand even a single sentence he spoke. Even worse, when I tried to say, "Welcome to Kumbum Monastery," he shook his head repeatedly, apologizing in broken Chinese, "Sorry, sorry. I don't speak Tibetan." Discouraged, I gave up my study of English, not knowing that I was only putting off the inevitable.

My other studies went better. I took courses in Tibetan language and literature and Buddhism. The intricacies of my own language had fascinated me since my long-ago stay at Tashi Lhunpo, when I had come across that book on rhetoric in the library. Studying grammar, composition, and literature remains a pleasure for me to this day, even as I struggle to improve my English. At that time, religious studies were still Communist controlled, and were therefore more about the history, doctrine, and evils of religion than about the teachings of the dharma. But I did not completely want for proper Buddhist teachings, because Shar Dong Rinpoche took me under his wing and gave me oral transmissions appropriate to a monk.

One day in the fall of 1979, I was ordered to attend an urgent meeting in Kumbum. Although at this point my role at Kumbum was minimal, I was still nominal abbot of the monastery and retained official responsibilities. When I arrived I saw that all of the monastery's monks, including Gyayak Rinpoche and Serdok Rinpoche, had gathered. Tashi Wangshuk, the Tibetan Communist who still played an important role in the Party, was about to make an announcement.

"The Party's good policy on nationality and religion has returned," he said. "Everybody has the freedom to believe in religion again. You monks should wear robes again, and return to your practice."

Although policy at that time had become looser, I still could not believe what I was hearing. What for decades had been considered "opium to poison the minds of the masses" was suddenly acceptable? Should I believe him? Or was this another Red Guard trick to uncover malcontents? I was incredulous, and not alone in my fears. Many others had the same reaction. No one said a word.

Tashi Wangshuk added, "Not only that, but soon you will receive important guests, representatives of the Dalai Lama. We will let them witness with their own eyes our great policy of freedom, and our openness of nationality and religion. They will report this to the Dalai Lama in India, which will encourage him to return to his own country." (By this time, the Dalai Lama was living in a flourishing government in exile in the Indian hill station of Dharamsala.)

Now we understood what was truly going on. These Communist-approved religious activities were merely intended to fool the Dalai Lama's delegation during their visit. But after they left, what would happen? Many monks feared that we would be punished. The local county and provincial Communist leaders seemed to understand our concern, so they tried to allay our fears by saying that "nobody should worry about anything. The Cultural Revolution has completely perished. The Gang of Four is gone. The central government's new policy is moving forward. Please, nobody should have the slightest worry."

Even with such reassurances, we did not completely believe Tashi Wangshuk. After the announcement, some monks did begin wearing robes again, some started chanting sutras and even lit butter lamps—but most of us were still very careful. I was given leave for two days to stay at the monastery since they wanted to receive the Dalai Lama's delegation at my residence (which would have been proper protocol if the last 20 years had never happened). The Communists arranged for a few friends and me to clean the guest reception areas of my former quarters, the drawing room, and the Buddha shrine room, which had been emptied when we were forced to move to other lodgings.

As we cleaned up, a local layperson, hearing that religion was now permitted, came to me and requested that I light 100 butter lamps in the shrine to purify the spirits of his parents. They had died many years before, but at that time no blessings had been allowed. I agreed to hold the ceremony, even though I felt quite nervous. Penalties for such things had been very severe in the past. To perform the ceremony properly, monks are required to chant as they light the lamps, but our practice during the ban had been to chant only a short sutra silently—and quickly—in an effort not to get caught.

This time we would do it properly. However, once we had finished and the dark shrine was lit by the warmth of softly dancing flames, we were surprised by the door bursting open. There was Gyaltsen Dragpa, the monastery security officer. Gasping for breath he said, "Comrade Dru Bum Gyal from the public security bureau is coming to examine the rooms to be sure that everything is ready for the arrival of the delegation. This is terrible! Where can we hide these hundred lamps?!"

At that moment, Dru Bum Gyal and others barged in. We were so frightened we had no idea what to do. But Dru Bum Gyal, seeing the expressions on our faces, only laughed and said, "Good, good, this shows you have started to trust our Party's policy, even though all of you are still a bit nervous." Then he turned to Gyaltsen Dragpa and said, "Please tell them not to worry so much. Everyone should open his mind, especially you. As team leader, you should be the first. Only in this way can you lead the masses." His face—insincere, reassuring, and intimidating all in the same moment—was a study in the absurdity of the times.

From the way Dru Bum Gyal spoke, it would seem that there had been no purging of the monasteries and no Cultural Revolution, that it was *we* who had chosen not to fulfill our religious obligations of our own volition, not because of the heavy, mailed fist of the Communist Party of the People's Republic of China. At any rate, the situation gradually improved, although we had been through too much to readily put our faith in it.

A few days later, under bright morning sunlight, eight rinpoches met happily, some for the first time in many years. Gyayak Rinpoche, Serdok Rinpoche, and I were joined by Gongya Rinpoche, Tashi Rinpoche, and three others

119

who had recently been released from work farms: Choeshi Rinpoche, Kegya Rinpoche, and Yang Gya Rinpoche.

We assembled in Kumbum Monastery with officials from the local county and provincial governments in a tree-shaded courtyard. Behind us rose the breathtaking blue-tiled Shapden Lhakang Temple, built in honor of a visit in the eighteenth century from the Seventh Dalai Lama. We were awaiting the arrival of the delegation sent by the Fourteenth Dalai Lama. Since the Dalai Lama had been forced to escape to India in 1959, he and his supporters had been constantly denounced by the Communists for betraying their country. And yet here we were, holding khatas in our open hands to welcome the "traitors"! This was indeed an unbelievable change in policy.

Having heard the news that a delegation from His Holiness was coming, people were arriving from all directions. Among them were many undercover policemen dressed in plain clothes, but immediately identifiable by the big straw hats and sunglasses that hid their faces. Except for a few monks who had been ordered to wear robes as part of the charade, the rest of us were in lay clothes. Even rinpoches wore the blue or gray Mao uniform to which we had all become so accustomed. The younger rinpoches, including me, who still had full heads of hair, looked like tractor drivers on a farm.

Eventually, eight jeeps drove up the road trailed by clouds of dust and continued into the monastery courtyard, honking their horns. Five members of the Dalai Lama's delegation descended from the vehicles, accompanied by a sizable retinue of officers, journalists, and security personnel. After the provincial governor delivered his introductions, Juchen Thubtan, head of the Dalai Lama's delegation, presented a khata to Gyayak Rinpoche. Juchen Thubtan wore a long, neatly tailored Tibetan chuba over his white shirt and slacks. He spoke formally in a soft, confident voice, conveying the impression of an accomplished diplomat.

Another delegation member, Lobsang Samten, the Dalai Lama's older brother, also wore a chuba, but hiked up casually above the knees, revealing flashy bell-bottom trousers. His Western appearance was very surprising to us. He also sported a mustache and unruly hair covering his ears and growing down his neck. The other three men also wore chubas, but as they always carried cameras, pens, and notebooks in their hands, they looked more like secretaries than delegates. Nevertheless, their bright silver cameras, so unlike the box-style Brownies we knew, caught the eyes of our young monks.

Accompanied by local authorities, we led the guests on a tour of the temples and halls of the monastery. Before entering each site, monks performed all the traditional rituals—prostration, lamp lighting, and chanting—that had long been forbidden. It was strange, doing what we were born to do, and yet feeling uncomfortable, even fearful, while doing it. With the exception of Gyayak Rinpoche and some of the older monks, most of us had forgotten which sutras to chant under which circumstances, and some of us had even forgotten how to chant at all.

At noon the delegation was invited to dine in my refurbished residence. Chatting and treating guests with food from my homeland was a far happier task than any I'd been assigned in the past 20 years. On the other hand, for our own safety we needed to be very careful while conversing with the delegates. Our Communist handlers had briefed us on suitable topics of conversation beforehand, such as our freedom to practice Buddhism and government support for maintaining the monastery. We had also been shown how to be noncommittal when dealing with certain issues, especially when it came to the difficulty of our lives over the past years. We were to pretend that everything had been just fine and hope that the delegation did not raise difficult issues. How ironic that to us this felt like freedom!

We sat around the table after lunch, drinking tea. The delegation began asking us more probing questions, but we were relieved that they did not ask the rinpoches many questions directly. Instead, they addressed our accompanying officials, as though they were aware of the strict limitations we were under, and of the severity of our punishment should we speak forthrightly.

The secretary of our county Party committee, Zhu Zi Min, spoke for the welcoming committee, peppering his speech with slogans. "Now a lot of changes are happening in our area. The people's standard of living is gradually improving; all is forgiven. You can come back and if you don't like what you see, you can leave again. On this visit, you should stay longer to see for yourselves how free our religious policy now is. As for what happened in 1958 and the Cultural Revolution, that was all done by Lin Biao and the Gang of Four, and has already become past history."

At the end of this monologue one member of the delegation suddenly asked, "Why aren't these rinpoches wearing robes?" Secretary Zhu turned to us, pretending surprise, and asked disingenuously: "Yes . . . why aren't you wearing robes?" We looked at each other, dumbfounded. A local officer from the United Front jumped in to smooth things over: "Of course they have the freedom to wear or not wear robes. They probably just don't want to."

And so it went: Delegation members asked questions and officials provided answers, but we rinpoches simply kept chatting, laughing, listening, and watching—feeling blessed just to be with a delegation sent by His Holiness. One delegate mentioned that when their group had first arrived in Beijing, they had met briefly with the Panchen Lama and Ngapo Ngawang Jigme. The afternoon flew quickly by.

After the luncheon, some of the cadres excused themselves to rest. Several members of the delegation asked me to accompany them up to the roof to take photos and videos of the panoramic views surrounding the monastery, which sits nestled in the hills like the center of a lotus. During our excursion to the rooftop, no officials accompanied us, so for a few minutes, I was free to talk. The delegates asked me to review briefly the history of Kumbum, a safe topic, which I discussed for their video microphones. But soon the talk turned serious.

Once the cameras were off, I described in some detail our lives in the recent past. As well as I could I told them the truth. When I mentioned that only 10 days ago Kumbum was closed as a working monastery, they were clearly surprised. The head of the delegation asked me, "Which do you think is better for us: to come back or to stay abroad?" I understood that he was talking about His Holiness, and perhaps all of those in exile. I told him that of course it was better to return, but it might still be too early, and we should wait to see how the liberalization policy evolved. They understood, and nodded to each other in agreement.

Before their departure, the delegation took pictures with the accompanying security officers. They also told the rinpoches to stand together for a group photo. We looked a sorry lot: beaten-down proletariats in our cheap

Mao suits. When it was time for the convoy to leave, we escorted the delegates to the parking lot, where the crowd had grown to thousands of curious onlookers, stretching all the way to Rusar, a mile away. Upon seeing the large group, the head of the delegation asked me, "Among these spectators, how many are Tibetan?"

"Very few," I told him, and went on to explain that most local residents outside the monastery were now Chinese or Muslim.

After seeing the delegation off I thought once again of the absurdity of this charade we were playing. My late teacher, Tsultrim Lhaksem, once said: "Politics is like a child's game: Sometimes people are enemies, and then they become friends." (And, as I would learn, one day they would become enemies again; it was not just a process, but a cycle.)

Not long thereafter a delegation led by the Dalai Lama's eldest brother, Tagtser Rinpoche (Thubten Norbu), came to Kumbum to visit. He was accompanied by his wife, Kunyang, and sons Lhundrup, Kunga, and Jigme, as well as a professor from Beijing. Tagtser Rinpoche was tall and very handsome with graying hair, wearing a reddish suit. His wife wore a traditional Tibetan dress with striped apron. The three sons were very charming.

A long line of people waited to greet Tagtser Rinpoche. He was very gracious and thanked everyone for coming. When someone wanted to prostrate before him, he protested: "No, no, don't do that. Humans prostrating to each other is not meaningful."

After the meal, Gyayak Rinpoche, Choeshi Rinpoche, various government officials, and I accompanied Tagtser Rinpoche on a grand tour of the monastery. As we walked around the Kalachakra stupa, Tagtser Rinpoche looked toward the hills where his home had once stood. He turned to the county director and asked, "Where's my old residence?" The director, knowing that it had been destroyed during the Cultural Revolution, was taken aback and immediately turned to Gyayak Rinpoche and said, "Yes, where is his residence?" Gyayak Rinpoche couldn't answer truthfully, so he attempted a lame excuse: "During the past years many houses have collapsed because of all of the rains. Your house was one of them." But Tagtser Rinpoche was not fooled. He turned to the county director and said, "Oh! So you people have destroyed my

123

residence." Later he confided to friends how horrified he was to see the destruction and neglect at Kumbum. He never got over it.

After a few days, before Tagtser Rinpoche left, I gave him the ashes of our mutual teacher, Tsultrim Lhaksem. Tagtser Rinpoche took them back to the United States, to the Tibetan Cultural Center in Bloomington, Indiana, and encased them in the Jangchub Chorten, the stupa where they remain. As fate would have it, this is where I now live, so I can circumambulate the Jangchub Chorten and honor my dear teacher whenever I wish, which is a constant source of comfort.

The Dalai Lama's delegation visited Tibet several times over the next two years. On what turned out to be their final visit to Lhasa, the delegation was led by Jetsun Pema, the Dalai Lama's sister. On that occasion they did not pass through Kumbum Monastery, but went directly to the Tibet Autonomous Region. News spread quickly among the people that the sister of His Holiness would be there, and officers of the United Front expressed repeated concern about the delegation's safety. Apparently believing their own propaganda, the government feared that the "emancipated serfs" in Lhasa would take revenge against their returning feudal lords. So as a precautionary measure they pressured local security officers to provide enough force to guarantee the group's protection.

What happened upon the delegation's arrival in Lhasa, however, was inconceivable to the Chinese Communist authorities. Thousands streamed to see the Dalai Lama's delegation, overwhelming the guards by their sheer numbers. But instead of a mob thirsty for vengeance, this was a crowd of enthusiastic people who wept with joy and asked for blessings and bestowals of good fortune. Some were so overjoyed that they shouted, "Long live the Dalai Lama!" and "Independence for Tibet!" knowing that they could face years in prison for their words.

Amazed that they had so misjudged the sentiments of the local people, the Chinese government swiftly expelled the delegation, claiming that it sought Tibetan independence and therefore lacked the sincere motivation necessary for negotiation. The truth was that this setback to the government's plans was brought on by a popular display of affection, and by the great fear the Chinese Communists feel when they can't control the will of the people. Such fear persists today.

CHAPTER 9

THE SACRED TREE
AND THE TIME MACHINE

The original intent of the Chinese clampdown on monasteries was not necessarily to destroy them, but to reduce the power of religion as part of an attempt to gain absolute control over Tibet. However, destruction was often the result, especially of those monasteries in mountainous and fortified positions, many of which had been taken over by Tibetan freedom fighters and would be flattened by Chinese shelling and bombing. The renewed destruction of monasteries during the Cultural Revolution was conducted for different reasons, but was no less devastating. With the blessings of Chairman Mao, Red Guard units joined by fearful or traitorous Tibetans—monks and laypeople—ransacked the temples and ravaged the buildings, destroying in weeks knowledge and culture that had taken 11 centuries to evolve.

Before the events of 1958 there were more than 600 Buddhist monasteries in our region. By the end of the Cultural Revolution in 1976, there were fewer than 20 left in the Amdo area, and most of them were partially destroyed—buildings in ruins, exteriors dilapidated, interiors vandalized and sometimes gutted. By the early 1980s the monasteries, although allowed to rebuild, were officially limited to 10 or 15 percent of their original populations. However, many Buddhist followers began donating money for restoration of their temples. Local bureaucracies were unsure of how to handle such matters, so they were slow to issue any administrative procedures—let alone give actual permits. In the vacuum created by this uncertainty, many people in our area assumed the responsibility of rebuilding temples, stupas, and sacred statues on their own, without waiting for government approval. Because of the surprising lack of direction from above, similar undertakings in other parts of the country soon amounted to a reconstruction boom.

This bureaucratic sluggishness was compounded because officials were unsure of the proper procedures for regulating religious activities. There had been no such activities at all for a generation. When inspectors from the State Administration for Religious Affairs of the People's Republic of China went to the countryside to see what was happening, they inspected only those monasteries that had been officially approved. Inspectors might come to the door of an unauthorized monastery and, not finding it on their list, quickly leave before they could be hustled inside and implored to grant formal paperwork. Monks preferred that their reconstruction be registered, so they made every effort to get the inspectors inside, but by entering a building, inspectors were giving de facto recognition that it existed.

Until a policy was finally decided upon, officials feared they might someday be accused of having made a wrong decision, so the existence of independent monasteries was simply ignored whenever possible. In our office we called this the policy of "three not-knows": not know how to regulate religion; not know how religion would eventually be regulated; and not want to know. In the end, although illegal, independently operating monasteries experienced greater liberty and flexibility. It was a confusing time of rapid recovery, caution, hope, and improvisation.

At the same time the government was trying to figure out what to do with monasteries, they faced an even greater dilemma. Tibetan Buddhism has a long-standing tradition of searching for the reincarnations of high lamas, or tulkus. As more monasteries began to function again, their monks realized how old they had become, and worried that at their passing there would be no rinpoches to hand down the teachings. An oral transmission of the dharma from teacher to student ceases to exist if the chain of teachings is broken. Herein lay the challenge: A full generation of trained young monks was missing.

Understanding the urgent nature of this need, monastic authorities from all over Tibet solicited the government to reestablish the tradition of finding tulkus. At first, the government was wary. Early in 1982 a Crimson Head document (headings of important documents were usually printed in red ink, hence the term) was released to clarify the government's policy. It left little room for ambiguity: "Reincarnated rinpoches are products of a feudal society, and are forbidden by the government."

In spite of this decree, believers still searched secretly. Reincarnations were found in other countries, and monks would travel to India to ask the Dalai Lama and other lineage masters to verify the authenticity of candidates they had identified. Upon receiving a satisfactory reply, they would return and privately hold enthronement ceremonies for the reincarnated rinpoches. This practice started slowly but gathered momentum. The government knew about these unauthorized activities, but this became another case of the "not-knows." Many monks believed that, just as unauthorized monasteries had been recognized after the fact, the newly discovered reincarnations would eventually be accepted. People began calling this the underground search for reincarnations, and those they identified were called underground tulkus.

Of course over the previous 20-plus years a great backlog of undiscovered tulkus had built up. This sometimes led to confusion, especially for the search teams. In one case, great effort was made by a monastery to locate their missing rinpoche, who had been born and identified in 1957 but was swept up in the wave of violence and chaos. When they found him—and many monks wished they hadn't—he was a married policeman with children! In this case things turned out happily; although he never became a monk, he actively participated in monastic affairs as a lay rinpoche.

As the number of recognized tulkus continued to increase, the State Administration for Religious Affairs of the People's Republic of China gradually woke up to the significance of these goings-on. If the department continued to ignore the searches for reincarnations and allowed the underground activities to continue, more and more reincarnated children would be found and moved overseas for their protection. And those who stayed in Communist China might not be raised to be obedient to the whims of the

127

State Administration for Religious Affairs, so the department's authority would become nominal, or even vanish completely.

For this reason, in the mid-1980s, the central government drafted a new policy: a Crimson Head document formally recognized the existence of reincarnations. A proviso was included that limited the number according to the size of the monastery to which they were attached. Ensuing propaganda claimed that this liberal policy regarding religion had proven itself effective, and at the same time had provided members of the religious community a chance to learn and appreciate "the greatness, superiority, and flexibility" of the Communist Party's policy on religion.

In two years I completed the university research program and graduated. After I attended a conference of the National Youth Alliance, the United Front in Qinghai Province arranged for me to work for the Buddhist Association of China in Xining. There I clerked in a liaison office, acting as a bridge between the Tibetan religious community and the government. I was uncomfortable with this position, knowing that I was being employed by the Communist government that had inflicted such atrocities on Tibetan monasteries, but something pushed me to take it anyway. I rationalized it by telling myself I was able to serve Tibetans, Mongolians, and other Buddhists in this way, which was certainly true. I'm not certain about all the forces at work inside me after two decades of Communist brainwashing, humiliation, and trauma, but I do know that I felt a strong impulse to enjoy myself, to take advantage of some new personal freedom, and to escape from the relentless Communist pressure to see myself as loathsome and evil. I lived in Xining in an apartment provided by the Communist government, and since there was not much work required, my life was leisurely—I had plenty of time to sit with friends gossiping in cafés—and not monastic.

I admit that after overcoming my initial reservations I found myself enjoying my new status. During my years as a farmworker, I had looked enviously at officials and the easy lives they seemed to have. After all, I had gone from a pampered child to a forced laborer in the fields, so this return to the high status of a bureaucrat seemed like a gift. My life seemed to have caught up with my dreams. I have to tell the truth: I became *proud* of my position, and I'm afraid I showed my pride in my strut and my attitude. I dressed and acted like a cadre, despite occasional qualms that I was betraying my heritage.

At this time monks in our region had not yet put on their robes, shaved their heads, or donned the other trappings of their vocation, so I was free to behave as a young man enjoying a lay life. This was a time of serious danger to my karma and my life's direction. The temptations of the material world (or *samsara*) were very strong, and threatened to sever my ties to the sacred vows I had taken.

After a while, however, I came to see that my position was nothing more than window dressing; through my work I made suggestions, but they were ignored by the Party, where all real power laid. Working as a liaison between the government and religious communities, I also had become much more aware of problems related to the reassertion of religion. As monasteries continued to revive, they faced great difficulties with restoration, finding reincarnated monks, and training them. As I learned more, my desire to actively help grew stronger.

I also saw firsthand how uncaring Party cadres could be when they dealt with monasteries. I found my sympathies increasingly turning toward my Buddhist roots and faith. In my ample spare time, I went more and more often to visit friends at Kumbum Monastery and my mentor, Gyayak Rinpoche. With his guidance, I moved steadily back in the direction of identifying myself as a monk. Ironically, it was the Chinese government that hastened my return to monastic life.

In the mid-1980s I was still working in my Xining office, looking like a Chinese cadre to the rest of the world. I had many friends, among them Comrade Ho, who came to visit me frequently. He was an amiable and courteous man, then in his forties. I learned from our conversations that he was Muslim, but Comrade Ho was also an official of the dreaded Ministry of

129

Public Security of the People's Republic of China. The political situation had improved, but I was still wary. Everyone had experienced an incident in which what seemed like a friendly visit by a security officer was really a probe for information—sometimes about you, sometimes about another person. One never knew. One always feared.

As it turned out, Comrade Ho did have a secret agenda, and one day he revealed it to me.

"The organization has sent me to persuade you to join the Party."

I was stunned.

"Me? Join the Party? You are inviting *me*?" I was trying to act calmly, but inside I was shocked and unsure of how to react. This was equivalent to converting to a different religion. But one doesn't refuse such an invitation lightly. Party members think that offering membership is a great honor, and no one likes to have a grand gesture refused.

Comrade Ho repeated himself, very slowly and deliberately this time, his face set. "Yes, we want you to join the Chinese Communist Party. Our country has opened up, and it is no longer the way it used to be. In your position you are most suitable to serve our country in its current state." His tone had become more confidential, but the words sounded rehearsed. "Of course, you can choose not to expose yourself after joining our Party. You can still engage in Buddhist activities and meet people of all walks of life. In fact, we prefer that you serve in secret. The only binding condition is that your *only* loyalty must be to the Chinese Communist Party."

As I listened to him, I was telling myself, *No! Never! They want me to be a spy. I will never join the Party.* But I did not dare utter this aloud.

"After you join the Party, your position and pay will be elevated immediately. But before you join you must tell the organization everything about yourself and what you have done, including all those bad things in the past. Afterward, you must obey the Party and formally swear to accept its assignments without question. Your loyalty and filial duty will be to the Chinese Communist Party, and not to your parents, teachers, or religion."

I wasn't sure, but I got the feeling that although he was officially inviting me to join, he was also warning me against turning my back on all that I believed. If so, that was very kind of him, but he needn't have bothered. I was not tempted.

Finally, he asked me directly: "Are you willing to join the Communist Party?"

I was absolutely certain that I did not want to do this. Still, not sure of what the repercussions might be, I asked, "Can I think about this before giving you an answer?"

"Of course," he replied. "I will be back in a few days. When you have made up your mind, we can arrange for you to go to Xining. We will set you up in a high-class guesthouse. You can rest there for several days. We'll give you the best room and attendants to serve your every need."

Once Comrade Ho left, I went to see Gyayak Rinpoche to seek guidance. Instead of giving advice, he asked me, "What do *you* think about this?"

I answered, "It is not possible."

"If that's the case, why didn't you turn him down right away? Why do you still have to think about it?"

I had no answer.

"You are still young, so allow me to give you this advice. Such things will happen again and again, and if you hesitate people will continue to bother you. Furthermore, they will think you went to someone for advice, and when you say no, that person will be blamed and get into trouble. Don't come to ask me in the future. Just remember this: Be pious and respectful of the Three Jewels; believe deeply in the law of karma; cultivate compassion and benevolence. Let these be your guides."

I called Comrade Ho, thanked him for his kind offer, and told him graciously but firmly that I was not interested in becoming a member of the Communist Party. I deflected his questions as to why, and remained firm until he finally gave up. Once again the guidance of Gyayak Rinpoche had proved timely—and invaluable.

Not all of my Chinese friends had hidden agendas. Because Zhang Xueyi was a doctor, we called him Zhang Menpa (*menpa* meaning "doctor" in Tibetan).

132 Zhang Menpa was a man of extreme integrity. He had been imprisoned twice, once for protecting his friends. He had paid a high price for his loyalty and devotion: 20 years in prison.

I met Zhang Menpa for the first time in 1965 during a campaign to cleanse the Party of corruption before the Cultural Revolution. That day Serdok Rinpoche and I had gone to visit Gyayak Rinpoche in his rooms. Upon entering, we noticed a man dressed in the navy blue Mao suit worn by Party cadres, sitting on the edge of Gyayak Rinpoche's platform. He had a ruddy complexion and facial features typical of local Chinese. We assumed he was a government official, so we meekly seated ourselves and kept our eyes averted, regretting having come to visit. But Gyayak Rinpoche—relaxed and playful— did not seem to mind this government official at all.

Gyayak Rinpoche explained, "This is Zhang Menpa. He is one of us. Don't be afraid." We answered, "Yes, yes," but secretly we remained distrustful. Zhang Menpa was a little embarrassed, too, and, after offering some excuse, left shortly thereafter. After his departure, Gyayak Rinpoche gave us a brief history of Zhang Menpa. His father was a famous veterinarian who had tended sick horses at our monastery in prerevolutionary days. The senior Mr. Zhang had sent his son away to become a medical doctor. In the 1950s, the young Dr. Zhang was imprisoned because he had his own office and was considered a capitalist.

He was supporting himself with a small business. At the time all trading was banned, and small businessmen were considered opportunists or bourgeois exploiters. The Communists accused Zhang Menpa of secretly purchasing a batch of Tibetan jewelry, such as traditional hair clasps for women, made of silver, turquoise, and coral. Trading was illegal, and so were crafts such as silversmithing and jewelry making. Their production was referred to as "business in underground factories."

After catching the unlucky Zhang on the outskirts of the nomad village where he had made his purchase, soldiers attempted to turn him into an informer for infiltrating the underground factories. The loyal Zhang refused to name any of the jewelry makers from whom he had purchased goods, despite being tortured. His home and property, with all its contents, were confiscated as a result of his refusal to cooperate.

While in jail, Zhang not only took care of ailing inmates, but was also diligent in pursuing knowledge for his own benefit. He became acquainted with a high Tibetan lama in prison and under his tutelage studied Buddhism. He soon became a dedicated practitioner, and after being released from prison continued instruction with Gyayak Rinpoche, under the pretext that he was visiting a patient. As Gyayak Rinpoche finished telling us this story, our doubts about Zhang dissipated. As we got to know him better, our admiration grew.

One day, Zhang Menpa invited me to his house, where I met his wife and two sons. After the meal, he asked me to create an ink and brush sketch for him. At the time, I was fond of drawing tigers, so I painted a common Chinese scene called *A Tiger Staring at the Moon,* which pleased him so much he asked me to sign it. Afterward, he took me to his bedroom and challenged me to discover a secret compartment hidden therein. I searched carefully but could not find anything.

Then he moved the headboard of his bed to reveal a mechanical lever, which he pulled. A small door opened behind his bed. We bowed our heads low and crawled on hands and knees to enter a large space. Inside was his private meditation room, beautifully furnished with statues, thangkas, and sacred objects—all of which were forbidden. He found some rice and asked me to chant and consecrate his shrine. After that, Zhang Menpa and I got together often. I asked him questions about Chinese medicine and acupuncture, and he asked me about Tibetan language and literature. We became very good friends.

As I mentioned earlier, one of my older brothers, Tenba Gyatso, was a member of Gyayak Rinpoche's household. Since Gyayak Rinpoche was his uncle, my brother had managed to stay and attend to him during the Cultural Revolution. My brother was clever and decisive, so that on several occasions when crises arose, Tenba Gyatso made critical decisions that saved all of us from serious consequences.

One day, my brother went to visit Zhang Menpa and, as was his habit, he approached carefully. Before knocking on the door, he peeked through a crack and saw security officials ransacking Zhang's house, while Zhang stood in handcuffs in the courtyard. The quick-witted Tenba Gyatso turned back

134   immediately and ran to the monastery to warn Serdok Rinpoche and me. He then rushed home to hide any thangkas, scriptures, and relics that Gyayak Rinpoche possessed. During the Cultural Revolution, we were careful not to keep any religious contraband in sight, but because monks typically carry chanting beads or pictures of the Buddha, at any given moment we were almost certain to be carrying some forbidden item.

Partly because of his prior record, Zhang Menpa nearly lost his life. In 1967 he was sentenced to his second 10 years in prison, where again and again he proved his goodness and loyalty, and thankfully, he survived.

In the following years I often visited Zhang's wife and two sons. His sons were good boys. Despite the hardships facing them with their father in prison—the loss of their home and their mother working in the fields—they helped with household chores and studied diligently. Zhang's sick mother, who also lived with them, waited anxiously each day for her son's return. She shared his letters with me, which were very moving. They were filled with love and pride in his wife as well as worry, regret, and sorrow for having put her in this situation. I resolved to visit Zhang in prison as soon as I could.

By 1975, the situation had eased sufficiently that I could engage in activities that were still officially forbidden but could be circumvented. I traveled to Xining to ask Choeshi Rinpoche for help in visiting Zhang. He said he had a friend named Lahting who could get us into the prison. Two days later, Choeshi Rinpoche and I took our bicycles to a street near Nantan Prison, known as the South Brick Factory. Rinpoche introduced me to Lahting and rode off. Lahting had told us to bring a carton of cigarettes. With that package in hand, he led the way inside.

Lahting was familiar to the prison staff. The guards at the gate greeted him and let us pass without any difficulty. Rows of armed guards stood at attention by the wall, stiff as statues. We wheeled our bicycles past them as if we were officers performing an inspection. Finally, we reached the last checkpoint. Lahting passed the carton of cigarettes to one of the work group leaders, and we entered the visiting room. Two minutes later, Zhang emerged. Lahting talked with the guard to divert his attention, so that Zhang and I could speak more freely.

Zhang had aged a great deal in eight years. The man I remembered had been carefully groomed, well dressed, and self-assured. Now, he was unshaven with a three-day stubble, and wore the clothes of a laborer; his hands were rough and calloused, and his skin was darkened by the sun. He looked changed, but fit and healthy. I gave him news about his family, and promised that I would help in whatever way I could. With tears in his eyes, he thanked me and said that one day, when he was released, he would repay my kindness.

Years later, in the mid-1980s, when circumstances had eased and I had returned to my residence in Kumbum, my attendant told me that a man was waiting outside with his entire family, insisting on seeing me in person. As the group entered, I realized it was Zhang Menpa, with his wife and two sons. He had grown a long beard. Upon seeing me, the family prostrated. Zhang rose and held out a pair of what appeared to be eighteenth-century teapots, both filled with water as an offering.

He said, "We don't have anything of value to offer you except this pair of old pots. We Chinese have a saying: 'Someone who throws rocks in the well where someone has fallen is a lowlife, but those who bring you charcoal for your fire on a snowy day are true friends.' I don't know how to repay the grace you have shown me in my time of hardship, so I am offering you this water, a symbol of the pure and sincere heart I have for you."

Still later, Zhang rebuilt his meditation room for all to see and remained a devout practitioner. His family prospered, and his sons came to be well-known entrepreneurs in Huangzhong County. How ironic that in the past Zhang almost lost his life for having a small business, and now his enterprising sons, engaged in a business many times larger than their father's, were being praised by government officials! It was remarkable how drastically things could change.

In 1979 I was invited to Beijing to attend a meeting of the All-China Youth Federation. I participated in the non-Party wing of the convention, made up of religious and laypeople of high social or professional standing. This was the first official meeting in many years, held to revitalize the organization after a

135

long period of inactivity. I was curious and excited about going to Beijing to attend a meeting as an honored guest, when only a few years before, people like me were considered evil parasites.

There were seven of us from Qinghai Province—all from very different backgrounds—attending this meeting. My roommate was Je-Ji, a Tibetan who hailed from Goluk, a district settled largely by nomads. This was his first time away from home. He was presentable enough, but unwashed and malodorous. His homeland in the Goluk region was an extremely cold place, perched high atop the mountains, where people seldom bathed. Except for falling in a river, Je-Ji might never have taken a bath in his entire life.

Since it was still summer, in self-defense I persuaded him to take a bath. He was a lively, easygoing young man, and in the end was extremely well liked by everyone. But perhaps because we shared the same language, he seemed to prefer spending time with me.

On our first afternoon of the meeting, we were eating in the spacious dining hall of the Xiyuan Hotel when a guest arrived and joined our table. Our visitor was Jamyang Shepa Rinpoche, the high-ranking abbot of the famous Labrang Monastery whose photo-processing chemicals I had discovered with my friends when we were children. Je-Ji, my roommate, became quite emotional when I introduced him to Jamyang Shepa Rinpoche. In Tibetan communities, meeting a high lama is a tremendous honor, a highlight of an entire lifetime. Je-Ji never thought that he would meet such a great lama, let alone dine with him. (I hadn't told Je-Ji that I, too, was a rinpoche, preferring to enjoy our relationship as equals.)

Throughout dinner Je-Ji stared at Jamyang Shepa Rinpoche in silent awe. When Jamyang Shepa Rinpoche finished eating and placed his soup bowl on the table, Je-Ji reached over, took the bowl, poured the few remaining drops into his palm, licked his hand, and rubbed it into his hair. I knew this was his way of receiving a blessing, but the others at the table were stunned, including Jamyang Shepa Rinpoche. After lunch, I scolded Je-Ji for being such a country bumpkin and embarrassing everyone. He said, "I will be more careful next time, really I will." Then he grinned contentedly, "But meantime I have received the blessing from Jamyang Shepa Rinpoche."

This was also my first time in the Great People's Hall on Tiananmen Square. Deng Xiaoping delivered a speech. Hua Guofeng (then chairman of the Communist Party, before being relieved of his duties) also attended and had his picture taken with us. On later occasions we had famous entertainers perform for us, and met famous leaders like Hu Qili; Wang Zhao-yu, a leader of the United Front; and Hu Jintao, who is now president of China. These men were part of the up-and-coming new generation of leaders. The All-China Youth Federation also organized many tours for us to other parts of China so that we could "open our eyes and receive a patriotic education by seeing the great strength of Communist rule." In the years following, I often went to such conferences, but this was my first appearance among people who were making big things happen in the secular world.

In 1980, when the Buddhist Association of China held its first nationwide meeting in Beijing, scholars and masters from different Buddhist traditions were excited and eager to meet. I heard that the learned translator of the Chinese *Lam Rim,* Master Fa Zun, was going to participate in the meeting as well. His translation is a classic that I use even today when I teach the Lam Rim in Chinese. To meet him would have been a great honor. Unfortunately, he passed away in the hotel, possibly due to his old age and the rigors of travel.

At this meeting the organization arranged several panel discussions. Some people spent their time talking about how grateful they were to the Communist government, but a few people expressed a different point of view. For example, my friend Yang Qing Xi, a veteran cadre, was on a panel with us. He expressed the idea that although these kinds of meetings were wonderful to establish good feelings about the new freedom of religion, they were not enough. He insisted that after the Cultural Revolution the government should have made an apology to the Tibetan people and given them rehabilitation to help them heal from their many wounds.

He told the story of an incident in 1958 in Go Ma Ying (Gomang) County, Qinghai Province. One night the cadres of the People's Liberation Army called the villagers to a meeting held in a local barn. After about 20 minutes, they announced that they had to execute all counterrevolutionaries and rebels. The cadres left the building, locking the door behind them, and then tossed hand grenades into the barn. The military had already surrounded the area, prepared to shoot anyone who tried to escape. About 200 people, including women, children, and elders, perished. Because they were considered "enemies of the people," their corpses were tossed into the fields where dogs and wild animals set upon them. The next year, when farmers came to plant their crops, they found arms and legs scattered everywhere. Their plows turned up intestines and other body parts.

Yang Qing Xi concluded this true horror story by saying: "Such a terrible happening in Tibet must be healed, or we will never be able to rebuild a good relationship between the Party and the people."

Yang Qing Xi's story shocked everyone. But in part because he and other brave cadres like him dared to tell the truth, the Beijing government eventually shifted its stance and decided to classify Tibetan and Mongolian political prisoners as "rehabilitated."

According to tradition, when Lama Tsong Khapa, founder of the Gelug tradition, was born, a sweet spring began to flow on the site and a white sandalwood tree appeared where the infant's umbilical cord had fallen to the ground. On each leaf of the tree appeared the image of Buddha. Later a monastery would be built here, called "Image of 100,000 Buddhas," or Kumbum. As late as the nineteenth century, French missionary Abbe Huc claimed to have witnessed the image of Buddha on the leaves, as well as mystic symbols.

After Lama Tsong Khapa was born in 1357, his father, Lumbum Gai, and his mother, Shingsa Achu, raised him like any other child. Then one day the Fourth Karmapa, head of the Kagyu sect of Tibetan Buddhism, was passing through the region when, according to custom, he gave an audience to the local residents. Tsong Khapa's parents joined the throngs of people who had come to greet the Karmapa. Immediately upon seeing their young child, the Karmapa recognized his special nature, shaved his head, and gifted him with the vows of a lay practitioner. On the spot where the child's hair fell, a cedar grew.

Lama Tsong Khapa became a monk at age 7 and, at 16, having learned all he could from the local monks, he traveled to central Tibet for further training. When he was 30 years old, his aging mother, who had missed him terribly during his long absence, sent a message asking her son to come home for a visit. Lama Tsong Khapa was so involved in his studies, however, that he could not fulfill his mother's desire. Instead he sent her small statues of Buddha and a thangka painting that he had made for her. He also enclosed a request that she have a shelter built over the sandalwood tree to protect the pilgrims who were already coming to pay homage at his birthplace.

Lama Tsong Khapa's mother raised funds from her tribal members, and in 1379 she built a simple refuge where people came to pay homage and quench their thirst with cool, sweet water from the spring. As Lama Tsong Khapa's fame grew, and more pilgrims came, a small retreat center was built on the site. After the Third Dalai Lama visited it, construction of what would become Kumbum Monastery began. Eventually, a large stupa, three stories high, sheathed in silver and decorated with turquoise and other jewels, was built to enclose the original shelter. At that time, one could enter to view the tree. Later the Great Hall of Golden Tiles of Kumbum Monastery was constructed around both the stupa and the tree.

In 1806, the 26th abbot of Kumbum monastery received a prophecy that the site was in danger and should be sealed. After preparing the interior, he and four monks exited the area for the last time before sealing it. On his clothes sat a leaf from the sandalwood tree, the image of Buddha still visible on its veined surface.

In 1985 the monastery made a decision that Lama Tsong Khapa's birth site, essentially the heart of Kumbum Monastery, should be thoroughly renovated. Although I still worked in Xining, I was now eager to reclaim my responsibilities as abbot so when Choeshi Rinpoche, khenpo of the monastery, asked me to direct the renovations, I accepted with tremendous joy.

I set about recruiting talented people to draft plans, raise funds, and hire the best craftsmen. The renovation, my first large project, took a year to complete and required me to find and gather many resources: time, energy, money, materials, goodwill, and political capital. The building's silver sheath was carefully removed to reveal a wooden substructure that was worn and cracked but remarkably free from rot. We repaired the wood and placed bands of

140 heavy bronze around the structure. Hundreds of people helped with the funding. They contributed money, jewels, and lots of old Chinese money in the form of little silver bowls that we melted down for the new leaf that would restore the stupa to its original glory.

We consciously chose not to penetrate the sealed inner recesses of the stupa to see the tree of 100,000 Buddhas, deciding that to search for it would have been a desecration of the sacred site. My joy lay in the completion of the external renovation. Organizing the effort was the first time in my life that I felt I was truly working to accumulate merit. (In Tibetan Buddhism, there are five paths to enlightenment. The first path is the Path of Accumulation. A person who does good deeds and says prayers and purifies his mind is creating good karma, or actions. The accumulation of this good karma will enable him to progress to the higher paths and eventually achieve enlightenment. When a person does good deeds through body, speech, and mind, he is said to be "accumulating merit"—he is on the road to enlightenment.)

This work so inspired me that I vowed to someday undertake the reconstruction of the entire monastery. With the blessings of the Three Jewels and the hard work of my colleagues, the renovation of the stupa was completed to the great satisfaction of the entire monastery.

The following year, Gyayak Rinpoche was moved to donate his entire life savings to build a large, three-dimensional Kalachakra (literally "time wheel") mandala as his tribute to the monastery. Gyayak Rinpoche assigned me to oversee the construction, requesting that I make a deep study of the Kalachakra and learn the significance of the mandala and the techniques for making its various forms. Unlike more typical two-dimensional mandalas made of sand or depicted in thangkas, he had in mind a realistic, three-dimensional representation of the palace of the Kalachakra deity. I happily accepted this honor.

The Kalachakra is an important component of the Tibetan cosmic view, in which humans, animals, and all life-forms have an intimate relationship with weather, environment, and other natural conditions. In humans the four elements of the universe—earth, water, fire, and wind (or solid, liquid, heat, and gas)—are connected to the formation of flesh and bone, bodily fluids, temperature, and breath, respectively. Karma, or cause and effect, operates at the universal level, the social level, and the individual level. A balanced flow of the four elements results in positive effects at all three levels. Human passage through the cycles of birth and death in our past, present, and future lives is called the internal wheel of time. Beyond the world, the movement of the universe has its own patterns and cycles; this movement is the external wheel of time, or external Kalachakra.

When the four basic elements of the universe are not harmoniously correlated, the result is disaster. For humanity as a whole, this conflict results in war, while internal disharmony causes sickness and dysfunction in the individual. In harmony, things flourish; flowers blooming are the result of harmony between plant, soil, rain, and sun. Obviously, people desire happiness and harmony and dislike suffering, but unfortunately the reality of *samsara,* or worldly life, includes both possibilities.

In my view the best way to stop war and sickness, to rejuvenate peace and harmony in the world as well as in the body, is to follow Buddhist teachings, especially within the Kalachakra tradition. His Holiness the Dalai Lama says that the practice of taming our minds to achieve inner peace is the foundation upon which greater peace is achieved. The Kalachakra mandala helps practitioners visualize, understand, and come closer to a living awareness of karma. This is a way to accumulate merit and gain greater personal happiness. Although the mandala itself does not directly teach people how to practice the Kalachakra, it is a visualization that helps people understand more clearly a profound aspect of Buddhist thought—how to achieve harmonic balance in our lives.

One year after Gyayak Rinpoche gave me the task of overseeing the construction of the three-dimensional palace of the Kalachakra deity, we completed the extraordinary creation. It stands 55 feet high and spans 85 feet in diameter; it may be the largest mandala in the world.

CHAPTER 10

BECOMING A POLITICAL BUDDHIST

In the early 1980s I became a board member of the Buddhist Association of China and also the vice chairman of its Qinghai branch. Unlike religious groups in other countries, Chinese religious organizations, although technically not affiliated with the government, are allowed to function only within strict limits set by the authorities. For example, at my office in the Qinghai Buddhist Association headquarters, a Party secretary was always present to keep an eye on rinpoches and other non-Party members.

In those years I had many opportunities to be with the Panchen Lama, helping him and Gyayak Rinpoche organize events in Beijing, and I sometimes took care of little projects, too, such as repairing sacred statues or thangkas. Once I helped build a folding table for the Panchen Lama that contained two shelves for sutras and relics and was designed so he could stretch his long legs underneath it as he sat on a dais giving a teaching.

In November 1986 I was at Kumbum when I received a notice from the National People's Congress requesting that I travel with the Panchen Lama to Nepal to participate in the 15th World Buddhist Conference. Our group was to consist of 30 people, including a security detail and foreign ministry representatives. Traveling with an important person such as the Panchen Lama is no simple matter, so I immediately fell into feverish preparations. Among other things, Panchen Rinpoche had asked me to gather copies of the Tibetan Buddhist canon and select a rare statue of Buddha as gifts for various Nepalese officials who were hosting the conference. I was also asked to prepare many yards of colorful silk cloth and other gifts for His Holiness the Dalai Lama, in case he should be there.

There was a chance that these two great Tibetan Buddhist leaders might meet at the conference for the first time since His Holiness's exile in 1959. If they did, it would be truly momentous. Not only would it mean much to the Tibetan people as a symbol that the spirit of our religion and culture had survived, but this meeting also might have some decisive impact on resolving the political, moral, and religious issues between Tibet and China. The matter might not be settled by our prayers, but we fervently prayed anyway.

Naturally, the Ministry of Foreign Affairs of the People's Republic of China weighed in with its opinions on the matter. Upon reading the ministry's *Rules and Regulations for Foreign Affairs,* a new policy handbook on how to engage with foreigners, the Panchen Lama gave up any hope of meeting with the Dalai Lama. The Dalai Lama's representatives would be allowed to attend only if they carried Indian passports, which the Dalai Lama lacked, and if he obtained one it would send a signal that he no longer considered himself Tibetan, which was untrue. Liu Long, a Muslim deputy director in the National Committee for Nationalities and confidant of the Panchen Lama, tactfully expressed his disappointment, saying, "The country needs to be more open and skillful about foreign policies. This would be a good opportunity to do so."

Before embarking on trips like these we had to undergo coaching, much like our preparation for the delegation from the Dalai Lama: learning the correct responses to questions on such issues as freedom of religion, the equality of ethic groups, and family planning. We were given booklets, brochures, and books to read so that we could quote the Party line, and yet we were expected to appear spontaneous and sincere when responding to questions.

At one of these training lectures I asked, "How do we handle questions about the Dalai Lama?" Our instructor's best advice was "When the question is about A, sometimes we must talk about B, and your translator will find ways to help you, too." When people ask me today how I felt about having

143

144   had to constantly avoid meaningful conversation in public situations, my answer is that, having lived since childhood in such a society, I became used to it; it was the Communist way.

For example, when I was sent to Israel for a visit in 1995, the mayor of Jerusalem, Ehud Olmert (who became the prime minister of Israel), said to me, "Jerusalem is the capital of Israel. The US is going to move its embassy from Tel Aviv to here. What do Chinese young people think of this move?" This was a subject for diplomats and politicians, not a monk. However, drawing on my years of training, I immediately replied to the mayor, "People in this beautiful city are like the beautiful weather here; they make me feel warm and welcome." I have no idea what the translator said, but the meeting went smoothly.

I am often asked if I ever thought about defecting on trips like this. The temptation was certainly there. Once I was actually offered an official opportunity to go abroad and study, but Gyayak Rinpoche, who was afraid I might break my vows and forget my responsibilities to Kumbum, said he wouldn't allow it. I could not disobey my teacher. The Panchen Lama certainly worried about defections before the Nepal trip; he told us that he had guaranteed the Chinese that no such thing would happen. If it did, serious consequences would befall him.

Once, in the Karachi, Pakistan, airport, I actually had an opportunity to escape if I had wanted to take it. Usually a security person took care of all the passports so we never had them in our possession. On this particular occasion, I saw our passports lying on a table in the VIP lounge. I could easily have taken mine and run off. I didn't take my passport, but I didn't say anything about what I'd seen, either. When we got to passport control, our security guard panicked. "Where are the passports?" he asked. "Did I give them to you?" I smiled to myself but said nothing, until finally he remembered where he had left them and raced back to the lounge. This was a less-than-compassionate thing for me to do, but from time to time I couldn't help but find little ways to get back at our handlers, who worked so hard to control our every move.

On another visit to Israel, my hotel room overlooked the American

Embassy. I could see people standing in line, probably for visas. It would have been easy to join them, but once again, the time didn't seem right. My presence was needed at Kumbum, and too many people would have suffered, including those in my travel group.

With our preparations complete, we boarded a flight to Nepal. As the plane flew over Lhasa and Shigatse, a crew member pointed out the Potala Palace and Tashi Lhunpo Monastery. Half an hour later, we flew past Mount Chomolungma, known in English as Everest. The temperature and landscape differ dramatically on either side of the Himalayas. On the Tibetan side of the mountains everything was wrapped in familiar, frozen whiteness. On the south side, where warm winds sweep up from India, we watched in awe as snowy, treeless plateaus gave way to dramatic river gorges and forested slopes before we descended into the unbelievably lush Kathmandu valley. As our plane dropped precipitously into the mist-wrapped mountains, I wondered if airplanes could land safely in these conditions. In our case, anyway, the answer proved to be yes.

When we arrived, a large crowd of Tibetan monks and laypeople in colorful attire had gathered to welcome the Panchen Lama with flowers and khatas in their hands. But they were held back by Nepalese policemen wielding batons. The Chinese government had insisted that Nepal not let the Panchen Lama have any contact with "separatists," meaning Tibetans in exile.

After leaving the tarmac, we were ushered into a small VIP lounge where the minister of Nepalese foreign affairs and officers of the Royal Army came to greet us. With assistance from the Nepalese police, we loaded ourselves into waiting vehicles and drove through the narrow streets of Kathmandu, which were noisy and disorderly, crowded with people, shops, and street hawkers. The city was pretty, with its temples, parks, and statues of kings and generals on horseback, but I was disappointed to see that it resembled old Lhasa more than a modern city like Beijing or Tokyo.

The opening ceremony of the conference took place in a sports stadium filled with 20,000 people, decorated for the occasion with Buddhist images, including giant statues of the Buddha. As if in the opening ceremony of the Olympics, young Nepalese women paraded around the track carrying banners with the names of our countries as they were being announced over the loud-speakers. Two or three hundred of us circled the track once before we climbed up on an elaborately decorated platform to take our seats with the monarch of Nepal, King Birendra.

The conference went smoothly, but outside one of the king's royal palaces where we stayed, more and more Tibetans were gathering as they learned of the Panchen Lama's presence. They demanded that he give blessings and a teaching. However, the attendants assigned by China's National People's Congress lied to the Panchen Lama, telling him that most of the people outside were not Tibetan and therefore he should not consider speaking to them. As usual, the Panchen Lama was aware of what was really going on, and who the people were. He sent me to observe the situation outside the walls firsthand.

When I returned and whispered to the Panchen Lama that these were indeed Tibetans waiting to hear him, he decided that he would do a teaching. The question was this: How to get the throng of Tibetans inside the palace grounds? Earlier I had observed that the stately gardens outside the Panchen Lama's rooms were large enough for thousands of people. The Panchen Lama commanded his Chinese staff one more time to let the crowd in so that he could see and address them. "No, no, no," they insisted. "It is too dangerous. These are not Tibetans." The Panchen Lama said nothing, but he nodded to us, indicating that we should find a way to let the people in.

Finally, the clever Liu Long devised a plan. News circulated by word of mouth that the gates would open and then the crowd should push its way in. Liu Long got into a car and asked the guards to let him pass through as if he was going on an outside errand. As the Nepalese guards opened the palace gate for the vehicle, several thousand Tibetans poured onto the palace grounds, knowing exactly where to go. Their wishes were fulfilled: the Panchen Lama, the reincarnation of the Amitabha Buddha, talked to them for more than four hours, giving a teaching on "long-life empowerment." After the teaching he greeted and personally blessed many of them. Our Chinese minders were enraged but helpless in the face of such a popular outpouring.

After this our activities were severely restricted around Kathmandu, and we were only allowed to visit designated sites. In our limited travels we could see some Tibetans and monks in the distance bearing khatas and flowers, lining the roads to pay homage to the Panchen Lama, but we could only wave to them. However, we were allowed to take a small helicopter to the town of Lumbini near the Indian border where Buddha was born.

When we arrived at the site of Buddha's birth, a strange thing happened. The Panchen Lama was taken into a gated area with a small pavilion. On one wall were spectacular bas-reliefs depicting the story of Buddha's birth. The Panchen Lama walked over to the sculptures to pay homage, and, at the very moment that his head touched the figure of Buddha's mother, water suddenly began to ooze from the wall and trickle down to the floor. People at the scene watched in amazement. Gyayak Rinpoche gasped and said, "Nectar, nectar," referring to the sacred liquid that flows from a deity in blessing. He told me to use my camera, and I have these precious photos to this day.

In 1988 I also accompanied the Panchen Lama on a trip to Mexico, Peru, Bolivia, Chile, Argentina, Uruguay, and Brazil. We participated in diplomatic and cultural events as part of an exchange program, but they had no religious purpose at all. Our delegation included a Tibetan official named Phuntsok Wangyal, an important figure in Tibet during the 1950s. He had been a strong supporter of the Communists after their occupation of Tibet, and because of this, I had considered him a puppet of the Communist regime, but when we actually met I found him forthright and open. As we traveled together, he often sought me out for conversation, even though I was younger than he. I learned that his sympathies stemmed from a sincere belief in the values of Communism, not from political opportunism. Although he had been imprisoned for more than 20 years, he had remained loyal to the ideology of the Communist Party.

I also met Li Zuomin, the deputy secretary of the national United Front, who spoke fluent Tibetan and English and was appointed political secretary to the Panchen Lama. The security officer in our group was Wang Houdu, a typical hard-line Party member in charge of logistics and keeping an eye on the Tibetans. He didn't trust us for three reasons: 1) We might defect to a

148 hostile country; 2) he was afraid we would leave sensitive or secret materials behind as we traveled; and 3) he was afraid that, as incompetent Tibetan monks, we would get lost in a foreign city.

An interesting thing happened while Mr. Wang kept a suspicious eye on us and not on his Party comrades. Mr. Huang from the Ministry of Foreign Affairs of the People's Republic of China forgot his briefcase in the lobby of a large hotel in Brazil. He didn't miss it until after the welcoming banquet was over, and the briefcase was gone by the time he went back for it. For the next few days he was so afraid of what might happen that he could neither eat nor sleep. Of course, the Panchen Lama, always very tuned in, noticed Mr. Huang's panic. As the titular chief of our delegation, he inquired about the briefcase, pretending innocent curiosity.

Mr. Huang and his roommate fabricated a story about it being stolen. When the Panchen Lama asked him what was inside the briefcase, he replied, "There are some classified documents, some letters, and some US dollars." The Panchen Lama handled the matter with compassion: "Old Huang, anyone can make mistakes. Please don't worry so much, but in the future, be more mindful. As the delegation chief, I'll speak in your favor to your superiors when we return to China." A relieved smile immediately came over Huang's face. From then on Wang Houdu, our security officer, felt obligated to the Panchen Lama, and, as a result, the burden of constant surveillance was eased considerably.

In 1987, the Tenth Panchen Lama established the High-Level Tibetan Buddhism College of China in Beijing, known as Xihuang Si (Western Yellow Monastery), to help offset three decades of systematic destruction of Tibetan Buddhism by the Communists. An entire generation of monastics had not received adequate basic training, let alone education in the more subtle and sophisticated aspects of sutra and tantra studies. I, too, was part of that woeful gap. Although now I had an advanced degree in Tibetan studies from a university, my Buddhist studies were still sadly incomplete.

By this time I should have completed all my vows and earned the advanced geshe degree, but the lama masters empowered to give essential teachings were now in their seventies and eighties, and many of the greatest masters had died, been killed, or escaped south to India and Nepal. Few qualified teachers remained to carry on the tradition of oral transmission. It was pure luck that Western Yellow Monastery, which had been built in 1651 for one of the Panchen Lamas by the Qing emperor, had survived. The army had been using it, but the Panchen Lama convinced them to return it to him so that he could train a new generation of rinpoches.

At the outset, the president of the academy was the Panchen Lama himself. From every region of Tibet he invited all the great masters who had survived from all four of the Buddhist traditions—Gelug, Nyingma, Kagyu, and Sakya—to take teaching posts. This notion of integrating the practices was quite innovative, and the system—known as Rimé—is supported today by His Holiness the Dalai Lama.

The curriculum at the academy was structured around both monastic training and conventional college courses. Besides the five traditional studies of arts and crafts, medicine, philology, philosophy, and cosmology, the academy offered modern science, history, Chinese, and English. Serdok Rinpoche and I were among the first students enrolled, but I'm sorry to say we were still at the bottom of our class, alongside other rinpoches who had also been deprived of proper monastic education. There were about 40 of us who, in one way or another, had maintained our vows and studies. Some of us went on to exemplify the highest standards. Jambo Rinpoche, for example, became a great scholar. He had survived persecution with the help of his local community in an isolated nomad area and was never bothered by the Chinese because he was the "caretaker of a poor old man" who, in fact, was Jambo Rinpoche's teacher.

But the academy was only a beginning. The Panchen Lama also began to prepare to develop other institutions, including schools that would offer Tibetan language programs in Tibetan regions where Chinese was the only language taught in schools. He knew that such projects required money, so he created a fund-raising organization called Ornaments for the Land of Snow (Kanggyan Gongsi). Its headquarters was to be somewhere in Beijing, and all 149

Tibetan districts would have regional branches. The Panchen Lama intended for the school to eventually become a corporation, which would include a large hotel with rooms designed to embody various cultures, so that Chinese, urban Tibetans, farmers, and even nomads could feel comfortable there.

Like my former roommate Je-Ji, nomads from Tibet and Inner Mongolia lived in a very harsh environment, and as a result, they seldom bathed. When they came to Beijing they were therefore discriminated against and refused rooms at hotels. The Panchen Lama's rooms for nomads would be styled after traditional nomad tents, and all the rooms would be equipped with Buddhist sutras, much the way Gideon Bibles are placed in Western hotels. When someone objected that the sutras would be stolen, he stopped, thought a moment, and exclaimed, "That would be good!"

The Panchen Lama's new ideas and activities were well received in Tibet, but the central government in Beijing was uneasy. While the High-Level Tibetan Buddhism College of China and other research institutions were meant to cultivate religious experts, establishing companies and building hotels were obviously ventures designed to create profit. For all the loosening of certain restrictions, ambitious plans were still almost reflexively met with misgivings. If this were allowed, what would the Panchen Lama do next?

The Panchen Lama's unstated goal was to set up a religious institution equivalent to a Chinese ministry. This organization, which he would run, would be in charge of all Tibetan monasteries and institutions, and when its businesses became self-sufficient, he would no longer need a governmental subsidy. The Panchen Lama argued that his plan was in keeping with Communist China's cultural policies and would be beneficial to the government because it would eventually reduce the budget for religious affairs.

The Panchen Lama appointed Liu Long (his Muslim confidant) and me to the planning committee. We were assigned to find the names and addresses of all the Tibetan monasteries in Beijing in order to select a location for the organization's headquarters. (We discovered that although there had been a total of 36 Tibetan monasteries in Beijing during the peak of the Qing Dynasty, only Yong He Gong Monastery and Xihuang Si Monastery remained.)

Kumbum Monastery in eastern Tibet, 1920s

Kumbum Monastery, 2006—a tourist attraction

With Gyayak Rinpoche, on the way to the enthronement of the Tenth Panchen Lama at Kumbum

With my parents at my birthplace, 1956

My enthronement at Kumbum, 1952

With Serdok Rinpoche at Kumbum, 1950s

With Serdok Rinpoche and monks, 1960s

With a monk after returning from a day at the Chinese school, 1960s

With my mom during the time of the Panchen Lama's visit, 1962

Return to work and school routine after the Panchen Lama's visit, 1962

Day off from working in the fields with Jamaga and other monks during the Cultural Revolution

With Gyayak Rinpoche, 1970s

With Tibetan friends, 1970s

With Qinghai youth members in Beijing, 1970s

During His Holiness's delegation visit in 1979, Rinpoches released from jail and fields gather together

With Choesang Rinpoche and Choeshi Rinpoche in Beijing for the Buddhist Conference, 1979

With Shar Dong Rinpoche and others at Qinghai University, 1979

With Gyayak Rinpoche, discussing the renovation of Kumbum, 1983

With my secretary Drashi, 1980s

With my mother at Kumbum after her illness, 1983

With Gyayak Rinpoche, Choesang Rinpoche, and others in Beijing for the Buddhist Conference, 1980s

Commemorating the 1959 Tibetan uprising with Serdok Rinpoche, 1983

The Panchen Lama, 1980s

With the Panchen Lama in Xining, 1980s

The Panchen Lama receiving blessing of water at Buddha's shrine in Lumbini, 1986

With the Panchen Lama and Kongtang Rinpoche on a flight to Nepal, 1986

The Panchen Lama with Nepalese officials and Chinese ambassador in Nepal, 1986

With Gyayak Rinpoche at the king's palace in Nepal, 1986

With high lamas in Kumbum, 1990s

At Kumbum with Wu Bangguo, Chinese congressional chairman, 1990s

Deng Xiaoping's son visits Kumbum, 1990s

High lamas praying together in Beijing, 1990s

Buddhist Conference in Beijing, 1995

With Hu Jintao, current president of China (2003–present), 1992

With Jiang Zemin, former president of China (1993–2003), 1993

With Zhao Puchu, chairman of the Buddhist Association of China, discussing my future position, 1995

Ceremony celebrating the completed renovation of Kumbum, 1996

Thai Sangha King in Bangkok, 1996

Layover in Amsterdam during escape, 1998

Leaving Guatemala for the United States, 1998

Our group has an audience with the Dalai Lama, 1998

With the Dalai Lama in the United States, 1998

Discussing Tibetan issues with the Dalai Lama, 1998

Our group with Mimi and Peter in California, 1998

With Rose and attorneys Peter and Pauline, 1999

With Tagtser Rinpoche in Bloomington, Indiana, 1999

With Tagtser Rinpoche after I became director of the Tibetan Mongolian Buddhist Cultural Center in Bloomington, 2006

Testimony for freedom of religion in Los Angeles, 2000

Saying prayers in Bloomington, 2006

Giving teachings

The Panchen Lama's plan, however, ran up against the Communist Party. If Tibetan Buddhist groups were allowed to unite, local Tibetan organizations might reassert themselves, and a financially independent entity meant freedom from control by the Communist government. Beijing could never allow that to happen. Not surprisingly, the Panchen Lama's dream was never fulfilled.

This moment marked the beginning of the end of the Panchen Lama's influence and support in Beijing. Welcoming hands were about to turn into clenched fists.

In 1987 I was in Beijing undertaking a research project for the Panchen Lama when I heard disturbing news from Lhasa. On September 27, monks from Drepung Monastery had staged a demonstration in central Lhasa, shouting, "Tibetan independence!" Several days after their arrest and reported beating, monks from Sera Monastery and nuns from other monasteries demonstrated in support and were also beaten and arrested in full view of spectators, some of whom were Western visitors. This led to still further demonstrations, in which 8 to 10 people were killed by Chinese gunfire. Tibetans were seething.

Within a week, at the request of Beijing, the Panchen Lama had organized work teams from the national United Front and the State Administration for Religious Affairs of the People's Republic of China to go to Lhasa to resolve this issue. There were, in fact, three groups. One was a religious team consisting of Tibetan monastic elders; another was made up of government cadres, mostly high-ranking officials from the national United Front; and the third group was a unit of the National Police Agency. A chartered plane was put at the disposal of the Panchen Lama for the transport of more than 100 people. I was asked to join the religious group, which along with the national United Front team was at least nominally led by the Panchen Lama. We lost track of the police unit the moment we landed in Lhasa.

It was afternoon when we arrived at Gonggar Airport, about 60 miles from Lhasa. On the way to the city we saw many heavily armed People's Liberation Army (PLA) soldiers, indicating the situation in Lhasa was very serious. The

151

Panchen Lama stayed at his residence, Shukling Dorje Podrang Palace, along with the other lamas and me. The minister of the Ministry of Public Security and other cadres went to the PLA's regional headquarters.

The next day we participated in an emergency briefing, led by a cadre from the office of the Tibet Autonomous Region (TAR). "A small number of extreme separatists have finally shown themselves. However, many people deceived by them have also demonstrated against the government. The government of the Tibet Autonomous Region, under the correct leadership of the Party, has tried repeatedly to dissuade them from their misguided efforts and has carefully explained the Party's policies on nationalities and religion. It has maintained its patience. In the meantime, the People's Liberation Army and the [People's] Armed Police have made great efforts to protect people's lives and the stability of the nation." The Panchen Lama sat silently, listening to this speech with obvious skepticism.

After dinner that evening, the Panchen Lama called for a meeting to watch a video recording of what had happened on the streets of Lhasa. Communist leaders of the TAR were to attend. When we arrived at the conference room on the second floor of his residence, all the team members who had accompanied us from Beijing were present, but as we were settling into our seats, the Panchen Lama asked, "Where are the leaders of the Tibet Autonomous Region?" Their absence indicated a profound lack of respect for the proceedings. A look of displeasure flashed over the face of the Panchen Lama.

The lights went off. The video was very long. The narrator constantly repeated the words "antirevolutionary diehards," while on the screen we watched monks and nuns raising their fists and shouting slogans such as "Independent Tibet" and "Long life for the Dalai Lama." Wherever the monks and nuns went, crowds of adults and children followed. Finally, when the demonstrators marched to Jokhang Temple, the video ended. From this version of events it appeared that the monks and nuns were clearly at fault for demonstrating against the government. From what he had seen there was no way the Panchen Lama could defend their actions.

When the lights came on, the Panchen Lama suddenly stood up, his eyes fiery. His voice exploded like a thunderclap that stunned everyone. "Is this the end of it? Is that all?" Those who were dozing snapped to attention.

"Li Zuomin, did you come here to sleep?" the Panchen Lama demanded, turning toward the deputy secretary of the United Front and his interpreter. The atmosphere in the room grew electric. The Panchen Lama rolled up his sleeves and strode to a short young man working the video projector. The Panchen Lama reached down and grabbed the front of the poor man's jacket and lifted him to his feet. It was like an eagle picking up a baby chick. I thought the Panchen Lama was going to strike him, but instead the Panchen Lama shook him slightly and let him drop to his seat. There was complete silence in the room.

"Everyone get in your cars and follow me!" the Panchen Lama commanded. We obeyed, although none of us knew where we were going. In less than five minutes we were congregated outside the residence of Wu Jinghua, the Party secretary of the Tibet Autonomous Region. Someone knocked on the gate. It was one o'clock in the morning. Wu Jinghua emerged in his pajamas. He said, "It's so late." And then, surprised, he added, "Your Holiness has come to me in person. What's wrong?"

Before he even finished his sentence, the Panchen Lama replied with rage, "If the leaders of the Autonomous Region don't trust me, I can immediately leave Lhasa." Without further ado, Wu Jinghua pulled the Panchen Lama into his home. Several dignitaries also went in. In the meantime, people began murmuring, "The original video was not shown to us . . . policemen shot at the crowd." Ten minutes later a car arrived at the gate. Wu's secretary rushed out of the car and into the house. A few minutes later the Panchen Lama strode out of the mansion with a new videotape in hand. We got back in our vehicles. Someone said, "That must be the original recording. The secretary locked it in his drawer, which is why we didn't see it."

It was two o'clock in the morning when we returned to the conference room. This time, the content of the video was far more graphic. Nobody fell asleep. In the darkness, people said things like "This scene was not included in that video," and "That one was also missing." Near the end we saw monks and nuns walking to the Jokhang Temple. A policeman standing near the

153

Jokhang Temple said the equivalent of "Sonofabitch, they're coming, fire! Fire!" Shots rang out.

The Panchen Lama stood up and ordered the viewing stopped. He put the videotape back in its case and said quietly, "Thank you, everyone, for sitting with me to this late hour. Have we all seen the police firing shots? Was I wrong to think there was more to this? You're all exhausted; please go to your rooms and get some sleep."

Before the 1980s the Chinese had created a policy: Whenever a conflict arose, officials were required to categorize it as either "external" or "internal." "External" referred to destructive acts from an outside source. Such acts had to be dealt with swiftly and with force. "Internal" referred to conflicts occurring among the people themselves, and had to be solved through investigations and education—not by force. The Panchen Lama always tried to show that conflicts involving ethnic groups such as Tibetans were internal, not external, so that the protestors would be protected from violence and not put in jail or tortured.

Today the situation has changed because there is no strong protector inside of Tibet to speak on behalf of its people. The Chinese always assert that conflicts involving Tibetans spring from the interference of the Dalai Lama, thus making such conflicts external ones—to be dealt with by guns, police, and even the army. Calling the Dalai Lama a separatist or terrorist enables them to crack down on Tibetan protestors with force.

The Panchen Lama's refusal to accept the first video required the Chinese authorities to regard the 1987 protests as an internal conflict. As a result, the cadres and lamas who had been flown in from Beijing were divided into five or six teams and sent to people's houses in and around Lhasa, as well as to the three large monasteries of Drepung, Sera, and Ganden. Study sessions were conducted to investigate the causes of the demonstration, and to listen to the opinions of laypeople and monks. My specific assignment was to interview monks at Ganden Monastery.

Ganden Monastery was the first monastery of the Gelug sect, built in 1409 by Lama Tsong Khapa, the first *tripa,* or head of the lineage. The tripa at the time of our visit was Bumi Rinpoche, the 100th monk to occupy this position. He had been arbitrarily selected by the Chinese after monasteries were reopened (the true tripa appointed by the Dalai Lama had fled to India years before).

In its heyday Ganden Monastery had housed more than 3,300 monks. In 1959 it was the site of armed resistance to the Chinese, whose artillery shells and aerial bombardment had reduced the walls to rubble. At the beginning of the Cultural Revolution, Red Guards and positivist monks smashed dharma halls and Buddha statues in the monastery with hoes and hammers. Along the way, they went into Yang Ba Jian Hall. When they pried open the golden stupa where the body of Lama Tsong Khapa was enshrined, they saw the Master's gray hair draped to the floor. His hands were crossed in the dharma-wheel mudra and his fingernails had grown so much that they were wrapped around his shoulders. Awestruck by the scene, even the revolutionary rebels dared not touch anything.

The Red Guards ordered Bumi Rinpoche to carry Lama Tsong Khapa's body out of the stupa and burn it. Rumor had it that no one was supervising the process, and that perhaps this was done deliberately to give the monks an opportunity to hide our founder's body instead of destroying it. However, the cowardly Bumi Rinpoche still carried the body to a hill on the east side of the monastery and burned it along with Lama Tsong Khapa's own sandalwood throne. As I describe this event, it still has the power to hurt me like a fresh wound.

I had been to Ganden Monastery once before, and on this latest visit I noticed the monastery looked much better. Reconstruction had begun, although I could still see rubble and broken walls. I met with the monks there for four days. The Chinese had briefed me as to how I was to proceed with my inquiries, just as the monks at the monastery had been briefed as to how they were to respond. As was typical of every meeting in Communist China, a cadre group participated. We all knew our roles well, but it was also clear that emotions in the room were running very high.

The Ganden monks who attended were uncharacteristically outspoken, especially the young monks. Many of them complained that although freedom of religion ostensibly had been restored, their religious activities were highly   155 restricted. They also felt discriminated against everywhere they went, and were forced to watch helplessly while monastery properties continued to be damaged and looted by Communist cadres. In these conversations the monks often used forbidden words and phrases such as "democracy," "freedom," and "human rights." However, between the intimidating pressure of Party cadres and the encouragement of the local rinpoches in the meetings, the monks finally managed to control at least the outward expression of their anger.

After we all returned to Lhasa, the Panchen Lama held a meeting at his residence, where we reported on what each work team had accomplished. Most team leaders made succinct reports, citing the numbers of demonstrators and describing how the monks had promised not to join them again. They also repeated the opinions of Lhasa residents and the complaints of the monks, describing the difficulty of getting young Tibetans to join monasteries and the lack of funding for monastic life and for restoration.

Finally Zhao, a cadre member from the State Administration for Religious Affairs of the PRC, began babbling generalities about how the situation was calm and the people were happy. The Panchen Lama looked displeased and interrupted him. "Old Zhao, I hope you'll present your report with more details at our next meeting."

Three days later, a follow-up meeting was convened, and the Panchen Lama asked Zhao, who was sitting in front of him, to present his report first. He began by apologizing so profusely for his last report that the Panchen Lama stopped him: "Okay, that's enough! By admitting your mistake, you've shown us that you're a good comrade. Please continue with your report."

This time, Zhao's presentation was more to the point. He was describing what he had found when, suddenly, he stopped speaking. His face turned pale and saliva ran from the corners of his mouth. The Panchen Lama yelled, "He's having a heart attack!" Three doctors rushed into the conference room and performed CPR. Zhao was taken by ambulance to a hospital, but a few hours later we learned that he had died.

We all attended Zhao's funeral. Someone eulogized him, in the process describing Zhao's life. He had always wanted to visit Tibet but had never done so, although he had traveled throughout China during his tenure at the State

Administration for Religious Affairs of the PRC. Just before his retirement, he requested that he be sent to Lhasa, and his superior granted his wish, fulfilling Zhao's lifelong dream. And now the spirit of Zhao was going to stay in the Land of Snow forever. As my fellow rinpoches and I viewed his body we silently offered prayers for this old Party member. Life and death are indeed ephemeral.

About 10 days later we had a large panel discussion to conclude the investigations into the Lhasa demonstrations and killings. Everyone from the Beijing contingent was present. This time leaders of the Tibet Autonomous Region and monks from the monasteries were there as well. The Panchen Lama began by showing us some religious artifacts that had been lost or "misplaced" during the Cultural Revolution. Among them was Lama Tsong Khapa's crown, which had been given to him by a Ming Dynasty emperor. There were also more than 100 Tibetan volumes of Buddha's Kangyur (canon) with their gold inlaid covers and text written in gold ink. Ever since the Panchen Lama had been released from prison, he had made every effort to locate missing Buddhist sutras, statues, and stupas. No one but the Panchen Lama could have undertaken this challenging task. Now he placed these precious relics on the table in front of him; after the meeting they were returned to the respective monasteries from which they had been stolen.

Wu Jinghua, the Chinese cadre leader, presided over the business part of the meeting, and as usual, cadres reported first to influence what subsequent speakers might say. Then it was the monks' turn. Prior to this meeting, cadres had met with monks to encourage them to toe the Party line. As long as the monks publicly agreed with the conclusions reached at the meeting, it would, as usual, end quickly and smoothly.

It seemed as if everything was going as scripted, but then to everyone's surprise a monk from Drepung Monastery suddenly broke the mood. "You People's Liberation Army soldiers and Chinese cadres, when you first entered Tibet, you came like beggars with only a cane and a small cloth bag. Now look at you; after retirement every one of you is shipping truckloads of religious artifacts back home. Aren't these riches from our Tibet? But what have you brought us? How many people were shot dead and how many monasteries were destroyed during your Democratic Reform and the Cultural Revolution?"

Some monks tried to restrain him before he ended his outburst. Everyone was horrified. Several undercover police had already entered the conference room, and their hands were in their pockets as if to pull out guns. Silence fell over the room. Many monks were so scared that they dared not look at each other. I assumed the monk who spoke would be whisked away, but he was not.

Wu Jinghua was enraged, and shouted, "What you want is Tibetan independence. Isn't that it? What is *this*?" He pointed at Lama Tsong Khapa's Ming Dynasty crown and continued, "This is proof that your Tibet was part of China even during the Ming Dynasty. With this kind of evidence, how dare you recklessly speak for the separatists! Under the wise leadership of the Communist Party, we liberated Tibet, overthrew feudal serfdom, and made farmers and workers the masters of Tibet. You just blind yourselves from seeing these changes!"

Wu's speech was translated into Tibetan word for word by Old Ma, a Muslim born in Lhasa. Wu Jinghua ranted for half an hour before the Panchen Lama finally interrupted him. "I had hoped the trials of these last few weeks would end soon. It seems that's no longer possible." The Panchen Lama's tone seemed to criticize the monk who had spoken, but it also expressed his frustrations with trying to resolve these irresolvable political problems simmering so close to the surface of our land.

Wu Jinghua's speech extended the work team's stay in Lhasa a few more days to allow time for further brainwashing of the monks involved. Another meeting convened. This time the brave monk did not show up. (Happily, a few days later he was back at his job working on the altar at Drepung Monastery.) The directors of the Democratic Management Committees of the three monasteries all spoke of the grace of the Communist Party and of the wonders of socialism. One after another the monks promised to stage no further demonstrations. Leaders of the Tibet Autonomous Region also delivered speeches, and presented ¥400,000 to each of the monasteries from the Beijing government to address some of the complaints of the monks.

And so at the end of several weeks our inquiry arrived at three conclusions (the first two of which are not uncommon): 1) Battling separatism would be a long-term struggle; 2) the masses were deceived by the demonstrators; 3) it was wrong for the police to open fire. That last finding was a tribute to the Panchen Lama's tenacity and courage.

We returned to Beijing.

By the summer of 1988 Serdok Rinpoche and I had completed our one-year program in dharma studies at the Panchen Lama's High-Level Tibetan Buddhism College of China. The Panchen Lama called me into his office to ask me if I wished to stay on with the academy as dean (not for my academic brilliance, but for my organizational skills). I thanked him but expressed my wish to return to Kumbum Monastery. He smiled warmly. "Being the abbot of Kumbum Monastery is also important. If you wish to take your rightful place as functioning head of the monastery, you have my blessings. But the department I am setting up also needs your help to manage the many plans we have under way. When we are ready, you must return."

The graduation ceremony for the first students of the Tibetan Language Department was very festive. Many Tibetan and Chinese dignitaries made speeches, including Zhao Puchu, chairman of the Buddhist Association of China. During the ceremony, the Panchen Lama personally conferred diplomas upon the graduates. I was chosen as one of the honors graduates, which was extremely gratifying.

But now it was time to return to Kumbum. I felt an enormous sense of satisfaction in finally stepping into the role that I was born to fill as the reincarnation of Arjia Rinpoche. This was the culmination of a lifetime of events that had begun for me when I was two years old and the search committee of monks emerged from the windswept steppe to stop at the entrance to my family's ger. I had some confidence in my ability to organize and run things, but I also knew that my training was inadequate to my position as khenpo of Kumbum. For nearly three decades, beginning with the Chinese Communist Great Leap Forward, I had lived a secular life—going to school, working in the fields, spending time with laypeople, living the life of samsara—not the

159

life of a monk. Before that, I had been too young to understand what a monk's robes or vows meant. Now, just before arriving at Kumbum, Serdok Rinpoche and I stopped to change into our robes. Other than for ceremonial occasions, this would be the first time I had worn robes since 1964, when we had been forced to give them up at Tashi Lhunpo Monastery, 24 years earlier. The robes felt awkward, slipping and sliding off my shoulders. They also felt ill deserved.

When Serdok Rinpoche and I returned to Kumbum Monastery, we were greeted in the great courtyard by the khenpo, Choeshi Rinpoche, flanked by many rinpoches and hundreds of monks, who held a festive welcoming ceremony for us. The sound of long horns, the sight of strings of prayer flags, and the smell of juniper incense made this a joyful occasion. Many older monks were teary-eyed, remembering a time long ago when I had played a role in such ceremonies as a little boy. Now I was finally coming home, and before long I would be assuming my rightful place as head of Kumbum.

Four or five months later, at the end of 1988, the Panchen Lama had arranged for an elaborate dharma event to consecrate a new temple at Tashi Lhunpo Monastery in Shigatse. The Panchen Lama had gathered the desecrated remains of his five previous incarnations, which had been scattered around the grounds by Red Guards during the Cultural Revolution, and had laid them to rest in a single stupa, located next to the newly constructed temple of Drashi Namgyal.

The discovery of some of the remains was nearly miraculous. During the Cultural Revolution, my friend Dondup Palden was working at Tashi Lhunpo as a cook for a cadre work team. He had always been a careful observer of what went on at the monastery. One day when he returned from grocery shopping, he noticed a large earthen urn that had not been there before, half hidden in a corner of a room near the kitchen. Out of curiosity, he opened it, and a mintlike fragrance arose; peeking inside the urn, he found the bodily remains of a white-haired lama. Dondup Palden could not describe the joy he felt at the discovery.

He immediately carried the urn to the office of the work team and quietly mentioned his discovery to Old Shue, a man he considered reasonable and sympathetic. Old Shue told him that they had just received directives from above changing the rules so that from now on all antiques, even broken ones, must be protected. So the urn sat outside the office of the work team for several months until it was confirmed that the remains were those of the Fourth Panchen Lama, Choeji Gyaltsen. Then it was re-enshrined in its original temple. Whoever had hidden it, whoever had discovered it, and whoever had placed it where someone would stumble across it never made their identities known.

My mother, who was now 81 and becoming frail, joined a group of us from Kumbum Monastery traveling to attend the consecration of Drashi Namgyal Temple at Tashi Lhunpo. On our way to Shigatse we stopped in Lhasa to pay our respects at several sacred sites. It was the only time in her life that my mother had visited Lhasa, but sadly, due to her failing health she was a bit overwhelmed by the trip.

When we arrived in Shigatse we saw a sea of people, horses, and vehicles. For local monks and laypeople the celebration had already been going on for several days, and now many dignitaries and high lamas were also arriving. Because of the extraordinary number of cars, there were a number of traffic accidents. Choeshi Rinpoche's car was hit and flipped over. He was not seriously injured, but my older brother Chipu suffered severe neck injuries and was sent to the hospital. On the same day, a car driving the khenpo of Tashi Lhunpo Monastery, Namgyal Tsewang Rinpoche, was in a head-on collision with a large truck. To our horror, everyone in the car was killed. These events were taken to be very inauspicious signs for the days ahead.

When we reached Tashi Lhunpo Monastery, Serdok Rinpoche and I found it so badly damaged that we could not even find the place where we had once lived. The only notable rebuilding we could see was the Panchen Lama's new structure, Drashi Namgyal. By the time we arrived, many rituals had already been completed, so we took part only in official events planned for those who had traveled some distance for the event. The ceremonies were splendid: Colorful prayer flags waved above; firepots of smoldering cedar leaves sprinkled

161

with tsampa offerings to local deities filled the air with their rich fragrance; with prayers, chants, and horns, monks performed sacred dances and local people performed folk dances. And of course there were ribbons cut, meetings held, and speeches filled with political messages.

During the ceremonies the Panchen Lama gave a long speech reviewing the sad history of the recent decades and offering directives for the future. This speech was sharply critical, and today all Tibetans remember his words. During our stay at the monastery, the Panchen Lama also gave a teaching on reincarnation and how to find tulkus. He even pointed out how to find a spiritual leader such as the Dalai Lama, or his own reincarnation. If we had been able to follow his advice, the ugly events surrounding his reincarnation would never have occurred.

After the consecration ceremony was finished, Serdok Rinpoche, my mother, other members of my family, and I set out on the long journey back to Kumbum. It was deep winter. The highway, now asphalt instead of rock and mud, wound through the mountains and grasslands from Lhasa to northeastern Tibet. Along the way we savored once again the grandeur of the Tibetan plateau, the snow-covered mountains visible through crystalline air at the very edges of the horizon, winds singing their symphony of mountain songs. Sometimes an eagle soared in the blue sky; sometimes horses, small and sturdy, galloped across mountain slopes. Except for the occasional convoy of military trucks, there were few other vehicles on the road. In the quiet of the car, I drank in the landscape and ruminated on the recent ceremonies.

Other than the tragic traffic accidents, politically, things had gone successfully. I could see the imposing figure of the Panchen Lama, and his forceful, inspiring voice still echoed in my ears. In that moment I had no inkling that this was to be the Panchen Lama's last teaching. Did he?

After several days of travel, we neared Kumbum. Our interim destination for that morning was Golmud, a new city built by the Chinese as a staging area for troops and transports moving into the Tibet Autonomous Region. The city lies at the southern edge of a great plateau at the foot of the mountains where the road rises toward an 18,000-foot pass on the grueling drive to Lhasa. We felt the joy and eagerness of nearing home.

But as we pulled into Golmud, we were hit with devastating news blaring from loudspeakers on the streets. "The outstanding religious leader, the great patriot, and the renowned positivist of national affairs, the Panchen Lama, has passed away at the age of 54 today at his residence in Tashi Lhunpo Monastery." We looked at each other in shock: "It's impossible!" We rushed to the front desk of a hotel where a TV was on. The date was January 28, 1989.

As we watched the newscast, tears silently streamed down our cheeks. We hardly knew what to say to each other. Even now when I recall that day, I feel the presence of the Panchen Lama. We tried to call Gyayak Rinpoche to get details on what had happened, but the phone lines were jammed with calls.

After eating a simple dinner, we discussed what to do next. I wanted to return to Tashi Lhunpo immediately, but Choeshi Rinpoche was calmer. He said, "Right now Tashi Lhunpo Monastery will be like a damaged beehive. Our arrival will only add to the chaos." So we decided to continue to Kumbum, hold a memorial ceremony for the Panchen Lama there, and return to Tashi Lhunpo in a week or so for his funeral.

All of Tibet was in mourning. On the last leg of our return to Kumbum, we passed by the azure vastness of Lake Koko Nor. At its edges farmers and nomads wept and prayed. The fragrant smoke from cedar leaves and tsampa smoldered in the fields farther along. We arrived at Kumbum to find the monks devastated. After the service we talked, and everyone, both Tibetans and Chinese cadres, expressed shock and agreed that the Panchen Lama was an irreplaceable loss. Some of them asked me, "You attended the consecration ceremony there. What happened?"

I told them I had no answers. I had heard rumors of a heart attack, but nothing had been confirmed.

Within 10 days, two cars filled with rinpoches and lamas, myself included, drove the long, tortuous road to Lhasa and on to Shigatse and Tashi Lhunpo Monastery—only this time our hearts were heavy with loss. As honored guests, we were permitted to enter the bedroom of the Panchen Lama to pay homage to his body, which was seated upright on a throne. The body was clad

163

in fine embroidered robes. Atop the Panchen Lama's head rested a golden crown with icons of the five Buddhas. His face was covered with a red embroidered fabric, and his large hands held a dorje and a bell.

I wept a silent prayer. "Master, you and the Dalai Lama both came to Kumbum Monastery in the 1950s to teach us dharma and instruct us in practice. Since then you have bestowed the cleansing rain of dharma upon us. I remember in the '60s, when we greeted you at the Xining train station, how you picked Serdok Rinpoche and me out of the crowd and called to us in Chinese. Your affectionate voice is with me still.

"And then, after you brought us to Tashi Lhunpo Monastery, when we had just begun our study of the dharma with you, I remember how the government labeled you antirevolutionary. On behalf of the dharma, the Tibetan people, and all sentient beings, you were as courageous as a roaring lion beset by cowardly foxes! They wronged you, defamed you, and threw you into prison for almost 10 years. You often said, 'The Dalai Lama is encouraging us from outside Tibet, while I am making the effort inside Tibet. Both of us naturally work together to protect Tibetan Buddhism and civilization.' Now you have left him behind. He is like an eagle with a broken wing. How can he soar into the sky alone?

"You are like a golden sun, covered now by dark clouds. Aieee, Master, I hope the birth of your reincarnation will soon be delivered." After my silent prayer, I looked around and saw Choeshi Rinpoche and Serdok Rinpoche crying and prostrating.

We had planned to visit the Panchen Lama's parents to pay our respects, but we were asked not to because of their age and because they could not endure more mourners. They were so overcome with grief that doctors had flown them by helicopter to a hospital in Lhasa. Instead, our group decided to visit Gyayak Rinpoche. At first he had refused to leave the Panchen Lama's body, insisting on guarding it himself, but afterward he had fallen ill from exhaustion and grief. Now he too was preparing to go to the hospital.

When we entered his room, Gyayak Rinpoche was lying in bed with a wet towel across his brow. While his attendants packed his things for the hospital, I had the opportunity to be alone with Gyayak Rinpoche for a few moments.

I quietly asked him, "Uncle, how did the Panchen Lama pass away?" He looked at me, paused, and unburdened himself of his story.

"After your delegation set off on your return to Kumbum, the celebration for the dedication of the stupa at the Drashi Namgyal Temple continued. Although most of the guests had already left, some who remained built a big bonfire and were dancing around it in joy. The Panchen Rinpoche stayed up watching with great pleasure," Gyayak Rinpoche said, "feeling obvious satisfaction for what he had accomplished. But later, he began to feel uncomfortable and complained of some pain. He decided maybe he should go to bed. His personal physician looked at him and gave him something to let him sleep.

"Very early the next morning someone came into my room, interrupting my prayers to tell me that the Panchen Lama had passed away. I was so shocked I just kept on shouting, 'What, what?'

"When I got to the Panchen Lama's quarters, the Panchen Lama seemed asleep. His face was so beautiful, his complexion was pale and clear, almost transparent. By this time people were running in and out of the room in panic. Someone tried to revive him; they thought he was still alive. They gave him CPR, violently compressing his chest. Panchen Rinpoche's face turned dark, gray as ashes. I shouted for the doctors to stop. I knew the Panchen Lama had passed on, but they wouldn't listen. In desperation I yelled, 'Stop, you're bothering our Master!' Still they continued."

Rinpoche did not remember exactly when, but sometime in the late afternoon a delegation from the central government in Beijing came to the Panchen Lama's quarters. It was headed by Wen Jiabao, who would become the prime minister of China. By this time the doctors had given up trying to resuscitate the Panchen Lama. An autopsy was ordered to establish the cause of death. Gyayak Rinpoche was told only that doctors had found an excess of liquid in his body and withdrew 12 bottles of fluid.

Shortly after my uncle told me this story, Serdok Rinpoche and I accompanied him to a military hospital in Lhasa. With the care of both Chinese and Tibetan doctors, his fever finally came down, but he was still weak and required ongoing hospital treatment.

One evening a yellow Nissan SUV pulled up to the hospital, unescorted.

A person wearing a blue down quilted jacket, looking like an ordinary cadre member, stepped out of the SUV. It was Hu Jintao, Party secretary of the Tibet Autonomous Region, who would later become president of the People's Republic of China. He paid his respects to Gyayak Rinpoche, and after they talked he also spoke briefly with Serdok Rinpoche and me. When he found out that we held official positions in Qinghai Province and that I was the vice chair of China's Buddhist Association and vice chair of the All-China Youth Federation, he told us that he had been chair of the All-China Youth Federation as a young man. After he became a member of China's Politburo, when I attended meetings in Beijing he continued to greet me with warmth.

Soon after Hu Jintao's visit, Gyayak Rinpoche and I received an invitation from Beijing to attend a memorial for the Panchen Lama. Gyayak Rinpoche was still recovering and could not walk very far, so I had to travel without him. It was a wet and rainy spring day in Beijing when I arrived for the memorial. This ceremony was taking place due to the Panchen Lama's political status, not out of respect for his religious eminence. I knew many leaders from the central government were attending only out of political necessity, but still there were also many people there offering khatas and bowing to his photo out of deep reverence. After the memorial I was frequently approached by people asking me, "How did the Panchen Lama pass away?" I told them what I knew, but it wasn't much.

A few days after the memorial service, the central government invited the Dalai Lama to preside over a prayer event for the Panchen Lama at Yong He Gong Monastery in Beijing, and—even more importantly—to participate in the search for the reincarnation of the Panchen Lama. The Dalai Lama declined to attend. Nevertheless, a search team was formed in China to seek the Panchen Lama's reincarnation. It was divided into two units: one political and one religious. The political division consisted of important figures from the central and provincial governments. The religious division was headed by Gyayak Rinpoche, with Chadrel Rinpoche serving as cochair; other high lamas on that committee included Jamyang Shepa Rinpoche, Kongtang Rinpoche, Ulan Gegan Rinpoche, me, and others.

The religious team quickly held its first meeting at the Mudan Hotel in Beijing to determine the procedure for the search. To our surprise, the central government reaffirmed the point that the Dalai Lama would be consulted during the search process, regardless of the fact that the search was under the supervision of the Chinese government. All the rinpoches agreed on the importance of His Holiness's involvement. Kongtang was so excited that he wanted to take the initiative, go to India, and discuss the search process with His Holiness in person.

That spring of 1989 Gyayak Rinpoche was transferred from the hospital in Lhasa to a hospital in Beijing, where Serdok Rinpoche and I helped take care of him. We stayed at a guesthouse in Yong He Gong Monastery, where our rooms were simple but adequate and transportation was convenient. Because Yong He Gong Monastery was now the only Tibetan monastery in Beijing, Serdok Rinpoche and I felt great affinity for it. It was our home away from Kumbum. But our mood was dampened by the Panchen Lama's passing and by worry about Gyayak Rinpoche's health.

One day, as we were on the bus going to the hospital, we saw hundreds of students carrying garlands of flowers toward Tiananmen Square. They were on their way to honor Hu Yaobang, who, as Party secretary in China, had blazed a liberal path in Tibet and had been the hope for democratic reform. For seven years, as a protégé of Deng Xiaoping, he had led Communist China toward liberalization, for which he had been removed from office in 1987. Now students mourned his passing.

This was all of special interest to me because five years earlier I had come close to having what would have been a difficult meeting with Hu Yaobang, who was then Party chairman. At that time I had been attending a meeting of the Qinghai Provincial Buddhist Association, and because of the bias against Tibetans, lamas, and non-Communists, I felt discriminated against and treated rudely. I was unhappy enough that I decided to resign my appointment to the association, an act that, in Communist China's political climate, was drastic.

I wrote the resignation, and knowing Party Chairman Hu Yaobang was coming to the area on a visit, I decided to hand it to him personally. Before I did so, I discussed my decision with Choeshi Rinpoche, who warned me against such a foolhardy act. He said Hu was honest and straightforward but had a temper. Then he told me a story about a recent visit Hu Yaobang had paid to Huangnan Prefecture. The Tibetan officials from that rural area arranged their reception for his visit in a traditional way, which meant paying honor to lamas before politicians. He waited and waited. When the time finally came to have a khata placed around his neck, he tore it off and screamed with rage. After hearing this story I decided to mail the letter instead.

Serdok Rinpoche and I usually passed Tiananmen Square on our way to visit Gyayak Rinpoche, so we noticed the crowd of students there growing larger each day. Soon newspapers and TV began reporting on the events in the square. Once we saw a huge portrait of Hu Yaobang, rivaling in size that of Mao Zedong—reputedly painted by students at the Central Art University—hanging on the Monument to the People's Heroes.

At first the students gathered only in the square and the streets nearby. As time went on, they took to bicycling the streets of Beijing to gather more demonstrators. Our friends Lobsang, Nima, and Tashi, Tibetan students in Beijing who supported the demonstrators in Tiananmen Square, sometimes wore white cloth bands around their foreheads with slogans in support of democracy written on them. I cautioned them to be careful.

After returning from a visit to Gyayak Rinpoche one day, I walked into Tiananmen Square and was struck by the optimism of the demonstrators. The square was now filled with a sea of people, including many professors and teachers. They were neatly dressed and wore armbands supporting the students, and the students in turn formed a protective circle around their professors. There were also children and parents in the crowd, waving banners.

Even though Gyayak Rinpoche was in the hospital, he was concerned about the events taking place in Tiananmen Square—specifically that they were getting out of hand. One day Zhen Ying, head of the United Front of the Tibet Autonomous Region, came to visit him. Rinpoche asked him exactly what the students wanted, and why the central government had not responded to their requests. Zhen Ying replied with a smile and a typical bureaucratic answer, "This is a student demonstration. Neither you nor I understand it. I believe the central government will resolve it."

The student demonstration had lasted for more than a month now and was showing no signs of diminishing. One morning on the way to the hospital, Serdok Rinpoche and I passed a semiconductor factory near the High-Level Tibetan Buddhism College of China and saw people lining up to leave work and take part in the demonstration. That day the demonstration reached its peak. The whole city was out, as many as two million people. Traffic was backed up, so it took us a long time to get to the hospital.

The hospital itself was also jammed. Ambulances were double-parked outside the hospital, as students sick from their hunger strike were moved into the emergency room. Even the hospital staff was getting ready to join the demonstration and to support a general strike. When we got to Gyayak Rinpoche's room he said, "My health is recovering, but the sounds of ambulances and sirens throughout the night have me worried. I can't sleep." He asked us to find out more about what was going on with the demonstration.

That afternoon we returned to Tiananmen Square. As we approached, columns of demonstrators filled East and West Chang'an streets. Crowds and banners were everywhere. One of the banners read, "The real boss is coming, public servants get out!" The Communists had always advertised that the "people" were the "boss" and the government was the "servant." Never had they acted that way, but the banner was reminding the world of the pretense. *Yes,* I thought, *whether you are a chairman or a party secretary, you are a servant of the people. And the people are the real bosses.* Yet in the perverse history of the People's Republic of China, when the people were not well served, it was they who paid the price. Still, I held out hope that this magnificent student movement might change this inverted master-servant relationship.

During the Cultural Revolution, Gyayak Rinpoche had taught me a type of divination using the *mala* (prayer beads) called Mo. He said that the Mo was simple but accurate. I have found that it works very well, and over the years it has served me faithfully when I have been in difficult situations.

One day during the height of the demonstrations, Rinpoche tested my divination skills by asking me to predict the result of the students' democratic 169

170 movement. After reading the Mo, I was afraid to tell him what I'd seen because it was so unthinkable. Rinpoche replied by advising me that I must trust the Mo or not consult it. He also told me that he too had read the Mo about the demonstration, and the result was so ominous that he wanted me and Serdok Rinpoche to leave Beijing immediately.

We bade good-bye to Gyayak Rinpoche, knowing he would be well cared for. As we prepared to drive back to Kumbum, the central government had already imposed martial law on Beijing. We left the city without seeing any signs of military movement. Four days later, we arrived safely back at Kumbum, only to learn of the tragedy that had unfolded behind us in Tiananmen Square.

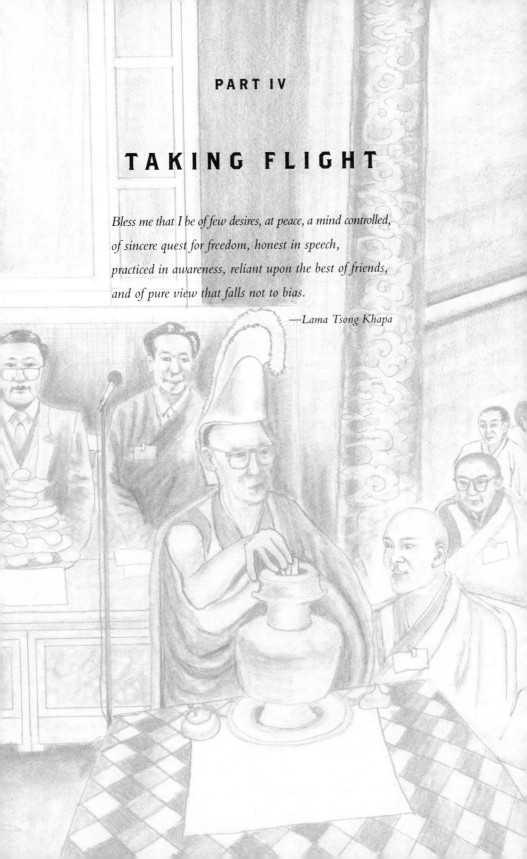

PART IV

TAKING FLIGHT

Bless me that I be of few desires, at peace, a mind controlled,
of sincere quest for freedom, honest in speech,
practiced in awareness, reliant upon the best of friends,
and of pure view that falls not to bias.

—Lama Tsong Khapa

CHAPTER 11

STEPPING INTO MY BIRTHRIGHT

Not long after my return to Kumbum, a festive celebration was held for my election to the role of khenpo, or director, of the monastery. Although we eliminated such "feudal trappings" as being carried in a sedan chair, we held a grand procession from my residence to the Golden Hall. Monks carried banners and parasols; incense swirled in the air; horns blew; drums banged. It was a joyful time for us all. In the days that followed, many prayers were said as I presided over the ceremonies from the khenpo's throne, just as Choeshi Rinpoche had done before me.

Heaviest on my mind as I took up my new responsibilities was the question of how I would reestablish and maintain the sanctity of a monk's sacred vows. Throughout its history, Kumbum Monastery had been famous for its discipline and dedication to Buddhist ideals. Since the 1930s, however, these values had declined, and dharma at Kumbum Monastery had dimmed like the setting sun. Several decades of Communist political campaigns designed to extinguish religion and subjugate its practitioners had further weakened the practice of dharma at the monastery. But now that people were allowed to follow their religious beliefs, many wanted to return to genuine monks' lives and fulfill their vows to strive for the benefit of all sentient beings.

Unlike any of my seven predecessors, I had been deprived of the years of academic discipline and rigorous studies necessary to be a khenpo in the traditional sense. Before 1958 the job of khenpo was similar to that of an academic dean of a university. Sitting on his high throne, the khenpo drilled students on religious texts by reciting one side of a dialogue in the textbook, to which the students were supposed to respond from memory. The job was a headache even then. Both teacher and student were pushed to study, and the khenpo even more so because he did not want to be embarrassed by seeming less knowledgeable than his teachers or students.

Understandably, some older monks did not consider me a real khenpo because I was not a learned scholar teaching classes, and because I had major secular duties, which was contrary to tradition. Also, the former khenpo, Choeshi Rinpoche, who had been released from prison, had never formally resigned. Proper procedure could not be followed because the government considered these routines and rituals to be part of feudalism. Historically, a khenpo had little to do with the day-to-day running of the monastery. His staff took care of all that. He was not concerned with building reconstruction and maintenance, financial matters, or counseling monks regarding their personal problems, as I was. For me, it was as if I were not only chief executive officer, but also chief operating officer.

From 1979, my predecessor Choeshi Rinpoche held the post of khenpo for 10 very difficult years while rebuilding the entire monastic system of Kumbum. The monastic system of education is based on 13 grades, but when Choeshi Rinpoche became director, he found only two or three grades still functioning, and no new teachers had been trained for many years. By the time I became director, Choeshi Rinpoche had successfully rebuilt the school up to eight grades. When Choeshi Rinpoche first took over, new monks did not even understand the precepts upon which their vows and obligations were based, and because many older monks had been forced to return to lay life or had died, again there was a scarcity of instructors. Confiscated monastic properties had not yet been returned, so there were not enough sacred instruments for ritual and ceremonial events, nor did the monastery have a stable budget for its daily operations.

Under Choeshi Rinpoche's leadership these difficulties had been greatly reduced, so that by the time I was appointed khenpo, the monastery's basic operations were reestablished. The teachings were slowly returning. However, some of Choeshi Rinpoche's assistants had undermined his efforts by allowing favoritism, profiteering, and bribery to seep into the administration of the monastery. In addition to these local problems, Deng Xiaoping's economic and cultural reforms were creating a new, more relaxed social environment; peddlers had gradually infiltrated the streets of the monastery, even setting up stalls near temples. Once again material wealth posed a growing temptation to the monastery's monks, exerting a strong, negative influence on those in and out of official positions.

Most monks were not involved in bribery or theft, however. Principled monks like Jamaga were far more common. When he was still young, Jamaga had been chosen to raise funds for our winter butter sculpture festival, for which Kumbum was justly famous. Well aware of those who had given in to the temptation to make extra money for themselves, he headed directly to a shrine to pray to the Buddhas and Protectors for guidance, and for protection from that bad karma. Then he went to his own village and told the residents that he didn't have friends in other places and asked if they could please help him with either money, or flour, or bread, or whatever else might be useful. The villagers said, "Fine, we'll do it!" Some ground flour, others made bread, and others sold something to make a monetary offering. Jamaga kept scrupulous track of where the money went, and anything left over went into the winter butter sculpture fund for the following year.

When I took office I was faced with problems of corruption, but there were many other smaller problems I had to confront, as well. One of the most delicate situations traced back to the Cultural Revolution, when a group of 35 mostly Islamic families—perhaps 100 people—had been moved into housing inside the monastery compound when their village was displaced by a road built by the Chinese government. After having lived on the monastery grounds for so many years they had come to regard it as home, and now that religious freedom was once again possible, they naturally wanted to build a mosque inside the monastery where they could worship. Such an idea was impossible for monks to accept, so it led to many discussions and negotiations, and several unpleasant incidents. Only after I took office and found the money to buy land and housing for Muslim families elsewhere was the issue resolved to everyone's satisfaction.

Another important task was to restore and preserve the precious antiques in the monastery. Some sutra texts and images of Buddha had survived the Cultural Revolution, but many had been lost. I knew that we had to do our very best to save the rare treasures that still existed, but we had only the most primitive means of protecting them. Theft was a chronic problem, with precious icons regularly appearing not only in our local shops but in the markets of Hong Kong and elsewhere. If we did not respond forcefully to this disgraceful situation, all of our treasures would soon be gone.

There were many other tasks as well, common to any large cultural organization, such as maintaining buildings and grounds, managing our finances, hosting visitors, arranging cultural exchange programs, and organizing a productive workday at the monastery. But among all these needs, renovation was paramount. Despite the earlier repairs I had managed under Gyayak Rinpoche's direction, and Choeshi Rinpoche's efforts, if Kumbum was to regain its status as one of Tibet's greatest monasteries it would need almost total reconstruction. Finding the money for this was the big challenge. In former days patrons supported monasteries and monks, but now, under a system that advocated self-reliance, monks and monasteries struggled to survive, much less pay for desperately needed renovations.

I agonized over the question of where to start, but I was encouraged by Gyayak Rinpoche's return to Xining from the hospital in Beijing. Not only was I grateful for his recovery, I was thankful to have his advice and support. Unfortunately, shortly after his return he ate some food bought from a street vendor and was rushed to the emergency room with food poisoning. He never made a full recovery from the violent illness, so I added his care to my daily monastic responsibilities. But his illness did not impair his ability to help me. One day while I was with him at the hospital, Gyayak Rinpoche noticed my anxiety and said, "We have a saying: 'The son of a horse needs to hurry, but the son of a man should take his time.' I think you are rushing yourself. This is not good. Remember, patience is the third perfection. Please go slowly, slowly. . . ." Once again, I benefited from his great wisdom.

In the winter of 1990 Gyayak Rinpoche's health worsened. Doctors used sedatives to help him sleep. His strong will to live had amazed them, but now he began slipping into unconsciousness more and more often. One day we were surprised when he awoke from his sleep clear-eyed and alert, recognizing people around him. We were thrilled. We thought his indomitable spirit had returned him to us. The doctors soon brought us back down to earth, telling us that we should begin to prepare for his passing. Soon he began to drift away once again. This time he faded further and further from us until he was gone.

Serdok Rinpoche and I began reciting prayers over Gyayak Rinpoche's body, while his two loyal attendants opened the door to mourners who had already gathered outside. The crowd began to move slowly past, saying prayers and draping khatas on the foot of Gyayak Rinpoche's bed. Their sobs brought home the enormity of our loss and infected us all with their grief.

We followed Gyayak Rinpoche's body in a funeral procession from Xining back to Kumbum, where it was received by grieving monks at the monastery. After they washed his body with saffron water, his students and attendants took paper inscribed with holy Sanskrit seed syllables, coated them with butter, and placed them over the openings on his face: his eyes, his nose, his mouth. Wrapped in cloth and dressed in his ceremonial robes, Gyayak Rinpoche was formally invited to join the funeral procession.

So highly respected was Gyayak Rinpoche that more than 100 delegations headed by high lamas from monasteries all over Tibet came to the funeral, as well as officials from many government bureaus, elevating the occasion's importance to that of a state funeral. Seated upright in the lotus position dressed in all his finery, Gyayak Rinpoche was placed on a sedan chair to which disciples and mourners had tied a long train of khatas, which they held off the ground as they followed the solemn procession. Prayers and chanting, drums, horns, and banners accompanied him to the courtyard for placement, chair and all, into the *dung kang*—the cremation furnace where Gyayak Rinpoche would make his final offering to the deities—the offer of his earthly body.

Tears welled in my eyes, and my heart felt like a fragile vessel at sea in a raging storm. Gyayak Rinpoche had been my uncle, my beloved teacher, and my protector; I loved him utterly, and I had felt unconditional love from him in return. His death left a devastating void in the center of my life.

After the funeral, we decided to build a stupa in his honor, and a strange series of events followed. Cedar, which is very difficult to find around Kumbum, is the traditional building material for the central structure of a stupa. My resourceful brother, Tenba Gyatso, whose devotion to Gyayak Rinpoche was unparalleled, decided to go in search of real cedar. His quest took him to a town more than a day's drive from Kumbum, where, after questioning local residents, he found some cedar posts in the yard of an old Mongolian. My brother offered to buy them, but when the man learned that they were to be used to build a stupa for Gyayak Rinpoche, he insisted on giving them as an offering. Three years later, when Gyayak Rinpoche's successor was found, he turned out to be the grandson of this old man who had offered the wood!

During this same time my mother's health also began to fail. She lived in a room in my residence—small but cozy—off the courtyard. I was very happy to have her near me, and I appreciated the help she provided in running the household. She was happy, too, in spite of chronic back pain. My mother and I didn't think a sore back was serious or very unusual for a person in her seventies, but when the Panchen Lama had visited in the early 1980s, he insisted she be examined at the hospital in Xining. Doctors discovered she had spinal tuberculosis, and thanks to the Panchen Lama's intervention and the fact that my mother was Gyayak Rinpoche's sister, she received excellent medical attention.

My mother was hospitalized for three months of testing, and although doctors gave her a series of shots to reduce her pain, my mother became completely bedridden. When she came home from the hospital I didn't know how to help her. We called in a Tibetan doctor, who gave her traditional treatment and recommended exercises to strengthen her body. We washed her legs with Epsom salts, massaged the soles of her feet with wooden rollers, and helped her so she could stand up to exercise. In a few months she could stand by herself, and after a few more months she was able to walk again.

Many people commented on her miraculous recovery, and some even came to me to learn what special prayers or mysterious medicine I had used to hasten my mother's recuperation. I told them that the secret of my mother's cure was her ability to emphasize positive thoughts. She had never once complained about the cruel blows that had filled her years since the Chinese occupation—the loss of my father, the public humiliations of our family, and the deaths of two sons from tuberculosis. She always placed unlimited faith in the Buddha, the Dharma, and the Sangha. These were her medicines.

By 1989 my mother had recovered sufficiently to join me on our trip to Tashi Lhunpo Monastery for the inauguration of the Panchen Lama's stupa. She seemed to enjoy the rugged car travel across the vast, open Tibetan landscape, and the company of her offspring. She was always happiest surrounded by her children and grandchildren. However, my mother had begun to lose some of her mental sharpness. She could no longer recognize some of her youngest grandchildren and great-grandchildren, although that was not altogether surprising; because she and my father came from such large families there were 200 or 300 of us, spread over three generations, who gathered for visits at her family home.

Her household responsibilities reduced, my mother had more time to focus on me, often scolding or lecturing me. "Where have you been? Someone came to see you and you weren't here; you have to show respect. . . ." Her scolding only made me feel more protective of her. I did my best to show my love for her, and I prayed that when the time came she would have a happy end to a life filled with hardship but also joy.

Even with the passing of the Panchen Lama and Gyayak Rinpoche, their influence followed my steady, if unbidden, rise in the religious and political hierarchies. Nor was it possible, member or not, to refuse such "honors" under the tightly controlled regimen of the Communist Party. The following spring, I was elected to the Chinese People's Political Consultative Committee

(CPPCC), an advisory group to the National People's Congress, the supreme law-giving body in Communist China. On the first day of the group's annual conference in Beijing, my family called to warn me that my mother was failing. My old friend Jamyang Shepa Rinpoche, from Labrang Monastery, reminded me of the old Chinese proverb that one can never simultaneously fulfill both duty to one's family and political duty to the court. He suggested that I ask to be excused to attend to my mother.

As I was leaving Beijing to return home, the phone rang: My mother had just passed away peacefully in the company of our family. I did not immediately break down, for Gyayak Rinpoche's words came to mind: "We should attend to people in their lifetimes and not shed tears of guilt and regret when they are gone." I also found comfort in a strong feeling of my mother's presence, which soothed my sorrow.

When I returned to Kumbum, I found monks reciting prayers for the dead. Drashi, my secretary at Kumbum, had lit many oil lamps for my mother in her room. I comforted my sister-in-law and oldest sister, who were crying, and then I walked over to my mother's body. "Why did you leave when I was not present?" I asked her. "I wanted to recite 'The Three Refuges' prayer for you. When I was a young boy, you and Father often visited me at the monastery, which made me happy, but every time you left, I felt this same sadness. This time I know you will never return." With that thought, the emotional realization that she was truly gone hit me, and I wept.

Images rapidly succeeded one another in my mind. My mother patching up the poster denouncing our family. My older brother's shame at having to grovel like a slave in front of the village's Communist leader. My oldest sister, accused of being antirevolutionary but somehow maintaining her liveliness and humor. My father not abiding any nonsense as he gave me a haircut. His embarrassing the changtso over my food and the lice in my bed. All these ties to my family came crashing down around my heart.

Monks continued their recitations. I also recited prayers, but when I closed my eyes again I saw before me in the interim realm of the bardo (the thin space between this life and the next) those who had been important in my life and had now passed through both worlds. I saw my first teacher, Tsultrim

Lhaksem, who had taught me to visualize all sentient beings as my mothers and all personal enemies as my brothers. I saw Jamaga, who quietly expressed the essence of his practice: compassion. I saw Gyayak Rinpoche, who had led me into adulthood by serving as my grandfather, father, friend, and beloved teacher. I prayed silently. "Dear Gyayak Rinpoche, although you were cautious of the political campaigns wrought by wolves and tigers, when calamity fell, you always helped others. Now you have passed away, along with my other teachers and loved ones—including now my mother. Now I am alone. In the future, who will guide me in times of trouble?"

A former temple near my residence, Gashima, had been empty for years except during the winter months when monks stored winter meat there—yak and sheep carcasses that nomads had given us as offerings. Pilgrims had begun to resume their visits to Kumbum, and on this day, as they made their way from temple to temple prostrating in front of each shrine, they came to Gashima and opened a side door to peek in. As I was walking by I overheard their shocked voices: "Oh, that's such a big temple, but there are no statues there, no holy things, only big piles of meat."

Their words struck me hard. I was shamed by the bloody image of sentient beings that rose in my mind, and I began some calculations: If one monk consumed the equivalent of one sheep per year, then 500 monks would eat 500 sheep a year. In 10 years, they would have eaten 5,000 sheep! How many karmic killings were committed each year just for the benefit of monks? When I thought of the problem in this way, my heart ached. At that moment I became a vegetarian, and I also knew that I had just found a home for the new college I had always dreamed of creating.

Every large monastery in Tibet consisted of four schools, the first of which all students entered as young nuns and monks. Many eventually gave up their studies for physical labor or administrative work in the monastery, but those who continued could earn the advanced degree of Geshe, or proceed to the third Geshe level of Lharampa (in Kumbum called *Ran Jahm Ba*), the equivalent of a doctoral degree.

In the traditional system young monks listened to their teachers, taking notes and asking few questions. If a student had questions, he had to figure out how to narrow them down to *one* with the fewest possible words. There were no written exams, but by listening to students recite their sutras and memorized commentaries, and by listening to their debates in the courtyard in the afternoons, teachers could observe their students' progress and discuss their performance in class the following day. This was the traditional way. But I knew that the teaching methods at Kumbum would have to adapt to modern times. Therefore, in addition to restoring the quality of the existing colleges, my colleagues and I decided to build a new monastic college for teaching in a more contemporary way. The Panchen Lama, by his willingness to embrace new ideas, had taught me well.

The school I had in mind would take new directions in education that were already being practiced in Buddhist monasteries in India. It would have daily classes with one day off each week, Western style. Lessons, also of a Western type, would offer such subjects as reading, writing, grammar, math, and logic. Gradually, more could be added—science, history, and so forth. Teachers would be young and enthusiastic. For the first time they would have blackboards to write on. In this new setting I hoped students would become motivated to learn out of interest rather than a sense of obligation. To advance this vision, however, I had needed a space for the school—and now, along with vegetarianism, I had found Gashima.

Within a few months the new school was ready to open its doors, and it became an immediate success. Modernization brought new excitement, and it encouraged more communication between teacher and student, who both benefited from the exchange. Along with a new curriculum, we tried new methods, including having teams compete in a quiz show format to test their knowledge of Buddhist thought. Students studied very hard so their team could win. Motivation was very strong in students and teachers.

Reactions to the project were more mixed, however, among older teachers. Some monks wondered why we needed a new college and new ways. Suspicion and skepticism among these older teachers ran high, but I was determined to prove the value of the new school. Once it was in operation, we chose an auspicious day for a celebration and invited the entire monastery to the opening.

The students put on a demonstration using the quiz show format to answer very difficult questions. They were asked to provide a specific commentary on a sutra, or to identify from which sutra a quote was taken. The students showed such a deep and wide knowledge that they won over many of the skeptics, including the gegue (disciplinarian) of the four colleges. To further soothe his feelings I presented him with a key to the college and a small endowment. This put Gashima under his control and blunted his criticism.

My teacher Shar Dong Rinpoche, who had given Serdok Rinpoche and me our first university instruction after the Cultural Revolution, praised me for taking a worthwhile idea to successful fruition. He said, "Your practice has improved." I felt gratified and hopeful. My confidence was enjoying a rainstorm after a long drought. I was becoming more comfortable in my role as khenpo—I was practicing the dharma through the path of action.

Having completed the new college, I decided that there could be no better spiritual practice than to help reverse the destruction wrought by the Communist occupation of Kumbum. I began to make drawings of all the buildings in the monastery, including plans for reconstruction. My experience of working on the Golden Hall, the Kalachakra Temple and Mandala, and now Gashima gave me the assurance I needed to take on this ambitious project.

However, rebuilding was not only a matter of will: My projects had to be financed. We hardly had enough money for day-to-day operations, let alone funds to restore Kumbum's former architectural glory. I knew this would be a long-term project, assuming I could ever make it happen. Then came an unexpected catastrophe with a silver lining. There is an old saying that with every disaster comes opportunity.

In the summer of 1990, a major earthquake rocked our region. The epicenter was only 150 kilometers from our monastery. In spite of great damage and loss of life, in Kumbum, thankfully, no one was hurt. The next morning, a group of us gathered to make a full inspection of the monastery. We found buildings that had collapsed and roads that were blocked by landslides. Immediately we began to make a detailed list of necessary repairs. Some of the young monks took photos. Local contractors and craftsmen came in to estimate the money, supplies, and labor needed for the job.

Throughout the region government agencies and public institutions petitioned for disaster relief from Beijing. I, too, filed a petition. When it comes to requesting money, the efficiency of bureaucracies suddenly asserts itself; agencies familiar with the procedures have large, trained staffs ready to submit an initial report of damage and estimates almost immediately. At this time, in 1990, we had no office equipment—not even a typewriter—and no office supplies. Nor did we have a secretarial staff. It took a week to handwrite the detailed report. I knew the report clearly explained our situation, but I worried because it was not typed and lacked bureaucratic language. I was afraid its old-fashioned appearance would fail to impress the appropriate officials, who were accustomed to receiving proposals with a more sophisticated appearance. We had developed the photographs ourselves, hoping they would make our submission more palatable to the bureaucratic eye, but I knew the photos looked amateurish.

A damage assessment committee from Beijing arrived in nearby Xining, so I rushed there, report in hand. The committee had already adjourned, however, so everyone was leaving as I walked in. Hoping against hope, I handed our report to the Qinghai provincial governor Jin Ji Peng, who studied it for a moment. "You've done a great job! But you are too late," he told me. I tried to reason with him, and then he surprised me: "Take this to the deputy secretary at my office," he said. "Tell him I sent you."

Although he was only recently appointed, I knew Governor Jin Ji Peng from his past visits to Kumbum, where I had received him warmly. As a minority Muslim from Central China, he may have had special empathy for our situation. He might also have realized that a restored Kumbum Monastery could bring greater prosperity to the region, and thereby benefit his own reputation. In any case, it was the middle of the night when I returned to Kumbum, empty-handed but hopeful; the governor's secretary had told me he would put my document into the hands of the damage assessment committee, and he had encouraged me to polish our material in advance of the next stage of evaluation.

The very next day I returned to Xining and bought an electric typewriter. I also sent a young monk to the store to take the two-week typing course being offered free with the purchase of the typewriter. For the next few days my assistants and I rewrote parts of our application, also redoing the photos so that we could submit a more professional document with the required carbon copies at the next stage of the process. I called the local Party secretary to gain his support. Perhaps our effort touched the dharma-protecting deity of our monastery, because soon after this, Qinghai Province established a special assessment team for our monastery alone, and they sent our new report on to Beijing for review, another stroke of good fortune. This change meant that whatever funds were approved would be specifically designated for our monastery and would not be shared with other agencies. It was good news, but still I knew that nothing came easily in Communist China.

For the next year, I made the three-day trip to Beijing almost monthly to plead our case. I became very familiar with the bureaucracy of the central government, and I made every effort to visit all the relevant departments as often as necessary. Thanks to my previous elections to various religious and political positions, I was already friendly with some of the government officials. Making *la guan xi* (personal relationships) is very important in China if you're going to get anything done. Now when I made an appointment and identified myself, or called at an office and offered my card, I would meet with someone of much higher influence than before. Ironically, because of these changes in my own status, local cadres in Qinghai who for many years had looked down on me now courted me to assist them in getting more funds from the central government. An even greater irony was that my robes now gave me an advantage by making me appear a little more exotic than other petitioners.

Finally Kumbum received a grant for a sizable sum. This was fantastic news. Inspired by the Panchen Lama's example of self-reliance and my own desire not to waste any money, I made the radical decision not to use any government-approved contractors. Their work was shoddy and their honesty questionable, so I decided that Kumbum would create its own contracting company. I put monks in charge of the overall planning, design, and logistics.

185

For jobs that required special skills we hired laypeople we knew and trusted, many of whom were often employed by the monastery and already involved with the artwork for which Kumbum is famous.

We sought the advice of engineers to analyze the special geologic problems we faced. Kumbum Monastery was built on fill in what had once been a ravine. Walls and foundations had to be redesigned and reinforced to avoid disfiguring the monastery. In the end we employed more than 100 workers, and I was involved in the work at every level.

We had other obstacles to overcome, too. None of the people who worked for city and county offices knew us. In the past if we wanted to build a house or a shop we just did it, so we had no history of relations with the local bureaucracy, or experience in how to get around it. Acquiring building and land-use permits was difficult. We had to set up offices in town, buy modern tools, equipment, and supplies. We even set up a shop to termite-proof our lumber, as required by law, and bought a truck—all this before work could even begin. But yet again my connections to the Panchen Lama, Gyayak Rinpoche, and my friends in Beijing oiled the wheels of our project. I have to admit to a feeling of satisfaction that came with every success. My political and social situations were beyond anything I could have conceived of in the time of Mao, but remembering those days sharpened my appreciation for the good I was able to achieve now.

After six years of intense effort our reconstruction project was complete. The monastery looked as it might have when it was new, which was tremendously gratifying to us all. We held a large ceremony, joined by high-ranking officials and monks from other monasteries. The police estimated attendance at more than 100,000! The news media was there in full force, including TV crews. Foreigners were invited; the occasion was perfect propaganda for "demonstrating religious freedom" and the "preservation of Tibetan cultural heritage." The only thing missing was the sun. The weather had been rainy and cloudy all day. But when the huge thangka—Sakyamuni Buddha made of sewn fabric, 25 by 30 meters (82 by 98 feet) in size—was unrolled on the smooth, steep mountain behind the monastery, the clouds suddenly parted, revealing the brilliant blue Tibetan sky. Everyone exclaimed, "The Buddha-light shines on everything!"

When I think back to that day, I realize that actions such as renovating Kumbum Monastery stood at the center of my life of spiritual practice. As much as I admired the contemplative life, it did not seem to be the path I was to travel.

Among the many influential Party members I met, Dundrup Gyal was one of my favorites. We were friends, but I also admired him as a Tibetan who had worked his way up through the ranks to finally become Party secretary of Hainan Prefecture. Unlike so many Communist Party members, Dundrup Gyal was not a political opportunist, nor was he a traitor to Tibet. He was faithful to Tibetan culture and the Tibetan people, and he was not afraid to speak his mind.

I first met Dundrup Gyal in 1985, when he was traveling with the Panchen Lama. He was elegantly dressed, wearing a heavy Russian-style coat with a fox-fur collar over his plain Mao suit. However, on his tanned face I saw traces of his rough life growing up as a nomad. Dundrup Gyal's bravery was inspired by the Panchen Lama. Once the Panchen Lama heard that the Chinese government was to give a portion of Tibetan land south of the Himalayas to India. He became upset and went directly to the office of the party secretary, banged his fist on the official's desk, and shouted, "During the Cultural Revolution, you denounced me as a traitor. Now you are giving our land to the government of India. How can you do such a thing? Who is the traitor now?" The Party secretary was shaken and pleaded, "Calm down, Master, please calm down."

The Panchen Lama's willingness to confront such a powerful official gave Dundrup Gyal courage to do the same. His feelings for his native land ran deep. He built Tibetan schools so children could learn the Tibetan language, established hospitals and clinics based on Tibetan medicine, and promoted Tibetan cadres to higher positions in the Party. He even insisted on adding some Tibetan styling to new buildings. He also encouraged local industrial development and private businesses, and implemented new farming projects and new dams. Dundrup Gyal was a devoted and high-minded reformer. 187

In June of 1993, Dundrup Gyal traveled to Beijing for a private meeting with China's president, Jiang Zemin. Later, when he told me about the meeting, he confided that, besides reporting on his plans for his prefecture, he had mentioned his ideas for resolving issues relating to the Dalai Lama. He had voiced his opinion that the Dalai Lama was not only the spiritual leader of Tibet, but was also renowned and respected around the world. If the government opposed the Dalai Lama, he had argued, domestic and international issues would become more and more complicated. Why not unite with him? I admired his courage to act so forthrightly. Dundrup Gyal told me that he had also presented his suggestions in writing. I didn't like the sound of this, remembering what had happened to the Panchen Lama after his 70,000 Character Petition.

Soon after this, there was a terrible accident in Hainan Prefecture. A dam broke, sweeping away several villages and killing several hundred people. In the government investigation that followed, Dundrup Gyal's enemies attributed the disaster to his incompetence and corruption. In the past, his style of governing had been praised as caring like a father, but suddenly it was being attacked as chauvinistic paternalism. His previously celebrated devotion to Tibet's well-being was now being reassessed as "local nationalism," and his praise of the Panchen Lama had become "an expression of superstitious thought." Even his building projects, with their emphasis on Tibetan-style architecture, were now being criticized as unpatriotic.

The most serious accusation, however, was that Dundrup Gyal was directly responsible for the dam break and for the resulting casualties—that his staff had embezzled public funds, received bribes, and bribed higher-ranking officials to avoid meeting construction laws and regulations. Many of Dundrup Gyal's friends were swiftly jailed or placed under house arrest. Shocked and no doubt terribly afraid of the personal repercussions, Dundrup Gyal completely broke down and was placed in a convalescent hospital.

I visited him there in an effort to offer him some comfort. Although he was being assailed from all directions, I knew him to be an honest and sincere man. I was shocked by his careworn face. The confidence he had exuded in the past had vanished. His office secretaries, assistants, drivers, and other attendants were gone as well. He had been utterly abandoned.

He poured out his bitterness to me. "The loss that the dam brought was certainly serious, and for that I'm willing to take full responsibility. However, it was a technical problem, not a criminal one." He told me that by the time the construction had begun, he had already been promoted to a higher position. He did concede that staff members might have been corrupt—he didn't know—but he was not directly responsible for the operation and maintenance of the dam. The Party had turned him into their scapegoat.

He breathed a long sigh of despair. "All my friends have become my enemies. All the good things I have done have been cited as evidence of my crime. Those who once begged for my help now avoid me." He paused and continued, "Frankly, I'm surprised that you would come to see me."

The Dundrup Gyal case dragged on for several months, until a large Muslim protest in Qinghai diverted the public's attention and the case slowly faded away. Eventually he was released and transferred to Xining, where he was reabsorbed into the anonymity of the bureaucracy. Like the Panchen Lama, Dundrup Gyal was a Tibetan of vision and courage who spoke too loudly, achieved too much, and shone too brightly. Despite his loyalty to the Communist Party, he was brought down by those he tried to serve.

Was not my star shining brightly, too? Could not the same thing happen to me? Both my life experience and my spiritual training served as constant reminders that it could. No force seems stronger than that of impermanence.

CHAPTER 12

THE FEAST OF PRIVILEGE
REVEALS ITS PRICE

One day in 1993, representatives of the Security Bureau of the central government came to Kumbum Monastery to check routes for a safe visit to the monastery by China's president, Jiang Zemin. Years before, when he was Party secretary of Shanghai, Jiang Zemin had been involved with religious affairs, so I considered him reasonably receptive to our needs.

We were still in the middle of renovations, and it was raining. The roads were muddy, but we did our best to prepare them for welcoming "our leader" by spreading gravel and keeping other cars away until he left. At around one o'clock on the afternoon that Jiang Zemin arrived, his motorcade, led by motorcycles and followed by vans, slowly wheeled onto the monastery grounds. Monks lined up with their long trumpets, flowers, incense, and a yellow parasol to offer him a traditional, noisy welcome.

Chairman Jiang stepped out of his vehicle as monks and local folks cheered dutifully. He waved back at the crowd, and I was surprised at how ordinary he seemed—quite modest, really. I presented him with a khata, which he graciously accepted. He then closed his palms and bowed in a traditional greeting to all the monks. As he was escorted into the reception room of the monastery, he looked around and remarked, "This is an exquisite place."

When it was my turn to speak I kept in mind what the Qinghai provincial leaders had told me: Chairman Jiang was not coming to Kumbum Monastery for the purpose of inspecting our renovations. He just wanted to tour some historical sites and learn about local customs. They told me I should speak for only 10 minutes, including a brief report about the work we had done to the monastery. They warned me not to mention any sensitive political issues, including the need for further funds for renovation.

I had planned on bringing up the benefits of talks with His Holiness the Dalai Lama. I had also wanted to discuss the search for the new Panchen Lama, which was still ongoing. However, taking heed of the official's warning, I changed my speech, but having avoided those sensitive political topics, I decided at least to bring up our need for more funding for the monastery.

When the time came I spoke to our visitors in Chinese, in honor of our guest, and ran through a brief history of Kumbum Monastery. Jiang Zemin listened attentively. He remarked, "Your Mandarin is better than mine."

I pressed this tiny opening. "During the Cultural Revolution, our beloved Premier Zhou Enlai ordered that this monastery should be protected. Today when people think of him, they are filled with emotions of gratitude. After you became chairman, our monastery received some funds for renovation, but there is still more work to be done. In the future, people will be as thankful to you as we are to Premier Zhou Enlai." Both guests and hosts clapped after I finished my comments. Jiang Zemin looked very pleased, and looked up to the ceiling momentarily. He said, "How much funding has been allotted you?" he asked.

"Initially, we were to receive ¥36 million, but after the terrible floods in southern China, our allotment was reduced to ¥20 million, but—"

Jiang Zemin interrupted and with an appreciative smile said, "My first stop after stepping off my plane was intended to be a pleasurable little tourist visit to your monastery. I only wanted to visit this ancient Buddhist site; now, I see you have given me my first work-related meeting."

Everyone laughed. Looking at Gan Ziyu, director of the National Development and Reform Commission, Chairman Jiang said, "Please consider Arjia Rinpoche's request for funding. Protecting national treasures is also

191

important." I was very pleased. Later I escorted Chairman Jiang on a tour of the monastery. Again our conversation was congenial and relaxed. When we stopped in front of the Golden Hall, he paused to adjust his suit before respectfully entering. As we passed the grand exhibition of butter sculptures, Jiang Zemin was very impressed, and praised it profusely. "It is better than Madame Tussauds wax museum in London," he remarked.

Later, while posing for group photos at the entrance of the Golden Hall, Jiang Zemin looked up and noticed two couplet boards above the front portal. Couplet boards are usually painted blue with gold writing in Sanskrit, Tibetan, or even Chinese, and placed over the main entrances of temples. Ours were blank. He asked why. I was at a loss for words, but a quick-witted provincial official replied, "We prepared them for you. Please fill in the blank boards with your *own* calligraphy." The monks in our little group gave me a puzzled look, but fortunately said nothing. Chairman Jiang seemed flattered and accepted the invitation, writing, "Butter Sculpture Gallery" in very passable calligraphy.

By four o'clock in the afternoon, Jiang Zemin and his staff had gone. I was relieved that the visit had gone so well. Mr. Li, the chief of police for Huangzhong County, came over and said, "I'm very pleased that we have perfectly fulfilled the task of the reception. In the old days, people described meeting their emperor as an honor. Our meeting with Chairman Jiang was like meeting an emperor."

Everyone laughed, thinking he was joking. He shook his head and continued, "Really, I think so. He is the emperor of today's China." Although we now live in the twenty-first century, and Mao is long gone, many Chinese still have this mentality. I fear this can only cloud their thinking and contribute to disastrous Chinese Communist policies that have resulted from too much power being placed into too few hands. Even in these modern times, the dragon is alive and well.

Despite the disastrous events at Tiananmen Square, the early 1990s was a very productive time for me. In addition to the work at the monastery, I also helped locate the first Red Cross hospital in Qinghai Province, which provided food and emergency medical relief programs to remote nomadic communities. In several instances I helped track down unscrupulous men—sometimes monks, and sometimes police officers themselves—who were stealing priceless religious artifacts from monasteries. I supported efforts—sometimes with my own money—to retrieve sacred objects from the black market and restore them to their original altars. I helped organize three international conferences to bring together, for the first time, Tibetan, Chinese, Japanese, and Korean Buddhist traditions. And I tried never to miss a chance to champion the rebuilding of the thousands of monasteries that had been looted and destroyed during the Cultural Revolution.

In the third century BCE, King Asoka stored *sarira* (relics) of the Buddha in 84,000 stupas throughout his kingdom in India. He hoped that they would forever stay accessible and thus benefit humankind, but very few sarira have survived to this day. According to some accounts there are still sarira in many locations, but it is difficult to say if they are true relics. However, the Buddha-tooth relics at Badachu Park in Beijing and in Sri Lanka are generally recognized as authentic. In 1955 these sarira had toured Burma, escorted by Geshe Lharampa Sherab Gyatso, a friend of the Panchen Lama and the same high lama who had visited Serdok Rinpoche and me at Kumbum in late 1961. In April 1994, at the invitation of Burma's military government, the Buddhist Association of China sent another delegation to Burma to display the sarira and receive offerings from the Burmese. I was to be a member of the delegation, and I was overjoyed by the honor of traveling with the Buddha tooth.

During the meeting in Beijing held to brief members of the entourage, we learned that the political situation in Burma was unstable because the military had usurped power, annulling the democratic elections of April 1992. The Burmese government was hoping to quiet the unrest by displaying the Buddhist relics and distracting the public. They also expected the sarira to generate a tremendous number of offerings, more than enough to cover the expenses of our delegation.

For this trip a special case was being built for viewing the sarira: a small stupa with a window, in which the tooth lay visible on a golden lotus flower cushion.

The day before our departure we had a public ceremony. As we were reciting sutras, several hundred people who had crowded into the hall suddenly knelt and prostrated, exclaiming, "The Buddha tooth is emitting light!" Unfortunately, from where I was standing, I was unable to witness this miraculous event.

The next day, as armed police waited to escort our delegation and the sarira to the Beijing airport, we held another brief ceremony. I was finishing my prayers when the miracle happened again. First, the color from the small opening of the stupa turned bright red, then it dimmed. A misty glow of white light rose from the sarira, like steam rising from a hot pool. We fell silent, and then a murmur grew: "Lights are coming, lights are coming; what's going on?" A few seconds later the white light began taking on colors, slowly fading from green to red to blue to yellow, and then gradually it receded, like a retreating rainbow. Suddenly, someone walked in front of the window for a moment, blocking our view. After he passed, the light had disappeared. The phenomenon lasted less than two minutes, but it was long enough for us to know with certainty what we had seen. I will never forget this vision. Whenever I think of it, I feel myself filled with renewed devotion, like a balloon filling with helium.

On our arrival to Yangon, Burma, we were greeted by a gloriously beautiful day and several thousand Burmese Buddhists who had been patiently waiting at the airport for the arrival of the sarira. Most of the people wore festive attire and were led by their local monks, whose looks differed greatly from ours; these Burmese monks were barefoot, dressed in dark saffron robes, and they carried begging bowls. They used fans decorated with Buddha's figure to cool themselves in the heat, which was already terrible in April. Everything was so different from Tibet!

Accompanied by sacred Burmese music and prayers, representatives from various monasteries and government officials carefully moved the sarira to a beautifully decorated platform full of fresh flowers. There it was placed under a canopy on a long, low wagon ornately painted in gold and red, with flowers draped over the whole thing like a colorful curtain. It was pulled by an elephant caparisoned in equal splendor. Monks and laypeople along the route sang songs praising the Buddha, the Dharma, and the Sangha. From the size of the crowds, we realized that everyone in Yangon must have been given the day off from work. We passed shrine after shrine along the way. Residents from nearby villages prostrated and scattered water and flowers on the streets ahead of the procession.

For more than an hour the procession crept through cheering, praying, bowing Burmese throngs until it finally arrived at the World Peace Pagoda, where the official welcoming reception took place. The sarira was "invited" into the large hall and placed on the dais. Burmese monks knelt on one side of the relic and prostrated before it three times, then prostrated three times toward us. General Khin Nyunt, military dictator of Burma, entered with his entourage and prostrated first to the sarira and then to both the Burmese high monks and our delegation.

When General Khin Nyunt left after a very impressive ceremony, the public was allowed to come in and view the relics. Inexplicably, an image flashed in my mind. I saw myself as a boy with my dear friend Serdok Rinpoche in Tashi Lhunpo, emptying privies, and I heard the voice of Gyayak Rinpoche saying, as he had so often, "The social status of a person is as light as a piece of paper, with little weight and easily blown away; however, compassion is a piece of gold, still shining even if it has been buried for a hundred years."

I very much wanted to visit a Burmese monastery and learn how monks lived in this dramatically different world. When we did so, however, I had a sense that the monks in this monastery were not truly settled there. The small sleeping rooms (where eight or nine monks slept crowded together on the floor) were devoid of amenities, except for pictures of movie stars pinned to the walls, which made me think the rooms had been hastily assembled for our visit.

We also went to a big monastic university, where, even though it was summer break, there were still 600 students. We ate a meal cooked outside the monastery in huge cauldrons. Bells rang when the food was ready. First monks, then novices came outside to stand in line with their bowls. In the bowls were four little cups for receiving the food, which included meat along with rice and vegetables.

Later we saw lines of monks in their deep saffron robes, holding their fans and begging bowls, walking toward town on the raised paths that separated the green fields in the countryside. Every monastery has its own specific

195

village where the monks beg. Each house in the village has a little shrine with a box out front, almost like a mailbox. Inside are small cups filled with food for which the monks exchange their empty cups. A newly ordained monk has to find a previously uncommitted family if he is to be fed.

I would have enjoyed staying at one of those monasteries. They were so serene. Tibetan monasteries seemed almost hyperactive by comparison: monks rushing here and there; believers chanting and performing prostrations; the endless stream of tourists. In Burma, we could hear birds everywhere. Before we left we met with political and religious leaders who greatly impressed me with their scholarliness.

Having grown up in Communist-controlled Tibet, reviled and punished for being an incarnate lama, I tried to remind myself every day how fortunate I was. I had no political power of my own, but my connections in Beijing were, at times, tantamount to wielding power. Whenever I thought of my standing, I gave thanks again to Gyayak Rinpoche for his lessons in following a spiritual path, to the Panchen Lama for his lessons in treading the political path, and to both of them for supporting my efforts to balance the two.

I could be proud of these things because they served to benefit others. But I never fooled myself. I benefited personally as well. I enjoyed luxuries that few Tibetans could even dream of. Living in the realm of samsara, I was not immune to being intoxicated by my associations with men of power (as relative and tenuous as I knew those associations to be). My main goal—to ensure the continuation of Buddha's teachings—remained constant, but I did like the life of privilege, there is no denying it. But here is my point: There were times during the 1990s when my privileged position and my advocacy for freedom of religion miraculously joined—like two streams merging to create a larger, more powerful river—and these were moments of great joy and great clarity.

However, Communist Chinese repression and coercion, like the breath of a restless dragon, were closer than I realized.

On May 14, 1995, I was stunned by the news that, in India, His Holiness the Fourteenth Dalai Lama had announced the name of the reincarnated Eleventh

Panchen Lama. My immediate fear was that the Chinese government would not accept his decision and would put itself at odds with Tibetan tradition. And I was right. Swiftly the government-controlled Chinese media moved to reject the Dalai Lama's choice. As one news commentator put it, "The Dalai Lama's biased announcement of the reincarnation of the Panchen Lama does not conform to the tradition of Tibetan Buddhism. His announcement betrays the constitutional guarantee of religious freedom and violates the national sovereignty of China."

The unusual thing was that the Panchen Lama had passed away in 1989, six years before. After he did, the government had quickly established a search team to find his reincarnation. Gyayak Rinpoche, as his dharma teacher, was placed in charge of the religious aspect of the search, assisted by Chadrel Rinpoche, head of Tashi Lhunpo Monastery. I was appointed to the selection committee. But because of the June 4th incident at Tiananmen Square in 1989, the Politburo had postponed the search for the new Panchen Lama. Liberalization—with its respect for Tibetan cultural traditions—was over.

To complicate matters, Gyayak Rinpoche and Chadrel Rinpoche hadn't agreed on where to conduct the search. Gyayak Rinpoche was aware that other parts of Tibet were unhappy that so many of Tibet's highest leaders (including the Dalai Lama and the late Panchen Lama) had come from the Amdo region near Kumbum Monastery. He proposed that at least one candidate hail from each province with a significant Tibetan population: Qinghai, Gansu, Sichuan, Yunnan, and of course the Tibet Autonomous Region. On the other hand, Chadrel Rinpoche insisted that the search should be limited to Shigatse, the area around Tashi Lhunpo Monastery, the primary residence of the Panchen Lama—or at least not extend beyond the boundaries of the Tibet Autonomous Region.

The Chinese government trusted Chadrel Rinpoche to do their bidding more than they did Gyayak Rinpoche, so they allowed Chadrel Rinpoche to continue the search, asking only that he report frequently to the central government on his progress. In the meantime, Chadrel Rinpoche's search team concealed what was happening from Gyayak Rinpoche, who was in the hospital. Chadrel Rinpoche resented Gyayak Rinpoche because, according to

197

tradition, he, as the Panchen Lama's tutor, had the authority to determine the Panchen Lama's reincarnation. Chadrel Rinpoche felt that it was he and the monks from Tashi Lhunpo who should have primary responsibility. So, with the backing of Beijing, Chadrel Rinpoche took up the task of presiding over observing signs at sacred lakes, collecting names of candidates, and coming up with the final three candidates who represented the body, speech, and mind of the Panchen Lama.

Gyayak Rinpoche's passing in 1990, only a year after the Panchen Lama's death, complicated matters further. This was followed in 1991 by "The Celebration of the 40th Anniversary of the Peaceful Liberation of Tibet," held in Lhasa. Li Tieying, the high-ranking bureaucrat given the responsibility of keeping an eye on the search committee, headed the central government delegation. Before the celebration began, Li Tieying, who was sitting on the stage, did a strange thing. When several children in Tibetan clothes presented Li Tieying with flowers, he stood up as if on impulse and tossed the flowers to Chadrel Rinpoche, sitting just below him in the first row.

A few hours later I ran into Li Tieying at an exhibit, and after we shook hands, he mentioned the moment I had noticed earlier. "This morning, I was overcome by an urge to toss the flowers to Chadrel Rinpoche, as if by some supernatural force. This is a good omen that the Eleventh Panchen Lama will be found under the leadership of Chadrel Rinpoche in the Tibet Autonomous Region, and not in the region of Kham, Gansu, or Qinghai." He added, making a request that was clearly something more, "Please cooperate with us."

Now I understood. Thanks to "divine inspiration," Chadrel Rinpoche would now have complete control of finding the reincarnation of the Panchen Lama, who would certainly be found near Tashi Lhunpo. From that moment on, the search team consisted primarily of the Tashi Lhunpo cohort, and I no longer participated seriously in the search.

Since the days when the search had begun, much had changed politically. The United Front, which oversaw religious activities, was now under new leadership, fearful and conservative, its former leaders having been involved in the Tiananmen Square protest on the side of the students. Cadres of the reorganized United Front, not really understanding the complexities of selecting the Panchen Lama, simply assured anyone who inquired that progress was being made.

Meanwhile, Chadrel Rinpoche had been secretly in contact with His Holiness the Dalai Lama in an effort to reach a decision that would avoid conflict. Unfortunately, travel was slow between Dharamsala, India, and Tashi Lhunpo Monastery, nor was there an efficient, secure means of communication with the Dalai Lama at the time. Unaware that Chadrel Rinpoche had written a "letter of promise" agreeing to obey Chinese government requests in the matter, His Holiness announced from India that he had made his choice for the Eleventh Panchen Lama. The timing could not have been worse. Cadres at the national United Front were enraged, and they immediately issued statements denouncing His Holiness.

As a matter of record, the Dalai Lamas and the Panchen Lamas shared a long and complex history. Both traced their lineage back to disciples of Lama Tsong Khapa in the fourteenth century. Historically they maintained a mutual respect for each other and had enjoyed close relations for many generations. Each became the other's teacher or disciple, depending on who was senior. Also, when one passed away, the other had the responsibility of searching for his reincarnation.

However, in modern times, relations between the two leaders had become strained for political reasons, and neither had participated in the search for the other's reincarnation. It was not the Dalai Lama and the Panchen Lama who were at odds with one another, but rather, influential followers on both sides who, for the sake of worldly vanity and the exercise of power, created political intrigue and feuds. Still, they continued to recognize the other's choice. As for the people of Tibet, no matter how politics changed, for them the Dalai Lama and the Panchen Lama remained the sun and the moon. To this day they believe that the reincarnations of *both* must be mutually recognized to be valid.

Tibetans clearly wanted the Fourteenth Dalai Lama to be the final arbiter of the identity of the true reincarnation of the Panchen Lama. But an ominous feeling was beginning to rise in me. I knew that if the state TV news was so quick to criticize the Dalai Lama, a political ill wind must be blowing. In order to avoid it, I arranged a trip to Inner Mongolia with one group of monks, and took another group up the Yangtze to the Three Rivers dam project. But in the end there was no escaping what lay ahead.

On November 4 I received two calls, one from the United Front in Qinghai Province and another from the State Administration for Religious Affairs. I was being ordered to travel immediately to Beijing along with other high lamas to attend an emergency meeting regarding the reincarnation of the Panchen Lama. I had no recourse, though I was filled with a sense of foreboding.

On November 9, 1995, the emergency meeting began. It was the first formal meeting of the full search committee since the Panchen Lama had passed on six years before. Normally, we would have received an official notice telling us where the meeting was to be held, but this time I received nothing beyond two phone calls. Upon our arrival at Beijing's airport, we lamas were met by cadres of the bureau of religious affairs, who drove us directly to the Jiangxi Hotel, located in a conference center reserved for military leaders.

At the entrance to the walled compound we noticed heavy security. As I was waiting to register, an acquaintance from the Tibet Autonomous Region came up to me in the crowded lobby and whispered, "This is serious. I'm told we'll need permission to leave the room during the meeting. We can only meet with each other in the lobby, not in our rooms. Surveillance cameras are hidden everywhere, and all the phones are bugged. Be careful."

As we were having dinner, I was surprised to see Ying Ke Sheng, the Party secretary of Qinghai Province. His secretary had told me that he would not be able to attend the meeting because of his busy schedule, but here he was. He, too, must have been ordered to attend. Then I realized that all the Party secretaries and chairpersons of the TAR and other Tibetan areas had also come.

The next day we had a number of preliminary group meetings. This was when I learned that Chadrel Rinpoche had been arrested for making secret contact with the Dalai Lama. Phrases we had heard years before when the search committee was originally formed, such as "soliciting the Dalai Lama's opinions" were no longer spoken. Instead, we were bombarded with statements like "We must not allow the Dalai's separatist clique to interfere in the Golden Urn Ceremony." Though not spelled out, the message was clear: His Holiness would not be involved in the selection process, and the Golden Urn Ceremony would be the method of choice.

The Golden Urn Ceremony refers to a practice (supposedly used by the Qing Dynasty in the eighteenth century) for selecting the Panchen Lama by drawing lots from a golden urn—instead of by shaking out tsampa balls, the traditional Tibetan method. By "reinstating" this purported Chinese practice after 200 years, the government hoped to legitimize its claims in opposition to His Holiness the Dalai Lama. Every aspect of the process was designed to bear a Chinese imprint.

After these meetings, high lamas were taken to the national United Front headquarters to be individually interviewed by Party officials. I met with Li Dezhu, a vice director of the national United Front, an ethnic Chinese of Korean birth. He politely briefed me on the progress of the search process, and invited me to offer my input. My first comments were candid. "The search should have been undertaken sooner," I began. "It should have been done when Gyayak Rinpoche was still alive. Now it is too late. And Chadrel Rinpoche's arrest is having a strong negative effect on all of us who are religious leaders. Please, cannot we consider the Dalai Lama's candidate? If the Dalai Lama's choice is not right, the Buddha will show us. If we simply stand in opposition to the Dalai Lama's choice, we will lose the heart of the Tibetan people. We religious leaders will lose our effectiveness as a bridge between the government and the Tibetan people. We'll never be able to recover from such a loss of credibility."

Upon hearing this, the kindly look on Li Dezhu's face evaporated, and his manner became serious and slightly ominous. "Chairman Arjia, it is because you are from Qinghai and ignorant of what some people in Tashi Lhunpo have been doing that you have come up with these suggestions and requests. We can agree with none of them, although we can understand why you made them. But I must tell you not to mention them anymore, for your own safety. We have no room for such ideas. I sincerely hope you will heed my suggestion."

After this none-too-subtle warning I understood my position. Where on earth had I gotten the impression that I, even as a high lama, could influence the decisions of the national government of China? If conveying the feelings of ordinary Tibetans was forbidden, I knew I would be allowed to have no impact on the proceedings of this meeting. I faced the conflict I so often faced: how best to help our Tibetan cause while obeying Party dictates— without being disloyal to the Dalai Lama!

When I returned to my room, I heard that Ying Ke Sheng, my direct supervisor, had called for me three times. Under normal circumstances, I found Ying Ke Sheng straightforward and easy to work with. That day he told me that after my meeting with Li Dezhu, Li had called him to instruct Ying Ke Sheng to do some "thought work" with me to make sure that my public opinion would align itself with that of Beijing; no glitches would be tolerated. Ying Ke Sheng met with me that very night to work on my thoughts.

The next day the main meeting took place. At the head table of the large conference table sat important officials from the central government. Three rows of seats for rinpoches lined one side of the room. In the first row sat Jamyang Shepa Rinpoche, abbot of Labrang; Tashi Kyil of Gansu Province; Bumi Rinpoche from the TAR; and me. Behind us were rows of important government officials, breathing down our necks. Ying Ke Sheng was sitting immediately behind me. Across from us along the opposite wall were lesser government cadres, who looked at us with obvious suspicion. Crews from the Chinese central TV and radio stations had set up their microphones and cameras and were poised to jump into the open space in front of us as the meeting began. We felt as tense as if we were under fire.

The agenda focused on three main points: 1) eliminating from contention the boy that the Dalai Lama had chosen; 2) denouncing and removing Chadrel Rinpoche from any official position on the search team; and 3) mandating a Golden Urn Ceremony. After these points were read aloud, the rinpoches were asked to express their thoughts as a TV camera panned toward our table. Would anyone have the courage to speak up in opposition? Images flashed in my mind of lamas in like situations who had disappeared immediately afterward. One after another, the rinpoches expressed their prepackaged sentiments, each identical to the one before. Some spoke loudly, some with obvious unhappiness, and some stared vacantly into space while mouthing the requisite words. Everyone spoke against the Dalai Lama and in favor of the government's decision. To my shame, I was no exception.

The meeting was swift and efficient. That same afternoon, central TV aired footage of the meeting throughout China and the rest of the world. That evening, the national United Front threw a banquet for all of us, delighted by the success of the filmed charade. Cadres praised the rinpoches and rewarded each of us with ¥10,000 in cash ($1,250), in those days a very significant amount. I received additional money for the travel expenses of my assistants. I was reminded of an old Tibetan saying: "Your mouth becomes smaller after eating other people's food, and your hands become soft after receiving other people's gifts."

Saddened, and frustrated by my feelings of powerlessness, I returned to Kumbum Monastery to await new orders.

No sooner had I returned to Kumbum than I received a message from Ye Xiaowen, in the State Administration for Religious Affairs of the PRC, who urgently wanted to speak with me. I told the monk who took the message to call him back and say he was unable to find me. Ten minutes later, the monk called again and pleaded with me, "You can't hide anymore. Chief Ye Xiaowen has called several times. He said, 'If Arjia does not return my call, I will lose my temper.'"

When I finally returned his call, Ye Xiaowen laughingly said, "Chairman Arjia, the next time I can't find you, I will have to report this to Party Secretary Ying Ke Sheng and let *him* scold you." What he tried to pass off as humor was, in fact, a serious threat of imprisonment, or worse.

Two days later, Ye Xiaowen met me in Xining to tell me in person that the government would be searching for the Panchen Lama's reincarnation in three areas: the Tibet Autonomous Region and the areas of Qinghai and Gansu. I was to help replace "the one that had been dismissed," meaning the Dalai Lama's choice. The search was to begin immediately. A few days later, along 203 with emissaries from Tashi Lhunpo, we selected the names of appropriate children in Hainan Prefecture as candidates and submitted them to Ye Xiaowen. Events were speeding up.

In November I received a notice to attend another meeting for determining the reincarnation of the Panchen Lama using the Golden Urn Ceremony, for which we would be flown to Lhasa. I was desperate to find a way to avoid this political sham, so I went to the doctor citing possible problems with my heart, and was admitted into the Chinese Navy Hospital in Beijing.

It turned out that many of us tried this same tactic to avoid participating in the Golden Urn Ceremony. Choeshi Rinpoche, my predecessor at Kumbum, even made arrangements for surgery. Our plans failed. Ye Xiaowen came to see me in the hospital. "For this event, everyone must be present. Nobody is allowed a leave of absence. If some rinpoches are suffering from serious illnesses, don't worry; we'll have the best doctors accompanying you." Under this unrelenting pressure, all of us converged in Beijing for the flight to Lhasa. Early the next morning, at the Xijiao military airport in Beijing, we Tibetan high lamas were joined by representatives from Chinese and Theravadan Buddhist groups—apparently to add the weight of numbers to our rejection of the Dalai Lama's choice.

We landed at Gonggar airport in Lhasa, which was tightly guarded by People's Liberation Army soldiers and armed policemen. Our column of buses, led by police patrol cars, took two hours to drive the 60 miles to the hotel. Soldiers were lined up along the entire route "for our protection." When we arrived at the Lhasa Hotel, things were even more oppressive; I saw squads of PLA soldiers with machine guns, as well as regular police, surrounding the hotel so that no one could slip in or out.

That same evening we gathered for an urgent meeting, where officials announced, "It has not yet been decided when the Golden Urn Ceremony will take place. It may be tonight, so please be prepared. Because this ceremony has not been performed for such a long time, arrangements must be meticulous. It has to be successful. If any unforeseen events should occur during the ceremony, please rest assured that we are prepared for any emergency. You need not be afraid. If a separatist clique attempts any disruption of the ceremony, everyone will be protected. However, if any among you support or participate in any such attempt, we will punish you without mercy."

Even if the Golden Urn Ceremony had been a time-honored tradition, which it was not, attending this particular ceremony in this political atmosphere was fraught with danger and intrigue. Someone guessed that the ceremony would occur in the middle of the night, and he was right; at two o'clock in the morning on November 29, 1995, we were called together and ushered into vehicles bound for Jokhang Temple. Although the night was dark, again we could see soldiers in their heavy bulletproof vests every few steps along the deserted streets.

It was three o'clock in the morning when we finally entered the Jokhang. The main hall was filled with Tibetans dressed in festive attire nervously whispering to each other. As we walked toward the statue of the Buddha, we saw undercover policemen standing in every corner and shadow. Lamas I had known from the Jokhang were not there. I had no idea where these new, unfamiliar faces had come from.

In front of the statue of Sakyamuni Buddha was a large table covered with a yellow silk cloth. Alone on the table stood a golden urn about 15 inches high, surrounded by seated high officials. In the center of the hall, Luo Gan, secretary of the Chinese State; Ye Xiaowen; and Gyaltsen Norbu (governor of the Tibet Autonomous Region) sat facing the statue of Buddha. Flanking them were cadres on one side and lamas on the other. Snacks and butter tea were set out on their tables.

One hour later, the secretary of the office of the Tibet Autonomous Region began the ceremony. Inside the gold urn was a small case, which contained three ivory lots, an inch wide and seven or eight inches long, with cloud scrolls etched at one end. The names of the three candidates were written on three separate pieces of paper and pasted to the ivory sticks, each of which was then slipped into a tightly fitted pouch of yellow silk. After being carefully examined by officials and raised above the preparer's head for all to see, the three ivory lots were placed into the Golden Urn.

Drawing of the lots was performed by Bumi Rinpoche, the government-appointed tripa (throne holder) of Ganden Monastery, presumptive leader of the Gelug sect, and chairman of the Tibet Autonomous Region's Buddhist Association. He first prostrated to the Buddha statue three times. I expected him to lift the vessel and shake one of the lots out of the urn, but instead he passed his hand quickly over the lots and pulled one out. He handed the yellow pouch to Luo Gan for verification. Luo Gan handed it to Gyaltsen Norbu, governor of the Tibet Autonomous Region, to announce the winner; ironically, the name of the boy selected was also Gyaltsen Norbu. This led to a widely circulated joke: "Gyaltsen Norbu chose Gyaltsen Norbu. The government chose itself as Panchen Lama."

The lamas recited prayers and cheered ritually, but with an obvious lack of enthusiasm. We returned to the hotel about five o'clock that morning, and later, when we turned on the TV, a newsman announced: "At ten o'clock this morning, the Golden Urn Ceremony was held at the Jokhang Temple." In the close-ups on TV it appeared that the ivory lot selected by Bumi Rinpoche stood slightly above the others, but the only lie we recognized for certain was the time of the ceremony.

Two weeks after the Golden Urn Ceremony, the counterfeit Eleventh Panchen Lama was enthroned at Tashi Lhunpo Monastery. We made the seven-hour journey from Lhasa in a long convoy, including police cars and two military trucks filled with soldiers. Again there were armed policemen and soldiers all along the way.

The enthronement ceremony itself was also unorthodox. The strangest and most awkward part was the way the Golden Seal of Authority, a six-inch block of gold, and the Golden Document (made of hinged gold sheets) were presented to the "reincarnation" of the Panchen Lama as symbols of his religious authority granted by the government. The presentation, made by Li Tieying, the highest government delegate at the enthronement, was neither a Tibetan custom nor an administrative one. It purportedly echoed the way Qing emperors had recognized reincarnations of the Panchen Lama in previous centuries, but there was no evidence to back that claim. In my view it just illustrated how the Chinese had always used feudal rituals to legitimize the appearance of their sovereignty over Tibet. One thing was for certain: It showed that this Panchen Lama was completely under the control of the central government.

The next item on the agenda was the one I was least willing to perform: We had to prostrate to the so-called Panchen Lama. Whenever high lamas bow to a master or prostrate to a rinpoche, we do so out of devotion. In this case we had neither respect for nor faith in this chosen child, yet we were forced to bow to him. I felt soiled by the gesture, but once again no one dared to defy our government handlers.

A few days later I boarded a chartered jet for the return trip to Beijing. On the airplane, Li Tieying, the Chinese delegate, called Jamyang Shepa Rinpoche and me into a private sitting room. Ye Xiaowen was also there. Both of them looked especially pleased with themselves. Li Tieying placed the event in the context of great moments in China's history, while Ye Xiaowen dutifully took notes. After a while Li Tieying, looking a bit tired, donned an oxygen mask in the unpressurized cabin and went to sleep.

Ye Xiaowen, a large, dark-complexioned man, continued to chat informally with us. Exuberant with the success of the past several days, he unwittingly revealed a shocking secret: "When the Dalai Lama announced the name of his chosen candidate, the government immediately sent out charter jets, usually reserved for members of the Politburo, to the birthplaces of the three final candidates in the Naqu district of Tibet. They put the boys and their families on the three jets and whisked them away into hiding." He proudly continued, "When we made our selection we left nothing to chance. In the silk pouches of the ivory pieces we put a bit of cotton at the bottom of one of them, so it would be a little higher than the others and the right candidate would be chosen."

We were dumbfounded! Certainly we had had our suspicions, but we never expected proof that the process was completely rigged. Goose bumps rose on my skin, but Jamyang Shepa Rinpoche and I kept silent, our heads lowered, pretending we had heard nothing unusual. After we were dismissed and heading back to our seats, Jamyang Shepa Rinpoche looked at me incredulously and shook his head. Then with a sigh, he said, "Maybe we can enjoy a little recess time now."

To this day Tibetans do not think of this Eleventh Panchen Lama as the
real Panchen Lama. Many monasteries do not put his pictures on their shrines.
Street vendors have difficulty selling his pictures to the faithful. He was hand-
picked by Communists, not ordained by Buddha. The Chinese State, aware
of this Tibetan skepticism, worked to come up with new strategies to legitimize their choice. It was not long before I discovered that I was to play an
important and shameful part in those plans.

In late summer 1997, several strangers came looking for me at Kumbum
Monastery. They presented a letter of reference written by a Mr. Shi. I knew
him. He had once been a Chinese bodyguard for the Panchen Lama, and now
he was head of a security department. They claimed that the purpose of their
visit was to arrange a large religious event (to be planned well in advance) to
commemorate the third anniversary of the Eleventh Panchen Lama's enthronement. Many other high lamas would be invited for the event, and, of course,
the boy they called the Eleventh Panchen Lama would be there, too. They
wanted me to sign a contract indicating that I would host the event.

Their proposal was very strange. Religious events are not business meetings; we don't sign contracts for planning ceremonies. Why did they want me
to do this? It also seemed strange that they had come on such an important
mission without an official letter of reference from the State Administration
for Religious Affairs of the PRC, or the United Front. Why was I dealing
with some obscure office of the security forces? Why had they not come with
a staff member of the provincial government? I could not guess what they
were up to, but I wanted to take no chances.

I asked them, "Do our provincial authorities know you're here?" They
looked at each other and replied, "They know, they know." Suspicious, I used
this absence of a provincial official as an excuse to avoid signing the contract.
They left the document with me, got in their car, and drove away.

That fall I was attending a meeting in Beijing when Li Guoqing from the
national United Front came over to me, beaming with pride. "I hear that you
will be the teacher of the Eleventh Panchen Lama! I think that's wonderful;
you are definitely the best candidate for the job." Stunned, I asked why I had
been selected. "It is because your uncle Gyayak Rinpoche was the teacher of

the Tenth Panchen Lama, and because you were close to the Panchen Lama, too. You are also a patriotic 'Living Buddha' (the Chinese translation of rinpoche), so you are being appointed as his official teacher." At the time, I thought, "Gyayak Rinpoche, no wonder you predicted I would leave politics by the time I was 50. I am only three years from your deadline, and things are getting very precarious."

That winter the security officers returned to Kumbum for a second meeting. This time, using the excuse that I was on retreat, I did not meet with them, so they forwarded a copy of the contract to me, requesting my signature. I told my secretary to relay my response: "In March of next year, when I attend the legislative meetings in Beijing with our provincial leaders, I'll sign the contract in front of them." As I put this promise in writing, I knew my days in Tibet and China were numbered—one way or another.

About the same time, the provincial United Front launched a new socialist education campaign, from which Kumbum Monastery was not exempt. This campaign had already started in some parts of Tibet several years before. It was terrible. Monks had been forced to stomp on pictures of His Holiness; photos of him were taken out of all the temples, and monks were required to sign an oath never to pray to him. They also had to vow never to participate in political demonstrations. Now the monks of the eastern districts would have to suffer the same indignities. Not knowing exactly what to expect, and remembering times past, we took what precautions we could. We warned monks at Kumbum to hide all photos of the Dalai Lama before government personnel arrived.

In the winter of 1997, 40 cadres descended upon Kumbum Monastery and set up camp. I spoke to the leaders, asking them why they felt the need to be here; Kumbum monks weren't causing political troubles. Their answer was that they were just following orders.

I did not argue with them, but I knew this was just the beginning. Unlike the days of the Cultural Revolution, these cadres were not fanatical ideologues; they seemed interested only in keeping their "rice bowls" (paid positions), and did not really care what we did, said, or believed. The topics of their meetings with the monks were mostly their own problems—delayed salaries, layoffs, and employment problems—not ideology. The cadres were local, so they went home every night to their families. Our monks knew that this entire program was a formality, but of course, everyone had to listen to those official speeches "improving their education."

There was no violence this time, but this campaign indicated a new political turn for the worse. After a little more than a month, it ended "victoriously," with every monk being forced to denounce His Holiness and sign a "patriotic agreement." I was supposed to be the first to sign, but I made up some excuse, and the cadres didn't press me further.

A ceremony held in the great courtyard marked the end of the campaign, during which I could not have been more depressed. Not only was this program reminiscent of the bad old days, but the location was the very same one where, in 1958, I had publicly suffered my first denunciation. That time I sat huddled on the ground. Now I was grandly seated on the stage. In 1958 they had denounced me as a "class enemy." Now I was the powerful deputy chairman of the Qinghai Provincial Committee of Chinese People's Political Consultative Conference, the equivalent of a deputy governor of a province. But in both instances the feeling of humiliation and helplessness was exactly the same.

Almost imperceptibly, my freedom of movement became more restricted. Spiritually and emotionally I felt I had reached a dead end. Denouncing His Holiness the Dalai Lama, being tutor to a counterfeit Panchen Lama, fearing the signs of renewed repression—all these things pounded me in debilitating waves. Sitting in the courtyard one day, I heaved a heavy sigh and gazed wistfully up at the overcast Tibetan sky. I longed for the peaceful blue sky on the other side of the clouds. Serdok Rinpoche, who knew me so well, leaned close to me and whispered, "What are you thinking? Do you want to escape somewhere?" Astonished, I didn't reply, but I thought to myself, *I think I do. How did you know?*

CHAPTER 13

FINAL DAYS WITH
THE DRAGON

My life was becoming intolerable. Over and over I replayed in my mind the last four decades, looking for answers. What had gone wrong? On the one hand, I was the reincarnation of Arjia Rinpoche, which charted my spiritual journey. Like a small boat on a great river, I felt destined to flow from my source along a naturally defined route to the sea, just as my seven predecessors had done before me. But against this natural current pushed a great and terrible wind, forcing me into eddies, rapids, and channels that threatened to swamp, smash, or misdirect my karma.

The politics of the Chinese Communist occupation had subsumed me. Instead of living the contemplative existence of a monk in a monastery, I was constantly navigating the treacherous shoals of Communist policy as it affected so many Tibetans. On a personal level, my suffering and success had each proved threatening in its own way. Every decision, every action required a choice between evils: to take direction from the Communists but use my influence on behalf of Tibetans, or to stand on principle and suffer the consequences. I had learned from the Panchen Lama and Gyayak Rinpoche to seek the middle way. I had sometimes felt uncomfortable with my prudence, but the safe choice was usually the one I made. Now I had reached a station in life that seemed the pinnacle of worldly success, and I found myself trapped in bureaucratic quicksand. In return for perks that made my life comfortable, I was obligated to participate in what was meaningless tedium at best, and at worst a charade that mocked everything I stood for.

In the end it came down to this: At 48 I was leaving my youth behind, and my life was turning from the adventures of discovery to the requirements of personal responsibility. My political life was betraying my religious and moral principles. Gyayak Rinpoche once said: "If I were allowed to choose, I should live in a cabin in the midst of a forest for the latter part of my life." I longed for that life, free of the worldly affairs, that Gyayak Rinpoche had imagined for my future. "When you turn 50," he had said, "you must excuse yourself from all political appointments and find a peaceful place to practice dharma." That didn't seem a likely possibility in Tibet or China, but perhaps Gyayak Rinpoche had known that, too.

Resigning from my many administrative appointments was impossible. It would only lead to endless harassment until I changed my decision, or until they simply reappointed me over my objections. Escape began to look like the only possible solution. As the Chinese saying goes, "Among all plans, escape is the best."

Once these thoughts entered my mind, they would not leave. But where would I go? Where could I go? Who else would travel with me? Could I really accomplish an escape? Was I willing to risk prison if I got caught? If I succeeded, what would happen to the people I left behind?

There were seven or eight people living in my quarters with me. It would be impossible to travel with all of them. The first person I thought of was my house manager and secretary, Drashi. Because he and I had gone through so many years of hardship together, we were very close. But I knew I could not bring him along with me. Nor did I dare even utter the word "escape" to him. Because Drashi was a cautious man, I could hear him saying how crazy my idea was, and how impossible. I struggled with my conscience about not telling him, but really I had no other choice. Better to keep him ignorant of my thoughts, so that after I fled he could truthfully claim he knew nothing of my plans. Serdok Rinpoche was involved with his own activities, and because I knew that he could see through my thoughts, I kept my distance from him.

Another person in my household was Chunpay Jiumei, my personal attendant. He was an outstanding monk, very kind and always considerate. I very much wanted to take him with me, but I worried that exile in the West might have a negative impact on his Buddhist practice; Chunpay prospered in monastic life. I broached the subject with him, knowing I could trust his loyalty and discretion. His first reaction was that the plan was too dangerous. After I convinced him that we could succeed, he reluctantly agreed to come, saying, "You are the lama, and my place is with you." But I could see he was not excited by the prospect of risking everything for an unknown life outside Tibet.

The third person I thought of was Lobsang, my bodyguard and driver. Most officials at my level were assigned two policemen as guards, but I had requested Lobsang instead. He was efficient, inventive, and loyal. When I told him about my plan, he was willing to travel with me, but only if his new bride, Meido, could also come.

The fourth person was my 13-year-old nephew, Chenlie Rejie. His birth had violated the two-child policy for minorities in the Chinese state, and since monks were allowed to legally adopt children, I had taken him into the monastery as my son. There was no doubt that he would join me, but I decided to keep my thoughts of escape from him for now, fearing that the wrong people might learn of my plans "out of the mouth of babes."

As winter ended, Lobsang and I went to Beijing for the annual Spring Festival Tea Party for Religious Dignitaries, held in the palace in the Forbidden City where Mao had once lived. Li Ruihuan, the chairman of the National Committee of Chinese People's Political Consultative Conference (NCCPPCC), and the leaders of the five major religions in China—Buddhism, Taoism, Islam, Catholicism, and Protestantism—were all there. On the second day, we attended a party in celebration of the Chinese New Year. During the party someone who always knew the latest goings-on walked up to me and whispered, "Congratulations!"

"On what?" I asked.

"Based on what I've heard, you will be appointed a standing committee member of the NCCPPCC, and chairman of the Buddhist Association of China. Congratulations!"

213

"Oh, really?" I said. "Thank you for telling me."

My heart sank. These were very high positions. Whoever occupied them was constantly surrounded by people. I knew it was now imperative that I accelerate the pace of my plans if I were to have any chance of escape.

Immediately after returning to the Beijing Hotel, I called a student of mine named Christine, who was in Beijing at the time. Christine was Chinese by birth but usually resided in Indonesia. She was a devout Buddhist, familiar with the ways of other countries, and spoke fluent English. Lobsang and I met her in the tearoom on the first floor of the hotel. I told her about my plans to escape. She was shaken. "Teacher, please think it over. This is a very dangerous plan. I don't think it will work."

"Please do not try to dissuade me, Christine. I have already made up my mind," I answered. In truth, although I sounded adamant about leaving, I was very aware of the enormous risks involved, and not just for me. If our little family unit was caught, each of us would face prison, and perhaps torture or death. I was willing to risk my own life, but what about the others? If I left him behind, Chenlie would forever be under suspicion. Lobsang would suffer drastically; as my guard he was allowed to carry a gun to protect me, but with the understanding that it should be used to stop me from escaping if necessary. And his young wife; what of her?

I worried also that if I got caught Kumbum would face the repercussions. Would new cadres invade the monastery and begin a whole new brainwashing program using more violent methods this time, demanding confessions for every activity that contributed to my attempted escape? More than anything I feared a resurgence of the horrors of the Cultural Revolution.

Christine pressed on: "Where are you going to go? What about Drashi and Chunpay? Aya, Teacher, you are too naïve. Wherever you go there will be unfamiliar customs to deal with, and you will have no friends. Have you thought about how you will make a living abroad? And how you will even get out of China? Have you thought about that?"

I had no reply. Lack of privacy was already a problem. My administrative positions now included deputy chairman of the Buddhist Association of China, member of the NCCPPCC, deputy chairman of the All-China Youth

Federation, chairman of the Qinghai Provincial Buddhist Association of China, deputy chairman of the Qinghai Provincial Committee of Chinese People's Political Consultative Conference, and dean of the Tibetan Buddhist College of Qinghai Province. I was constantly expected to be on stage. And soon I would be appointed head of the Buddhist Association of China! If I waited until then, I would have no unsupervised moments at all.

My first thought was to escape to India. But to do that, I would have to go through the Tibet Autonomous Region. Traveling through the TAR—especially as head of the Buddhist Association of China—would require an entourage of many people, some of whom would be secret agents. For the moment, however, I still had a chance. I began to clear time on my calendar, beginning with a leave of absence from the NCCPPCC and the United Front to go on retreat in Guangzhou in southern China.

I told Christine, "Whatever happens, I don't have much time left. If I continue to rise in the government hierarchy, I won't ever be able to escape. If I stay, I will no longer be able to play my role in the Communist charade; I've reached the breaking point." I showed her my passport and explained, "I already have a diplomatic passport. Chunpay and Lobsang, as my personal attendants, also have passports; so do Meido and Chenlie."

Christine still looked puzzled. "Of course you must have passports to travel," she replied, "but from which embassy are you going to obtain visas? What would you give as the reason for your trip abroad?"

Visas? Of course. Christine was right. I had thought the passports were the most important documents in attaining our freedom, but gaining a proper visa from another country would be much more difficult. Then Christine had an idea. She said, "Once you mentioned that you had a friend in Central America. Do you have his address? Perhaps he can help you."

"Yes, his name is Peter," I answered. "He is a kind man, and every New Year we exchange cards. We met in 1988 when I visited Central America with the Panchen Lama."

I found Peter's business card, and Christine immediately called him in Guatemala. Peter told her that Guatemala had diplomatic relations with Taiwan, but not with the People's Republic of China. If a Chinese citizen

215

wanted to visit Guatemala, he or she needed only a letter of invitation from a Guatemalan resident; then an entry visa could be granted. Peter promised to send letters of invitation to everyone in my group.

Everything started to come into focus: We would travel to Guatemala under the guise of being a tour group. I felt tremendously relieved. At least I had a destination.

After the traditional tea parties celebrating the New Year, Lobsang and I flew from Beijing to Guangzhou, ostensibly to begin my retreat. According to plan, Chunpay brought Chenlie and Meido to meet us there. All around us people were in holiday mode, celebrating the New Year. Few people knew our whereabouts or cared; for the time being we were off the radar screen. A few days later we quietly flew back to Beijing to make our flight arrangements. Once we arrived, Chunpay and I exchanged our robes for regular clothes and checked into a small hotel on the outskirts of the city. Only Christine knew we had returned to Beijing. She met us at the hotel on Friday.

When Christine and I were alone, she cautioned me once more: "Teacher, do you really have to leave? The chances of a successful escape are very, very small. Have you done a divination? What does the Mo say?"

"Success," I answered.

Christine gave a resigned shrug and handed me an envelope. "Here are the invitation letters from Peter. I just received them. Also, I have learned that KLM has a direct flight between Beijing and Guatemala on Monday leaving at 11:30 a.m. There are no other direct flights."

I asked her, "Can we book the plane tickets?"

The always-efficient Christine answered, "When you left for Guangzhou I tried to book tickets, but it was already too late. No tickets are available for the flight next Monday, but we can get on the standby list. If seats open up, you will be able to take off in three days. Otherwise, you will have to wait two weeks."

"Let's try for standby seats this Monday."

For the next two days, I could not sleep. I was praying for the blessings of the Buddha, the Dharma, the Sangha, and all the Protectors. The young people around me, usually very happy, had also become anxious; they felt my concern. They too must have been vividly aware of what lay ahead if we failed, but they kept their fears to themselves. Only my nephew, Chenlie Rejie, who knew nothing of our true plans, was enjoying his stay in a hotel.

Finally, Monday came. We got up early. Snow was falling. We prayed. After the prayer, we split up. Christine and Lobsang set out for the KLM office downtown, hoping to buy five tickets. They were to use money from the sale of a car that a student had given to me. The rest of us—Chunpay, Meido, Chenlie, and I—looking like tourists in our hats and sunglasses, took a taxi to the airport. Slush was so thick on the streets that our progress was painfully slow. The taxi seemed to crawl.

When we arrived at Beijing International Airport, it became obvious that there were fewer travelers than usual because of the snow. We hoped this would increase our chances of getting seats. As we carried our luggage to the waiting area, I suddenly spotted Wang Zheyi, a staff person at the State Administration for Religious Affairs of the PRC. I immediately turned away from him and folded up my collar to avoid being seen. Luckily I did not have my robes on, and I had grown a mustache, so he did not recognize me. We saw another man, seemingly on vacation, filming airport activities with a video camera. We tried to avoid him, but it felt like he was everywhere, filming, filming, filming. Suddenly every stranger posed a potential danger.

With two and a half hours to go, I called Lobsang on my cell phone asking, "What's going on? Where are you?" He had just arrived at the ticketing office; the traffic had slowed them, too. A few minutes later, I called again. He told me that a large crowd of people was in line waiting for the office to open. My nerves were frayed; Chunpay and Meido felt the same way. Only little Chenlie was relaxed, innocently asking us, "Where are we going?"

An hour later I called Lobsang again. They were still waiting for tickets and asked us to pray for them. So we prayed and we waited, and we waited and we prayed. The giant clock in the terminal struck ten o'clock. Only an hour and a half left before the flight. I called Lobsang and Christine again. The girl at the ticket counter was questioning them. Why had they come so late to purchase tickets? The good news was that tickets were available.

Lobsang and Christine were doing their best to expedite the transaction. The cost of round-trip tickets for five people was ¥80,000 ($10,000). They handed the girl the money, fervently hoping she would not delay them further by counting it all. The cash was still in bundles from the bank, so the girl decided to trust them. Finally the tickets were secured and they were on their way to the airport, although traffic was still heavy. At 10:30 the loudspeaker announced the boarding time for our 11:30 flight; it was on schedule. Finally, at 10:40, we saw Christine and Lobsang running toward us in their heavy coats. We took the tickets and quickly said good-bye to Christine as we headed to the security checkpoint.

Here more dangers awaited us. First we had to get through customs, and then we had to make our way through passport control, where I feared we might be on the blacklist and all this would have been for nothing. But our Protectors were with us at customs: no problem. I showed the official our passports; our tickets and luggage were in order, so he let us pass. We needed to hurry, for the plane was now boarding, but we still had to get through passport control.

Again we pretended to be a tour group. I pulled down the brim of my hat to conceal my face and stayed in the middle of our group, hoping to pass through inconspicuously. We offered our passports for inspection, all of us saying prayers. My diplomatic passport was in the middle, in blue plastic to disguise the fact that its cover was red—different from the others. I had none of the necessary authorizations to go with it.

While the Chinese customs officer looked through our passports, my heart raced. He glanced at each one—I held my breath—but without much interest. Whether it was the blessings of the Dharma Protectors or the officer's negligence, our passports were finally stamped and we boarded the plane just minutes before takeoff. With sighs of relief, we took our seats. After a few minutes, however, we noticed there were no preparations being made for takeoff. The plane's door was still open. Five minutes passed; then 10. Passengers became restless and began to complain about the delay. We tried to remain inconspicuous, slouched in our seats.

I didn't know how much more of this I could take. Horrible images were running through my mind: the flight attendant announcing our names and leading us off the plane, ominous-looking undercover policemen putting us in handcuffs. I tried to block the thoughts by pulling out my prayer beads and rapidly reciting mantras. I also quietly consulted the Mo: "Auspicious."

Just at that moment, several passengers boarded the plane. The flight attendants apologized for the delay, explaining that these passengers were late arrivals due to the snow, and the plane had been held for them. As soon as they were seated, the door was shut, and we taxied down the runway. The engines roared, the force of the plane lifting off pressed me against my seat, and my heartbeat finally began to slow. We were in the air!

The plane rose, breaking through the dark snow clouds that seemed to mirror my years of imprisonment as it nosed up into the bright blue sky above. In my heart I felt a blessing and a promise. Although I hadn't been able to catch a glimpse of my beloved Amdo as we lifted out of the storm, I took comfort in knowing that the same brilliant sun warming my face was at this moment shining above the dark clouds covering Tibet.

The jetliner flew west over Siberia, which looked like an endless, desolate sheet of ice. We continued on to Europe, landing in Amsterdam, where we spent the night sleeping on benches in the terminal. I was no longer an important person. The comfortable airport VIP rooms were now closed to me. No more welcoming flowers and khatas wherever I went. To my surprise, I felt enormously relieved. My heart was light in a way that I had never before experienced.

The next morning we crossed the Atlantic Ocean and flew over North America, stopping briefly in Mexico that afternoon. We finally landed in Guatemala as the sun was setting. We passed through customs smoothly, and on the other side of the barrier we saw a man waving at us. It was Peter's friend. As we walked toward him, we became aware of a military checkpoint looming directly ahead. Unknown to us, Guatemala was under martial law. 219

Perhaps because we were the only Asians in the terminal, the military official examined our passports closely. He spoke swiftly to an officer, who gathered our passports and walked off with them. The man turned to us and said, "You cannot enter Guatemala because of your diplomatic passport. It is possible you will be sent to the Taiwanese embassy, or even deported to China." As he spoke, armed soldiers with an intimidating German shepherd surrounded us, while Peter's friend looked on helplessly from the other side of the barrier. My blood froze.

To make matters worse, although we were capable of understanding what was going on, none of us spoke English or Spanish, so there was no way for us to plead our case. I recalled Gyayak Rinpoche's first instruction for using the Mo beads. He had cautioned me not to consult them except in an emergency. Well, yesterday at the Beijing airport had certainly felt like an emergency. And so did this. I consulted the Mo once again.

Smooth.

There was nothing to do except stand, wait, and wonder. Every second increased our anxiety and tested my faith in the Mo. Peter's friend had disappeared, and we could only hope he was working on a way to help us. An hour and a half later, the military officer finally reappeared with our passports. Peter had sent someone to deal with the authorities, and money had changed hands. (Peter later explained that it was quite common for soldiers to detain hapless travelers in order to wring money out of them.) The officer nodded to the soldiers. They dismissed us. We began to breathe again.

As we walked out of the airport lobby, I saw a tall young man walking toward us. He introduced himself as Peter's younger brother, Mario. With his help we checked into a small hotel in Guatemala City.

The next morning we took a walk to have some experience of this country and its people. Guatemala looked as though it might be fairly similar to my homeland: The pace of life seemed slow, and the streets were not very clean; cars and trucks drove dangerously fast down narrow streets; before a bus reached a station, the conductor would skillfully dangle out the window, waving to attract new passengers—antics identical to those I'd seen in Pakistan and Nepal.

We met Peter for breakfast. He asked us about our plans.

"We have round-trip tickets, but because we left Tibet and China for political reasons, we can't go back. If we returned, we'd be arrested. So we're thinking about staying in Guatemala indefinitely."

Peter was surprised, but he expressed his willingness to help. He said, "It's not safe on the streets here; please be cautious. Please also eat clean food." He suggested that Guatemala was not the right place for us to stay long. In his opinion, the United States or Brazil would be better.

I decided to call home. Drashi answered, thinking I was still in Guangzhou on retreat. "Where exactly are you?" he asked. "Is anything wrong? Why does the phone sound so strange?" I answered ambiguously, telling him everything was fine with us. Although I could sense how lonely he was in the house, I did not want anyone to know about our escape for as long as possible.

Usually at this time of the year I would be busy with dharma events and planning a trip to Xining for the Qinghai provincial conferences. I would also be making preparations for attending two upcoming annual conferences in Beijing, so I decided to call Hu Qijiang, general secretary of Qinghai Provincial People's Consultative Conference. Hu asked me where I was and when I would be arriving in Beijing. I said, "I'm still in Guangzhou for my solitary retreat. I may not be able to come to Beijing this year." Upon hearing this, Hu expressed anxiety. "Deputy Chairman Arjia, you must attend the conferences in Beijing. Chairman Han Yingxuan has repeatedly told me to find you, and he has requested that you come to Beijing for the conferences."

Hu gave me a time frame for my arrival in Beijing, and assured me that he would take care of the conference registration for me. After hanging up I wondered if I should also call friends in Beijing, to try to glean what, if anything, they knew or had heard about my "solitary retreat." In the end, I called no one, simply because I didn't want to create trouble for them later on.

A few days later, Peter introduced us to Mrs. Feng, Mr. Lu, and other friends of his. These people became our family in Guatemala, inviting us often to visit their homes. Time flew like a darting arrow; 15 days passed, at the end of which we needed to extend our visas. Now we encountered new

221

trouble. The immigration officer told us that visa extensions for everyone else were no problem, but he could not grant one to me, given my diplomatic passport. If I wanted to extend my visa, we had to visit the Guatemalan foreign ministry. We were at a loss, but Peter tried to comfort us by saying, "Rinpoche, don't worry. If there's any trouble, I'll drive you to El Salvador." His encouragement only added to our worries. If trouble befell us, we would have to become illegal aliens.

Peter asked, "Have you contacted the Dalai Lama? Perhaps he has some ideas that might ease your situation." Suddenly I felt as if I were awakening from a dream. I couldn't believe that I had been so passive. I immediately called Christine in Beijing, asking her how to get in touch with the Dalai Lama. She told me there was no news about us in Beijing, and explained that the Dalai Lama had many liaison offices throughout the world. She promised to find out how to contact his office in the United States.

Two days later she called back, telling us she'd heard that Chinese police were making inquiries as to my whereabouts. She also told me that the Dalai Lama had offices in Washington, DC, and New York City, and that she was working to contact them. In the meantime I came up with a way to try to calm the anxiety of Hu Qijiang. I have a habit of collecting stationery from hotels when I travel, so I wrote Hu a letter explaining my absence on Guangzhou hotel stationery, which I had in my bag. I sent the letter to a friend in Shenzheng, asking him to forward it. The envelope to him contained my letter inside an envelope with the Guangzhou logo and a Chinese stamp on it.

Easter in Guatemala is a major holiday, so Mrs. Feng invited us to her house to view the Easter procession and celebrate. People had carpeted the streets with colorful sawdust, while others carried a huge statue of Jesus past devout Catholics kneeling on the decorated pavement. I was intensely moved by their obvious devotion. After the procession ended, we discussed visa applications to the United States with Peter's friends. Every one of them had a story to tell, all of them disheartening. As we returned to our hotel, several policemen walked by; Peter told us not to get out of the car until after they passed. That night in our rooms we were afraid to turn on the lights. That familiar sense of fear, never far away, had returned in full force.

With Christine's help, we finally got in touch with the Dalai Lama's Washington office, and I succeeded in explaining my identity and my intentions. The representative there told me, "His Holiness will hold a dharma event in America in April. I'll ask the organizers to issue you an invitation. The problem is that it is very difficult to secure a visa to the United States in a third-world country."

When the invitation arrived we hired an English interpreter and set out for the consulate. I had never applied for a visa, but I remembered the view of long lines from my hotel in Israel. I was very nervous. Our invitations from the Buddhist center in New York had come with a letter to the US Consulate explaining our circumstances and who I was. I found out later that Robert Thurman and other Tibetan scholars had also written on my behalf. Feeling some hope mixed with our apprehension, we joined the long line of waiting people. When the consulate finally opened, a staff member announced: "Today is Secretary's Day. We will not be accepting visa applications. Come back tomorrow." As our group turned to leave, the staff member stopped us: "The US consul general wishes to interview you. Please follow me."

Thinking that meeting the US consul general would involve a formal introduction in some sumptuous office, I was surprised to walk into a large, drab room with seats at a long counter set beneath thick glass windows, like a bank without any amenities. The consul general sat opposite me, wearing a white shirt but no tie. He grilled me for 45 minutes through a translator: who was I, what was my position in Tibet and China, where was I going, why was I going there, and so on. Had I ever had contact with the Dalai Lama before? His tone was very professional, neither pleasant nor unpleasant. I explained my status in Tibet and China, and told him that I had never had an opportunity to be in contact with the Dalai Lama before this time.

His final question was "Sir, are you still planning on returning to China?" I replied, "Of course, I have a round-trip air ticket." With the slightest hint of a smile, he continued, "You hold a diplomatic passport, and you intend to meet with the Dalai Lama. Do you really think you can return to China after that?" He had not been fooled. Then he handed me back the passports, and I could see that he had granted us six-month visas. I was so relieved I felt I should offer him something, so I slipped a white silk khata under the glass that separated us. He was startled. "What's that?"

The girl in the next booth smiled and explained it to him in Spanish. He picked up the white scarf and inspected it carefully before tossing it to the girl. She looked very happy to receive it.

We called Christine in Beijing, asking her to meet with us in New York. With the help of many friends, we had survived our first two months out of Tibet and China. Gratefully, we boarded the plane to New York.

CHAPTER 14

FROM KUMBUM
TO KUMBUM WEST

When we landed in New York, Christine was waiting for us at Kennedy Airport, and together we drove to Manhattan. Years before, in 1988, when I had traveled with the Panchen Lama to Central and South America, New York had been on our itinerary, but that trip was canceled. This time, as we crossed the bridge connecting Queens to Manhattan and I saw the famous skyline, I thought about how much my life had changed since last I had planned to come here. This time I was hardly in tourist mode. I was preoccupied with two conflicting feelings: I worried about the safety of my friends and family back in Tibet and China, and I cherished the joy of knowing that I was about to have an audience with His Holiness.

The Buddhist center in New York had arranged for us to stay at a hotel where our privacy was assured. Once we were settled, I asked Christine to call Wu Bing in China. I was very worried that Drashi and others at the monastery were in trouble over our disappearance.

Wu Bing was very anxious over the phone. "I don't know where Arjia Rinpoche is!" he told Christine. "Policemen have visited me many times, and they keep accusing me of lying: 'The director of Kumbum Monastery's liaison office doesn't know where the abbot is. Do you think we can believe that?' They have ordered me not to leave Beijing and to discover the whereabouts of

225

Arjia Rinpoche. They have sent people to look for Arjia Rinpoche in Guang-dong and Putuo Island. Where are you, Christine? I can't even find *you*."

I felt terrible. I knew that trouble was coming down on my friends, and I was in no position to help. I felt particularly powerless because ever since we had arrived in Guatemala, we had felt like fugitives. We rarely walked on the street. We wore lay clothes. I had kept my small mustache as a disguise. Looking back, my fears seem unnecessary, but at the time they felt very real.

Our visit with the Dalai Lama was a thrilling occasion. He was the hon-ored guest at a large award ceremony for a group of leading scholars and experts, after which he had granted us a private audience. Chunpay and I changed from our Western clothes into our best monastic robes. The others donned traditional Tibetan attire.

We were met by Dawa Tsering, the Dalai Lama's representative in New York, who led us into a richly decorated hall packed with 2,000 people. I found a seat reserved with my name on it in the middle of the first row, a place of honor. I was surprised and a bit uncomfortable to be so conspicuous. I glanced around nervously, searching for the ubiquitous Chinese secret police, but instead I found myself surrounded by neatly dressed Westerners who greeted me with kind looks.

A few minutes later His Holiness the Dalai Lama emerged in his maroon robes, with a simple monk's bag hanging from his left shoulder. Two attendants accompanied him. When the audience rose to its feet and gave him a standing ovation, he joined his palms together and, bowing left, right, and center, greeted everyone with his dancing smile; the humility of the simple gesture deeply touched me. As the audience sat down, His Holiness waved to his friends and acquaintances, reminding me of the time I had met him when I was a little boy in 1954. Suddenly I realized that he was looking directly at me and greeting me with that same great smile and a small gesture of welcome.

As His Holiness spoke and conferred various awards, he did so in fluent English, but unfortunately my own English was not up to the task. It seemed strange to be so close to him and not understand what he was saying.

After the meeting, we were led to his room. Christine joined us. As we entered, we immediately dropped to the floor, prostrating according to custom. His Holiness attempted to stop us with happy chuckles. After a photo opportunity, everyone else retreated from the room, and His Holiness and I began a private conversation.

The first thing he asked was "How is Kumbum Monastery? Are the monks doing well?" He told me that he had seen the reconstruction of the monastery on TV, and had appreciated the enormous effort we had made. We talked about the passing of the Panchen Lama, and the choice of the new Panchen Lama and his Chinese surrogate. He seemed to be fully aware of current events in Tibet and China. Toward the end of our conversation, he asked, "How did you manage to leave the country?" As I gave him an abbreviated version of the story, he nodded frequently, murmuring with obvious concern, "Dangerous . . . very dangerous. . . ."

His Holiness then shared his own thoughts on Tibet's future. "Since the 1970s I have abandoned the idea of Tibetan independence, but I've never stopped demanding true autonomous status for Tibet. I hope Tibet will keep its language and customs, and that the Chinese will respect them. Tibetans must have a genuine religious life. However, the Chinese government has interpreted my requests as part of a plan for 'indirect independence.' Well, no matter what happens," he continued with his usual optimism, "I have confidence in negotiating with the leaders of China, and I hope to have the Tibet question resolved soon.

"Based on my understanding, after me you are the highest-ranking Tibetan figure to leave Tibet since I did in 1959. What was your title before you left China?"

When I answered, he nodded, "Yes, yes, that was indeed a high position. You must have enjoyed many benefits. Why would you want to leave?"

It was neither the time nor the place for a complete answer, so I spoke briefly about my growing difficulty maintaining the political charade. I explained to him that the immediate reason was that the Chinese Communists were intent upon my tutoring their surrogate Panchen Lama. I could not bring myself to do that, so flight seemed the only choice.

"There must have been enormous pressure there," he responded.

At the end of our meeting, His Holiness offered his counsel. "You have been mistreated and naturally have much discontent, but please don't be driven by your emotions to make angry public statements. Please maintain a low profile. Recently, I have been trying to establish a dialogue with Beijing, and I hope your exile in the West will not hinder my attempt to do so. It would be a shame if that dialogue broke down. I hope you will make positive contributions to the dialogue. That would be much better." He stopped and thought for a moment. "Maybe you can somehow help to bridge our differences."

Given my concerns about our safety, I was only too happy to follow His Holiness's instructions to keep a low profile. Before he left New York I was fortunate enough to see him again. This time I requested teachings from him. He bestowed on me Lama Tsong Khapa's Three Core Principles, and he asked me what I had practiced all these years. I replied that I had read Lama Tsong Khapa's *Treatise on Steps toward Becoming a Bodhisattva,* and sometimes recited mantras.

I was ashamed to be such a shallow monk, but His Holiness responded with praise and encouragement. At my request, he recommended a spiritual teacher for me, Geshe Sopa, a retired professor at the University of Wisconsin. As our time together came to a close, His Holiness said: "You must keep in touch. Remember, please, to maintain a low profile." His final words, however, gave me a touch of anxiety: "Please consider writing a personal letter to the Chinese government. Perhaps they may heed your voice."

Write a letter to the Chinese government? Up until now my only thought had been to stay clear of the Chinese government. This was something to contemplate. Nevertheless, His Holiness had given me a task, and there was no question that I would do as he asked.

But how?

What should I say?

Where would I begin?

The most pressing thing on my mind every day was the safety of my friends and family in Tibet and China. Again I asked Christine to call Wu Bing in Beijing. This time the news was very bad. The Chinese secret police had discovered that I was in New York, and that I had met with the Dalai Lama. They were determined to find out how I had escaped and who had helped me. I knew that they would be especially vicious, and that someone in the security office would have to take the blame—unless they found another scapegoat; I was considered too big a prize to be ignored. My return to Tibet and China would be considered essential to save Chinese face.

I also learned that the police's investigation had already turned brutal. All my friends had been arrested and questioned, then released and brought back for further questioning. Anybody who had anything to do with me was being investigated, followed, and harassed. I felt thankful that I had involved none of them in my plans. I was especially glad that I hadn't let Drashi, my secretary, in on the secret. Even so, the police didn't believe him. I felt sick with regret and concern. I could only hope that the fact that Drashi was telling the truth would help his situation. I didn't dare call Serdok Rinpoche for fear of how he might be affected. It would be two years before we talked, and it would be a conversation marked more by tears than by words.

I have always enjoyed visiting other countries. Living in America was every person's dream, and we were deeply grateful for the opportunity to do so. But my circumstances were different from anything I had ever experienced. We were living in America as immigrants—no, it was more difficult than that, we were political refugees. Our initial excitement upon arriving in the States was gradually giving way to dismay and uncertainty. The questions Christine had raised as we talked in the Beijing hotel now took on the weight of reality. Where would the five of us live? What would we do?

Our saving grace was the generosity of Americans with whom we came into contact. We met Ms. Rose Boyle, a warmhearted woman living on Central Park West, in New York City. She invited us to stay in her apartment for 10 days and then extended the invitation after she came to know us a little bit better. We didn't speak the same language, so we had great difficulty communicating with her, but Rose saw how diligently we practiced and how well we all got along together. As the weeks went by, she asked us to stay indefinitely. 229

For our part, no matter how much we appreciated Rose, we felt hemmed in by the comfort, the unfamiliar lifestyle, and the communication barrier. We could not talk without a dictionary. We studied English with Rose, and with her friends John and Walter, which was helpful, but still our sense of isolation weighed on us heavily.

Two months passed. So many changes had come upon us so suddenly. We missed our monastery, our homes, and our families and friends. I could not help thinking of my life in Tibet, how it flowed in the thousands of tiny unnoticed patterns that could make a day predictable, from the morning tick of my clock to the feel of my cushion as I said my evening prayers. Along with our loved ones it is the absence of these countless little things that makes us feel homesick. Despite Rose's generosity, we ached for a more familiar life.

A few years before this I had met Stephen, a Chinese-American Buddhist businessman who later became my student and often made pilgrimages to Kumbum Monastery while I was there. I thought of him now, but I had failed to take his American address with me when I escaped from Tibet and China. I thought he lived in Los Angeles, so I found a telephone book and was amazed to quickly locate his address and phone number. I called him, explaining how I came to be in the United States, and then I asked him if he could help us. Stephen immediately offered us his house until we could find our own lodgings. He insisted that we move to Los Angeles as soon as possible.

This was very good news. We were eager to set out for Los Angeles the very next day, but first we needed to make our feelings clear to Rose. With our poor English it was difficult to convey that we were leaving, and why. Finally Stephen talked to her, explaining how strange life in New York was for us, and how in Los Angeles there was a Chinese community where we would feel less strange. Rose understood and personally escorted us to Los Angeles.

What a relief it was to be in a neighborhood that felt so familiar: Chinese food and shops, a language I could understand, and behavior that I knew. Even the noise and the crowds of people elbowing their way along the streets were reassuring. We felt ready to settle down.

The day before Stephen was leaving for China to look after his business ventures, he asked if he could do anything for us while he was there. I said, "I am worried about you on this trip. I don't want you to get into any trouble with the Chinese government because of us." Stephen assured us that because he was an American citizen no one would bother him. His trip happened to coincide with President Bill Clinton's visit to China in June 1998.

Clinton's trip raised our hopes that American and Chinese leaders would reach some agreement on the Tibet question, so we watched the television news every day. If real progress was made, we would all be able to return to Kumbum. Then one day the news showed a meeting between President Clinton and Jiang Zemin; the last issue President Clinton raised was the question of the Dalai Lama. Jiang Zemin repeated the same old Party line: "If the Dalai Lama sincerely wants to have a dialogue with us, he must abandon his idea of Tibetan independence. . . ." Then Jiang asked Clinton in a disparaging tone, "Why do you Westerners trust this leader of Lamaism?"

Clinton retorted, "If you meet with him, you will like him, too."

I was disappointed by how far apart the two men were on this issue. The Dalai Lama's return to Tibet seemed a long way off. Meanwhile, we heard that the Chinese secret police were looking for us. Our paranoia returned. Now when we ventured into Chinatown, it seemed as if every Chinese person was regarding us with suspicion—or worse. We didn't know. Outside our house the smallest unusual sound after dark made us jump. At night I dreamt of being chased, or trapped, or tortured.

Then Stephen rang us from Shanghai. Two undercover policemen had interrogated him the moment he landed and had ordered him not to leave his hotel. Stephen was audibly shaken. And so were we. Two days later, he called again. A high-ranking police officer had just questioned him. "Do you know Arjia Rinpoche? Was it you who assisted him in leaving China? Where does he live now?"

Stephen told the interrogator that he knew nothing. Two days later, the police also detained Stephen's business manager, who was very upset with Stephen for being indirectly associated with the Dalai Lama. Then the factory Stephen had been doing business with suddenly canceled its contract. With so much pressure coming down on him from the Chinese government, and concerned for our safety given how much the secret police knew, Stephen suggested that we leave Los Angeles as quickly as possible. We didn't need convincing. We were packed and ready to go in no time. The only question was, where would we go?

Rose was very worried about us, too. I don't know how she found out about our newest predicament (maybe Stephen phoned her), but she suddenly appeared in Los Angeles. For the second time she came to our rescue. With her help, we headed north on a Greyhound bus. It was June, and our destination was San Francisco.

San Francisco was filled with pleasant ocean breezes and skies as clear and blue as those of Tibet. Helpful friends of Rose's—Kath and Eric—invited us into their home across the beautiful Golden Gate Bridge. San Francisco sparkled just behind us as we saw the still-green hills of Marin County for the first time. Kath and Eric were wonderful hosts, but our arrangement was temporary. How long would we stay on the move? I decided to put my fate in the hands of my karma and turn my thoughts to something I could control.

Over the next few days I considered how to write the letter to the Chinese government as requested by His Holiness the Dalai Lama. Until now I had cut all ties to my past political life, and part of me wanted to keep it that way. Writing a letter in itself might seem as if I were having second thoughts about my decision, which I was not. I had little confidence that my letter could facilitate any dialogue between the Tibetan government in exile and the Chinese government in Beijing, but I put my personal qualms aside and wrote directly to President Jiang Zemin. My letter began with an apology for causing embarrassment to the government and a reminder of our pleasant day together in Kumbum.

I wrote a less conciliatory letter to the national United Front. I cited their insensitivity and their arrogance, but more importantly I took them to task for the way they had handled every aspect of the Panchen Lama affair, from faking the Golden Urn Ceremony to demanding that I tutor their surrogate incarnation. I mailed both letters to a friend in Beijing and asked her to forward them on.

Some time later, a registered letter arrived in the mail from Wang Zhaoguo of the United Front.

Dear Arjia Lobsang Tubten Jigme Gyatso Rinpoche:

Since we met at the tea party for religious leaders in Beijing during the Chinese New Year, we haven't been in touch with each other. Recently, I learned that you have arrived in the United States. This news indeed surprised everyone who cares about you.

If it is because of dissatisfaction with worldly matters that Rinpoche decided to cross the ocean, this decision was a bit hasty and deserved more careful consideration. All previous Arjia Rinpoches made significant contributions to the well-being of the nation. You, as the reincarnation of the previous Arjia Rinpoches, bear the high hopes of lamas and lay Buddhists. Your uncle, the sutra instructor of the Tenth Panchen Lama, loved the nation and Buddhism. He also placed high hopes in you. In February this year, you were elected a permanent member of China's National People's Political Consultative Conference. This showed how much the Party and the government care about you. It is indeed incomprehensible that you left us without saying good-bye.

The international status of China, with its internal unit, is rapidly increasing. The recent meeting between American and Chinese leaders has attracted attention from all over the world. All Chinese, abroad and overseas, are overjoyed by these exciting events. Among them, Tibetans outside China also miss the motherland and desire to contribute to the well-being of their hometowns. The Dalai Lama is personally seeking contact with the central government and hopes to return to China soon. Your own political position in China is high, too.

What does the Dalai Lama think of you? The root of Tibetan Buddhism is in China, and Ta'er [Kumbum] Monastery is in China, and your disciples are in China. Rinpoche may leave China, but it is not possible to move Ta'er Monastery to the United States. You are becoming water without a source and a tree without roots, as you've left your own monastery and your countless disciples. I hope Rinpoche will carefully evaluate the situation and make right decisions.

The letter that Rinpoche sent to President Jiang has been forwarded to him. President Jiang hopes for your early return to China.

If Rinpoche can return to China in the foreseeable future, all your political status will remain the same without any change. I hope you will come back and devote yourself to your religious study and practice, see the true nature of enlightenment, pay homage to the motherland, and benefit all sentient beings. If you are unable to return to China because you are caught in a situation that you cannot extricate from and find difficult to explain, I hope you'll remember your successive predecessors' tradition of safeguarding the nation and benefiting sentient beings, and bear in mind Jiaya Lama's [Gyayak Rinpoche] patriotic words. If you have difficulties, we will offer best assistance. You may contact our consulate near where you live.

Wishing you a peaceful summer,
Wang Zhaoguo
July 1998, in Beijing

The letter had been faxed to Wu Bing and forwarded to me. I responded but never received a reply. The matter was closed.

Finally, I received a response to my letter to the president of China, Jiang Zemin. I wasn't prepared for a poem, but that is what he had written me.

Dear Arjia Rinpoche:
   Ta'er's Three Arts shine in the full of the moon,
   One Hundred Thousand Buddhas gather round the sandalwood tree.
   Awaken to your homeland where you belong!
   The beautiful lotus, by the River Tsong Chue.
   —Jiang Zemin

It was a touching reminder of Kumbum—its beauty and the depth of its connection to all the past Arjia Rinpoches. But I also felt the poem's ominous undertone. I had acceded to the request by the Dalai Lama. I had also effectively cut my ties with the dragon. That world was gone. Beneath my feet however, the seeds of a new life were about to be planted.

Fortune again smiled on us. Through yet another friend of Rose's, a Bay Area writer, we met Peter and Mimi Buckley, who generously offered to share their house in Stinson Beach, where the Pacific Ocean crashed at our doorstep. Asia lay across that ocean: Home seemed just below the horizon, but also impossibly far away.

Peter and Mimi were very kind, but once again we were living among strangers with whom we could hardly communicate. Although they did not espouse a particular religious belief, Peter and Mimi were more compassionate than many religious practitioners. Seeing our struggle to adapt, Peter let us know that he would provide the means for us to find our own permanent place, so that we could really, truly, finally build a new life for ourselves in the United States. With this promise of stability we regained our faith that we could adjust to the aspects of culture, language, and daily living that lay ahead.

That was the real beginning for us—a new start for which I was, and continue to be, extremely grateful. I sat that evening on the beach at the foot of Mount Tamalpais feeling optimism for the first time in months. I watched the waves rush to the shore, one after the other, like friends from afar who had come to visit me in my new world.

Renewed, we were able to take on several projects. First and foremost, we seriously began our study of English. The generosity, dedication, and expertise of our tutors, Katherine Lemon, Julie Jones, and Ann Williams, gave us hope that eventually we could learn this demanding language. Then one day Peter announced that he had found suitable housing for us. He had recently purchased property in Mill Valley—a picturesque town on the eastern side of Mount Tamalpais. The 1900s Craftsman-style house was located on 10 acres of redwood forest. On either side of the house a delightful creek flowed year-round. I knew immediately that this was the home Gyayak Rinpoche had encouraged me to seek by the time I was 50, a place to have a life free from political turmoil.

Our joy and gratitude knew no bounds. I had a room large enough to serve as my study. Chunpay had his own room, as did Chenlie, and Lobsang and Meido had their own private quarters. I felt something shift inside me.

For four years, since I had first started to consider the idea of leaving Tibet, I had suffered from two recurring dreams. In the first dream I am in prison, shuffling back and forth in my tiny cell, wearing shackles that clink

235

in a rhythm that accommodates whatever outside noise surrounds my sleep. In the second dream I am walking down the aisle of the airplane that will fly me to freedom when I see lots of people I know from my political life. They greet me, saying, "Hello, Arjia Rinpoche. What are you doing here? Where are you going?" I open my mouth to reply, but no words come out. I cannot tell them.

The night we moved into the Mill Valley house, I slept peacefully for the first time in memory, undisturbed by dreams of any kind.

We had a home! It was private and protected enough that all my fears of kidnapping or murder began to ebb away. Although the possibility of Chinese retribution felt more and more remote, we continued to maintain a low profile just to be cautious. Lobsang and Meido found local work; Chenlie enrolled in school; I found a teacher, Geshe Ngawang Drakpa in San Francisco, to help me continue my oft-delayed dharma studies. I still hoped that one day I would take all the vows expected of a rinpoche. For the moment I was a secluded monk, free to pursue my studies and my practice, which filled me with a giddy joy that I hadn't felt since childhood.

In March of 2000 I went to Los Angeles to testify before a committee studying freedom of religion in Tibet and China. The committee was eager to speak with me due to my former rank and how recently I had arrived in the United States. For my part, I worried that if I told my story to the committee, I would be breaking my promise to His Holiness to keep a low profile. Not wanting to bother the Dalai Lama directly, I talked to the International Campaign for Tibet (ICT) office about the matter. They said that if I spoke the truth without anger and bitterness, I could be faithful to both Tibet and the Dalai Lama. The question was moot in any case because by this time my whereabouts in California had already been published in a *Newsweek* article. My life had suddenly become very visible.

Anyone could find me now, but that felt okay. By becoming a public figure I hoped it would no longer be so easy for Chinese secret police to kidnap me without political repercussions, which might discourage them from trying. Chunpay and I began taking walks in the neighborhood for the first time. Not surprisingly, our maroon robes drew a lot of stares, but they also prompted people to say hello, or stop to talk. One day a nice young man asked if he could join us in our morning prayers. I said, "Of course." Wayne became my first American student.

Another time we were in Circuit City when a tall, athletic man introduced himself and talked to us about his interest in Buddhism. We invited Jerry, a San Francisco fireman, to join us as well. It wasn't long before more people than we could properly accommodate were coming for daily morning prayers, so we found a larger space and set up a regular schedule for prayers and teachings. Suddenly we had a center, the Tibetan Center for Compassion and Wisdom. I continued my studies with Geshe Ngawang Drakpa while I struggled to give serious dharma teachings to my new students. I say "struggled" because everyone insisted that I not use a translator but teach in English. Sometimes when I couldn't find the right word, our group would play guessing games to find what I meant. Never before in the history of Buddhism was there such interactive teaching of the dharma!

All these blessings took place thanks to our benefactors Peter and Mimi, as well as new friends like Peter Sandmann and Pauline Tessler, who guided us through the byzantine bureaucracy that leads to establishing legal status in the United States. Once again I had a home, and friends, and a mission. I became very busy offering special prayers for Tibetan and Mongolian families, preparing lessons, and giving talks at local schools, including Stanford University. There were also religious groups—Christian as well as Buddhist—that invited me to their centers. I opened an extension of our center in downtown Oakland. I gave Tibetan language lessons to a few eager students, and began teaching in both English and Chinese the *Lam Rim*, the root text of the Gelug tradition. The sangha became our extended family, and I knew that my life had taken on new meaning. My sense of being where I belonged had not been so strong since my childhood in Kumbum.

Then I decided to write my life story. One of my close friends and English tutors, Bernard della Santina, was very enthusiastic about this project, and selflessly worked with me for years to write these pages. During this eight-year cycle our lives took on form and structure. We settled into a very satisfying pattern. I felt more fulfilled than at any other time in my life. But for

237

238   me—the eighth incarnation of Arjia Rinpoche—that number seems the maximum time allotted for any one stage of my life. And so it proved to be.

The telephone rang at our home in Mill Valley. It was the Dalai Lama's office in New York calling to tell me that the Tibetan Cultural Center in Bloomington, Indiana, was in serious trouble. Tagtser Rinpoche, the oldest brother of His Holiness, whom I had met at Kumbum, had suffered a series of strokes and could no longer oversee the wonderful project he had established in Indiana many years before. At Indiana University he became known as "Professor Norbu" (his common name); he taught there for 22 years, and had built a center for the preservation of Tibetan culture on 108 acres of rolling meadows and thick forest.

The voice on the phone brought me back to the present moment. "Could you please take over management of Tagtser Rinpoche's center?"

I politely refused. If, as His Holiness often says, happiness is what every sentient being wants, why would I want to leave the happy life I had in Mill Valley?

The New York office of the Dalai Lama called again, and still I refused.

The third time, they said the magic words: "His Holiness has specifically named you as the person he wants to take over the management of Indiana's Tibetan Cultural Center. He fears that otherwise it will be lost."

So here I am in Indiana, having ventured forth on yet another journey. Once again my life is linked to a monastery that needs renewal and restoration. Gyayak Rinpoche told me that by age 50 I should leave politics and concentrate on the dharma. In fact, at 50, I did exactly that. Mill Valley was an idyll. But although my dream may be to follow a quiet life of retreat, reinvigorating monasteries appears to be my path. In this way I have come full circle, at least for now.

I have some sandalwood seeds in my robe that I saved from Kumbum. I will plant them here, in Indiana, at Kumbum West.

What will arise from them?

We shall see.

EPILOGUE

Like my own life, the history of Tibet can be seen in cycles marked by hope, patience, despair, and finally hope renewed. As the first decade of the twenty-first century nears an end, the view is bleak. The Panchen Lama is dead. Tashi Wangshuk and others like him are gone. The Dalai Lama is our biggest hope, and prospects for his return to Tibet are dim. In their hearts, Tibetans still rely on him, but they are suffering under the weight of so many burdens: the repressive policies of the Chinese government, the settlement of the Tibetan plateau by an overwhelming influx of Han Chinese, unequal job and education opportunities, and new reeducation programs harassing the monasteries once again.

Having painted such a dismal picture, how can I continue to believe that Tibetans have reason for hope? My native Tibetan optimism leads me to expect that as the wheel of life turns, the change that inevitably lies ahead will be for the better. Are we to expect that Tibetans are meekly willing to accept Chinese rule and allow their culture and religion to disappear from the Tibetan plateau?

Before the 2008 Olympics, Tibetans rose up in protest. Their demonstrations reminded the world of the true situation in Tibet. The Communist Chinese say everything is wonderful, yet there are protests not only in Tibet but throughout China. Nothing is what it seems. The situation is frighteningly unstable. And this the world must understand: Communist China has restive armies in every province, which the government must constantly redeploy to deal with insipient insubordination. Civil unrest among Han Chinese is increasing, too, perhaps to dangerous levels.

The Tibetan and Chinese people alike want democracy and freedom, but they have not forgotten Tiananmen Square, so how can change happen peacefully? One hope lies with a new generation of educated, professional leaders—lawyers, scholars, and scientists, some of whom were educated in the West—who can see the dangers ahead and respond with optimism, not fear. Many of them see the situation with clarity, and are speaking out. Some leaders understand and support the dreams of Tibetans and other ethnic people. That is a good sign. Recent changes in the law are applying term

239

240   limits to government officials. Perhaps new leaders will bring new points of view, and move Tibet and China in the direction of confidence and freedom. The movement for reconciliation in South Africa and the moral power of the Dalai Lama's insistence on nonviolence offer accessible models for positive change.

The current regime in China is uneasy with political and social changes of any sort. But if a federation of autonomous regions were ever to be established, if a democratic way of life were ever to prevail, then His Holiness the Dalai Lama's dream of the Middle Way, his hope for a genuine autonomy for Tibetans and other minorities, could be fulfilled. At last minorities could be free to follow their particular religious beliefs and celebrate their unique customs. The five stars on the Chinese flag could truly stand for the equality of China's ethnic groups—the Han majority and the Tibetan, Manchurian, Mongolian, and Muslim minorities—just as the 50 stars on the US flag stand for 50 separate but united states. Like those white stars in a field of blue, China's golden stars would shine for free peoples who share the daunting but glorious duty of governing a free country. Then the dreams of His Holiness the Dalai Lama will come true for Tibet—and for the world.

This too is my dream; this is my hope; this is my prayer.

APPENDIX

HOW BUDDHISM CAME TO TIBET, AND THE LINEAGE OF THE ARJIA RINPOCHES

Today there are three main linguistic branches of Buddhism. They are all firmly grounded in the words of Buddha Sakyamuni, 563–483 BCE, who preceded Jesus Christ by five centuries. However, because each branch evolved in its own language and in its own region, there are differences rooted in their unique cultural perspectives.

The Theravadan Buddhism that spread from India to Southeast Asia maintains the original style of Buddha's day. Theravadan temples are simple, and monks who practice Theravadan Buddhism have a reputation for strict discipline, excellent meditation practice, and renunciation of wealth that requires begging for alms and food.

Buddhism also spread from India into China, where it flourished in a complex form called Mahayana, influenced by the Chinese Imperial style. Today the best-known forms of this tradition are Pure Land and Zen, which gained new characteristics when they spread to Japan.

However, when Buddha's teachings spread from India to Tibet, which was isolated from surrounding areas by towering, snowy mountains, this natural barrier limited the third branch of Buddhism from influencing other countries and from *being* influenced. Tibetan Buddhism therefore developed in some unique ways, as we shall see. However, it did maintain a conventional emphasis on tantric or "secret" practices, in addition to sutra studies, which focus on Buddha's spoken words passed down directly to his disciples and to their students. The authenticity of this oral transmission is essential to spiritual realization, which is why what we call lineage is so important in Tibetan Buddhism. Also, in this process master and student become like father and son, a relationship that becomes a rare and precious part of the teaching itself.

The famous Indian guru Padmasambhava visited Tibet in the eighth century at the invitation of the king of Tibet, and the guru's teachings were so successful that eventually they eclipsed the native Tibetan religion, known as Bon. This continued for several generations. However, after the king's death, the king's grandson suppressed Buddhism and restored Bon to its earlier primacy. Buddhism continued in a diminished role in Tibet until the eleventh century, when the great master Atisha came from India to solidify Buddhism's hold and expand its practices. It has been the dominant religion in Tibet ever since.

From that time, Tibetan Buddhist teachings formed four main schools: Nyingma, Sakya, Kagyu, and Gelug. The Nyingma School, sometimes called the Old School, is based on the original teachings of Padmasambhava, who first brought Buddhism to Tibet. Identified by the colorful head coverings worn by monks of this sect, it is called the Red Hat Sect. The Gelug tradition, which I practice, derived from a combination of the original teachings of Padmasambhava and the later teachings of Atisha. It was founded by Lama Tsong Khapa (1357–1419), a reformer who stressed the importance of monastic virtue and discipline. The yellow hats worn by the monks have led to its being called the Yellow Hat Sect. Each of these traditions, schools, and lineages has its own subtle variations that honor the teachings of specific masters, but they are all clearly part of one great tradition.

Buddhism is based on a belief in reincarnation—that we are all endlessly reborn into new bodies until such time as we achieve the enlightenment of a Buddha, which is the ultimate goal. The continuity of practice in some Tibetan Buddhist traditions is achieved through a system that seeks out the reincarnations of deceased teachers so they can be restored to their rightful positions of honor and continue their teaching. Remarkable and deeply moving stories of reincarnated beings have served as precious spiritual food for many generations of Tibetans. One example is the history of the Arjia Rinpoches, the line of high lamas in the Gelug tradition of which I am the current living form.

Naturally enough, my story begins with the founder of the Gelug tradition itself, Lama Tsong Khapa. In opposition to standard practice, Lama Tsong Khapa insisted that in the Gelug lineage his reincarnation *not* be continued through a reincarnation recognized by his disciples. Instead, he ordered that the position of leadership go to the abbot of Ganden Monastery. Honoring his request, the students of Lama Tsong Khapa never searched for his reincarnation.

Nevertheless, a school needs a line of masters to continue the oral transmission of Buddha's teachings, so they searched instead for reincarnations of Lama Tsong Khapa's disciples and family members to pass on his teachings and to administer the many Gelug monasteries established during his lifetime.

One such monastery, Kumbum, was built at the birthplace of Lama Tsong Khapa in Amdo Province, a region of northeastern Tibet, near the Chinese capital city of Xining (in Tibetan, *Siling*). Starting in the sixteenth century, the position of abbot in this monastery was traditionally offered to the person identified as the reincarnation of Lama Tsong Khapa's father. (In the Amdo dialect, *arjia* means father, and *rinpoche* means "precious one," so the title Arjia Rinpoche translates as "precious father.") To honor their abbot, the disciples of Arjia Rinpoche have traced stories of his reincarnations all the way back to the time of Buddha. This legendary history honoring my predecessors is 21 generations long, but I am only the eighth incarnation of whom there is a written record.

Each incarnation of Arjia Rinpoche has been respected as a knowledgeable and resourceful leader working to protect the dharma (the teachings of Buddha) and the people of Amdo Province. The first formally recognized Arjia Rinpoche was Tsultrim Jongni Jung Ni, supposedly born in the sixteenth century; the 15th abbot of Kumbum Monastery, he was given the name Arjia Rinpoche posthumously. He was a learned and much beloved scholar, so when he passed away his distraught disciples were eager to find a reincarnation to ensure the continuity of the lineage. They searched among the estates owned by the monastery in an area called Five Valleys, and eventually they found the abbot's reincarnation in a family who lived in the small village named for the wild cloves that grew nearby.

The second official incarnation was Arjia Sherap Sangbo (1633–1707), who was elected managing abbot (*khenpo*) of the monastery when he was 54 years old. (Monasteries in our region often have two abbots; one serves as spiritual leader, and the other runs the monastery's day-to-day affairs.) Besides being a sutra and tantra master, Arjia Sherap Sangbo was a gifted administrator who formulated rules and regulations for the monastery and set up a curriculum for learning and practicing dharma. He also added to the magnificence of

243

Kumbum Monastery by restoring it and extending it so that it overlooked the valley formed by the Lotus Mountains.

The third Arjia Rinpoche was the abbot Arjia Lobsang Denbi Gyaltsan (1708–1768), a noted scholar who wrote many important books and articles about cosmology, the metaphysical study of the origin and nature of the universe that plays an important role in Buddhism. He was even honored by Emperor Qian Long of the Qing Dynasty, who invited him to Beijing.

Arjia Lobsang Jamyang Gyatso (1768–1816) was the Fourth Arjia Rinpoche. As a young man from Amdo who attended Sera Monastery near Lhasa, he studied and trained in the five major disciplines of Tibetan classical studies (arts and crafts, medicine, grammar, logic, and philosophy). Acclaimed by the Eighth Dalai Lama, he was bestowed the Mongolian title of Pundit of the Three Jewels and was also given the title Virtuous and Talented Master Arjia, the Hutuk htu, by Emperor Qian Long. Later he accepted an invitation to serve as tutor to the Mongolian Lama-king, who held a position in Mongolia similar to the Dalai Lama's in Tibet.

The Fifth Arjia Rinpoche, Yeshe Kalsang Kedrup Gyatso (1817–1869), practiced the martial arts of war in addition to more scholarly pursuits. During this time the Muslim minority in Amdo became violently opposed to the royal Qing government. Muslim rebels burned houses, robbed temples, and terrorized the people. At the request of local citizens, the Fifth Arjia Rinpoche militarized monks and trained villagers to protect the temple and their villages. At the same time, he wrote letters to the royal government in Xining requesting aid.

The Qing government replied that although it was very concerned about this matter, it preferred that Arjia Rinpoche solve the problem through peaceful means. Of course the Fifth Arjia Rinpoche agreed that cultivating loving kindness was the best way, but the situation was dire. Monks and villagers were forced to take up arms and fight for their families, homes, and temples. Eventually, the government dispatched troops to aid them and suppressed the rebellion.

The Sixth Arjia Rinpoche, Lobsang Tenbe Wanshuk Sonam Gyatso (1871–1909), was also a military monk. Adept with sword and spear, he too was called upon to fight when the Muslim rebellion resumed in 1895. He was accorded great favor by the Qing emperor Guang Xu, who sent Arjia Rinpoche to Japan in 1900 on a religious mission to meet with the Japanese emperor. While there, Arjia Rinpoche was invited to a sword match in Kyoto to demonstrate his skill. He won admiration from the Japanese emperor, who honored the Sixth Arjia Rinpoche with gifts, including a statue of the Buddha and a precious sword. These gifts and photographs of the event were kept in my residence at Kumbum. I still vaguely remember from my childhood that on New Year's Day, they would be taken out and put on display. Sadly, they were destroyed by the Chinese in 1958, during a violent political purge at Kumbum Monastery.

My predecessor, the Seventh Arjia Rinpoche, Lobsang Lundak Jigme Tanbe Gyaltsen (1910–1948), devoted his life to Buddhist teachings. As abbot, he ran the temple according to strict rules and regulations. Despite his efforts he presided over the monastery's moral decline at a time when the Qing Dynasty collapsed and was replaced by the Republic of China, and a sense of Western modernism swept the land, further undermining discipline among some monks. I heard one story of a monk who stole an iconographic painting (a *thangka*) from the monastery and put it in the private altar of his own family's home. Somehow the Seventh Arjia Rinpoche found out, and although he was a very gentle person, he became so angry that he struck the monk. The following day Arjia Rinpoche's hand swelled, never to truly heal. The Seventh Arjia Rinpoche died a year later, in 1948, when he was only 38 years old. His cremation took place in the courtyard of the residence where I played as a child.

The Eighth Arjia Rinpoche, Lobsang Tubten Jigme Gyatso, was born in 1950.

I am this Rinpoche.

GLOSSARY OF TERMS AND NAMES

TERM OR NAME	EXPLANATION
70,000 Character Petition	1962 document compiled by the Tenth Panchen Lama reporting on the Chinese Communist government's mistreatment of Tibetans, their religion, and their culture
A History of Confucian Scholars	Chinese literature read by Arjia Rinpoche at Kumbum during the Cultural Revolution to improve his Chinese
Abbe Huc	French missionary of the nineteenth century who witnessed the image of Buddha on the leaf of the sandalwood tree of Lama Tsong Khapa
Ajita	Maitreya—Supramundane Being; Buddha to Come
Aku Jigme Tsang	Monk at Labrang who gave Arjia Rinpoche his religious name
All-China Youth Federation	Group that Arjia Rinpoche represented during his official trips abroad; he was its deputy chairman when he left Tibet and China
Amdo	Eastern region of Tibet where Kumbum Monastery is located; known as Qinghai in Chinese
Amitabha Buddha	A Supramundane Being and Buddha of the Pure Land
Apah and Amah	Familiar names of the parents of the Tenth Panchen Lama
Asanga	Indian Buddhist philosopher (fourth century), exponent of the Yogacara School
Asoka (Ashoka)	Emperor of India, 304–232 BCE, who embraced Buddhism
Atisha	Indian Buddhist teacher (982–1054), whose most famous work is the *Lamp for the Path to Enlightenment*. Upon the invitation of King Lha Lama Yeshe Yod, he traveled to Tibet where he taught the Dharma for 17 years, reintroducing the teachings of Buddha to the Land of Snows.
Badachu Park	Cluster of eight temples in Beijing now used as a park; the Buddha's relics were displayed in the second temple
Bakshi	Family pet name of Serdok Rinpoche; "teacher" in the Mongolian language
Baldan	Arjia Rinpoche's father
bardo	Intermediate state where the subtle consciousness wanders seeking rebirth
Barkhor	Path around the Jokhang Temple used by pilgrims and Tibetan merchants
Beijing	Capital city of China
Black-Nose Xu	Communist Chinese official at Tashi Lhunpo, who protected the urn containing the remains of the Fourth Panchen Lama, Choeji Gyaltsen
bodhisattva	A Supramundane Being who pledges to remain in samsara to help all sentient beings attain enlightenment
Buddha	The founder of Buddhism, Siddhartha Gautama (563–483 BCE); any enlightened being
Buddhist Association of China	Religious organization of which Arjia Rinpoche was vice chairman at the national level and slated to become chairman when he left Tibet and China

TERM OR NAME	EXPLANATION
Bumi Rinpoche	Monk at Ganden Monastery who helped desecrate Lama Tsong Khapa's body; lama who participated in the selection of the Chinese Panchen Lama
Buton Rinpoche	One of Tibet's most renowned scholars and translators (1290–1364), who purportedly copied the complete set of the Kangyur (Tibetan Buddhist canon) seven times by hand
cadre	Soldier or representative working for the Chinese Communist government
Campaign of Three Educations	Propaganda classes taught to the monks at Tashi Lhunpo: Marxist Internationalism, Marxist Patriotism, and Marxist Socialism
CPC	Communist Party of China
CPPCC	Chinese People's Political Consultative Conference; it has central, provincial, and county levels. Arjia Rinpoche was slated to become a standing committee member of the central level.
Chadrel Rinpoche	Abbot of Tashi Lhunpo and original cochair (with Gyayak Rinpoche) of Eleventh Panchen Lama search committee; later arrested
Changchup	Monk whose corpse was disposed of in the Yarlong Tsangpo River
changtso	Manager of an estate and household in a monastery
Changya Forest	Woodland where Arjia Rinpoche cut jute for renovation of the meditation hall at Kumbum
Chen Yong Hua	A retired cadre and friend who helped repair Kumbum after the earthquake of 1990
Chenlie Rejie	Arjia Rinpoche's nephew and adopted son who escaped with him to Guatemala and the United States
Chibo	A lay brother of Arjia Rinpoche who was with him at Kumbum
Chief Director Du Hua Nan	Chief director of the Qinghai Province United Front who officiated at public accusation meetings in 1958
Choe Gyang Jep	Changtso of Arjia Rinpoche's estate and household at Kumbum before 1958
Choesang Rinpoche	Artist monk and devout Buddhist who was imprisoned for 20 years
Choeshi Rinpoche	Khenpo of Kumbum when it was reopened in 1979 after his 21 years of imprisonment
Chomolungma	Tibetan name for Mount Everest; refers to a place where a female Protector resides
Christine	Devoted Buddhist who helped Arjia Rinpoche and his party escape to Guatemala and the United States
chuba	Tibetan outer garment resembling a coat
Chunpay Jiumei	Arjia Rinpoche's personal attendant who escaped with him to Guatemala and the United States
Chushar	Remote area 50 kilometers from Tashi Lhunpo where black thistles grow; east side of the Yarlong Tsangpo River
Comrade Ho	Muslim official of the Ministry of Public Security of the PRC sent to persuade Arjia Rinpoche to join the Communist Party

TERM OR NAME	EXPLANATION
CPPCC	Chinese People's Political Consultative Committee, an advisory group of the National People's Congress
Crimson Head documents	Important Communist documents whose headings were usually printed in red ink
Cultural Revolution	Period in Communist China from 1966 until the death of Mao in 1976, during which time religions and traditions were destroyed in all of China and its ethnic regions
Dagpa Gyatso	A holy monk who lived in the early twentieth century and taught his students how to die well
dai maozi	Notation on identification papers revealing the stigma that he or she had been given a "paper hat"
Dalai Lama	Spiritual and political leader of the Tibetan people. The name Dalai Lama is usually translated as "ocean of wisdom."
Dawa Tsering	Representative of the Fourteenth Dalai Lama in New York City at the time of Arjia Rinpoche's escape
Dechen Podrang	Palace of the Panchen Lama at Shigatse near Tashi Lhunpo
Delinkha	Prison where Uncle Chungchu Oser was detained
Democratic Management Committee	Organization with branches representing Drepung, Ganden, and Sera monasteries in the meeting concerning the 1987 uprising; also name of the organization that managed Kumbum during the Cultural Revolution
Deng Xiaoping	De facto leader of the PRC from 1978 to the early 1990s
Dharamsala	Hill town in northern India and location of the Tibetan government in exile
dharma	Teachings of the Buddha; the second of the Three Jewels of Buddhism; an object of spiritual refuge
Dolma	Eldest sister of Arjia Rinpoche who was humiliated during the Cultural Revolution
Dolon Nor steppe	Area in northeastern Tibet near Lake Koko Nor where the Eighth Arjia Rinpoche was born; later was the site of Communist Chinese nuclear activities
Dondup Palden	Monk and cook at Tashi Lhunpo during the Cultural Revolution who discovered an urn containing the remains of the Fourth Panchen Lama, Choeji Gyaltsen
Dong Qiwu	Grandfather of Li Jie, who married the Panchen Lama
dopdo	Worldly monks in a monastery who are sometimes part of a gang
Dorji Shara	Positivist monk at Tashi Lhunpo
Drashi Gyaltsen	Arjia Rinpoche's secretary when he was khenpo (director) of Kumbum
Drashi Namgyal	Temple at Tashi Lhunpo near the stupa that contains the remains of the previous Panchen Lamas
Dream of the Red Chamber	Chinese literature read by Arjia Rinpoche at Kumbum during the Cultural Revolution to improve his Chinese
Drepung Monastery	One of Tibet's largest monastic universities near Lhasa. In the 1980s, its monks put on a show of resistance against the Communists.

TERM OR NAME	EXPLANATION
Dru Bum Gyal	Officer of the Ministry of Public Security of the People's Republic of China (similar to the US's FBI)
Dundrup Gyal	Party secretary of Hainan Prefecture, a Tibetan who benefited other Tibetans during his tenure but was later disgraced
dung kang	Cremation furnace for high lamas
Ehud Olmert	Mayor of Jerusalem during Arjia Rinpoche's trip to Israel; later prime minister of Israel
Empowerment	Tantric ceremony in which an initiate is given meditation instructions to aid him on his path to enlightenment
four pests	Sparrows, rats, flies, and mosquitoes in the Qinghai area
Fourteenth Dalai Lama	Born in 1935, Tenzin Gyatso fled Tibet in 1959 and established a government in exile in Dharamsala, India. A world-renowned leader for universal peace and harmony, he received the Nobel Peace Prize in 1989.
Gan Ziyu	Director of the National Development and Reform Commission when Arjia Rinpoche was director (khenpo) of Kumbum
Ganden Monastery	The first Gelug monastic university founded by Lama Tsong Khapa. It was destroyed during the Cultural Revolution and partially rebuilt in the 1980s.
Ganden Tripa	Throne holder (leader) of the Gelug sect of Tibetan Buddhism
Gang of Four	Four high Communist leaders, including Mao's wife, who are blamed for the Cultural Revolution
Gansu	Province in eastern Tibet
Gashima	Temple near Kumbum, part of Arjia Rinpoche's residence, where he established a Western-style school
Gegue Gendan Sopa	Disciplinarian monk whom little Arjia Rinpoche denounced at a public accusation meeting
Gelug	One of the four sects of Tibetan Buddhism, founded by Lama Tsong Khapa; the sect to which the Dalai Lama, the Panchen Lama, and Arjia Rinpoche belong; the Yellow Hat Sect
ger	Dome-shaped dwelling for Mongolian nomads
geshe	Degree bestowed on a Tibetan monk upon the completion of the mastery of Buddhist philosophy (13 to 16 years); equivalent to a master's degree
Geshe Lharampa	Degree bestowed on a Tibetan monk upon the completion of the mastery of Buddhist philosophy (22 to 26 years); equivalent to a PhD
Gheypa	Uncle of Arjia Rinpoche, humiliated by the Communists during the Cultural Revolution
Gnuchoe Rinpoche	One of the Panchen Lama's spiritual teachers
Golden Urn Ceremony	Method used to select the Eleventh Panchen Lama; purportedly used during the Qing Dynasty to recognize the Dalai Lama and the Panchen Lama. This claim has never been accepted by Tibetans.
gongdak	Hereditary abbot and owner of a monastery; Arjia Rinpoche is gongdak of Kumbum Monastery
Gonggar Airport	Airport 100 kilometers outside of Lhasa

249

TERM OR NAME	EXPLANATION
Gongo Tseten	Name of the Tenth Panchen Lama, given to him by his parents
Gongya Rinpoche	Tibetan lama who was with Arjia Rinpoche when the Fourteenth Dalai Lama's delegation visited Kumbum
Great Hall of Golden Tiles	Serdung Chenmo, in Tibetan; a place in Kumbum that houses the spot where Lama Tsong Khapa was born, and contains the stupa that encloses the sacred sandalwood tree that grew on his place of birth. Also referred to as the Golden Hall.
Great Leap Forward	An economic and social plan used from 1958 to 1961 that aimed to rapidly transform China from a primarily agrarian economy into a modern agriculturalized and industrialized Communist society
Green Tara	Female Buddha of Compassion
Guangzhou	Place in south China where Arjia Rinpoche pretended to go on retreat when he escaped
Gyaltsen Dragpa	A security guard at Kumbum when the Fourteenth Dalai Lama's delegation visited
Gyaltsen Norbu	Tibetan governor of the TAR during the time of the selection of the Eleventh Panchen Lama
Gyaltsen Norbu (aka Gedhun Choekyi Gyabo)	Child chosen by the Chinese Communists in 1995 to be the Eleventh Panchen Lama
Gyayak Rinpoche	Spiritual teacher of both the Panchen Lama and Arjia Rinpoche; also Arjia Rinpoche's uncle
Hainan	A prefecture in Qinghai Province in Amdo, Tibet
Han Chinese	Majority ethnic group in China
He Hai	One of little Arjia Rinpoche's best friends in his Chinese school
Heart Sutra	Buddhist sacred scripture that enunciates the doctrine of emptiness; also called the Wisdom Sutra
Heroes of the Marshes	Chinese literature studied by Arjia Rinpoche at Kumbum during the Cultural Revolution to improve his Chinese
High-Level Tibetan Buddhism College of China	Highest Buddhist academy in Beijing, established by the Tenth Panchen Lama. School where Serdok Rinpoche and Arjia Rinpoche studied the dharma in 1988.
Hu Jintao	Party secretary of the TAR when the Tenth Panchen Lama died; presently president of the PRC
Hu Qijiang	General secretary of Qinghai Provincial People's Consultative Conference
Hu Qili	Once a high-ranking member of the Communist Party of China, Hu Qili is still affiliated with the CPC and serves as a national symbol of intelligence, leadership, technology, and political idealism
Hu Yaobang	Protégé of Deng Xiaoping; Liberal Party secretary removed from office in 1987; hero of students in Tiananmen Square
Hua Guofeng	Immediate successor to Chairman Mao during the Cultural Revolution
Huangzhong County	County in Qinghai Province in eastern Tibet where Kumbum is located

TERM OR NAME	EXPLANATION
Inner Mongolia	One of the ethnic regions adjacent to the Mongolian People's Republic. It is controlled by the Chinese Communists.
Investiture of Gods	Chinese literature read by Arjia Rinpoche at Kumbum during the Cultural Revolution to improve his Chinese
Jamaga	A simple monk who became Arjia Rinpoche's protector and caretaker in 1958
Jambo Rinpoche	Monk at the High-Level Tibetan Buddhism College of China who became a great scholar
Jambudvipa	A continent of the Terrestrial World in Hindu and Buddhist geography
Jamyang Shepa Rinpoche	Abbot of Labrang Monastery and member of the All-China Youth Federation; member of the original search committee for the Eleventh Panchen Lama and involved in the selection of the counterfeit Panchen Lama
Je-Ji	Tibetan nomad from Goluk and friend of Arjia Rinpoche during the meeting of the All-China Youth Federation in 1979 in Beijing
Jetsun Pema	Younger sister of the Fourteenth Dalai Lama who was part of a delegation that visited the TAR in the 1980s
Jiang Qing	Mao's wife and one of the Gang of Four
Jiang Zemin	President of the PRC from 1993 to 2003
Jigu	Area in northeast Kham, a western region of Tibet
Jin Ji Peng	Qinghai provincial governor at the time of the earthquake in 1990
Jokhang Temple	Most sacred Buddhist shrine in Lhasa, built in the seventh century by Songtsen Gampo
Juchen Thubtan	Head of the Fourteenth Dalai Lama's delegation that visited Kumbum in the 1980s
Kalachakra	"Wheel of time"—Empowerment and mandala that depicts the Tibetan cosmic view and the interdependence of all phenomena and the workings of karma
Kalachakra Temple	A temple at Kumbum
Kampa Basang Norbu	A positivist monk who was a group leader at Tashi Lhunpo
Kanggyan Gongsi	Fund-raising organization ("Ornaments for the Land of Snow") created by the Panchen Lama to raise money to support the Tibetan culture and religion
Kangyur	Buddhist sacred scriptures that are the direct teachings of Buddha Sakyamuni
Kagyu	One of the four sects of Tibetan Buddhism
Karlchen Dawa La	Khenpo of Shartse Dratsang in Tashi Lhunpo and teacher of Arjia Rinpoche and Serdok Rinpoche
Karmapa	Founder of the Kagyu sect of Tibetan Buddhism
Kashag	The Tibetan Cabinet; a member of the Kashag is a powerful minister of the Tibetan government
Katika Monastery	Monastery in Amdo that houses the original thangka intended to be given as a gift to his mother by Lama Tsong Khapa

251

TERM OR NAME	EXPLANATION
Kegya Rinpoche	Khenpo of Kumbum who was imprisoned when the monastery was taken over and dissolved in 1958
Khampo Gyamda	A desert area near Shigatse where the Chinese Communists planned to establish a farm
khata	Silk scarf—usually white (Tibetan) or blue (Mongolian)—given to another to show honor and respect. Represents the "sense offering of touch."
khenpo	Usually the administrative abbot of a Tibetan monastery; renamed "director" by the Chinese Communist government; sometimes used as a political title
Khin Nyunt	General and military dictator of Burma during the visit of Arjia Rinpoche in 1994
Kongtang Rinpoche	A high lama from Labrang Monastic University who was a member of the original search committee for the Eleventh Panchen Lama
Kumbum	Monastery of Arjia Rinpoche located in Amdo, Tibet. "Kumbum" means "Place of 100,000 Buddhas." In Chinese, it is called Ta'er Si.
Kumbum West	Monastery on the grounds of the Tibetan Mongolian Buddhist Cultural Center in Bloomington, Indiana (formerly the Tibetan Cultural Center)
Kuomintang	Political party founded in 1911 by Sun Yat-sen; it governed China under Chiang Kai-shek from 1928 until 1949, when the Communists took power. It is the current government in power in Taiwan.
Labrang Monastery	A monastery in eastern Tibet where Arjia Rinpoche took his first vows (Labrang Tashi Kyil)
Labrangze	Auspicious Palace at Kumbum, a residence for abbots and a place for spiritual leaders such as the Dalai Lama and the Panchen Lama to stay
Lake Koko Nor	Lake in the region of Amdo, Tibet; Arjia Rinpoche's birthplace was near this lake
Lam Rim Chenmo	*The Great Treatise on the Stages of the Path to Enlightenment,* the root text of Lama Tsong Khapa
Lantern Festival	Gelug festival that honors the passing of Lama Tsong Khapa
Lhasa	Capital city of Tibet, located in the central region
Li Dezhu	Chinese Korean vice director of the United Front Work Department of the CPC Central Committee during the time of the selection of the counterfeit Panchen Lama
Li Guoqing	Official of the United Front Work Department of the CPC Central Committee who spoke to Arjia Rinpoche about being the tutor to the counterfeit Panchen Lama
Li Jie	Granddaughter of Dong Qiwu who married the Panchen Lama
Li Tieying	Head of the Chinese delegation during the selection of the counterfeit Panchen Lama
Li Yin	Serious student and classmate of little Arjia Rinpoche in his Chinese school
Li Zuomin	Deputy secretary of the United Front Work Department of the CPC Central Committee, the Panchen Lama's Chinese interpreter during the 1987 uprising investigation, and member of the Panchen Lama's party who traveled to Central and South America in 1988

TERM OR NAME	EXPLANATION
Lin Biao	A high-ranking Chinese Communist leader and second in command to Mao during the Cultural Revolution
Liu Long	Communist Party member who advocated openness; worked with Arjia Rinpoche to establish a Tibetan version of the Chinese ministry that was planned by the Panchen Lama before he passed away
Liu Shaoqi	Chairman whose policies helped reverse the Great Famine. He died in disgrace.
Living Buddha	Familiar Chinese name for a rinpoche, an incarnate lama or tulku
Lobsang	Arjia Rinpoche's bodyguard who escaped with him to Guatemala and the United States
Lobsang Chunpay	Positivist monk at Kumbum who embraced Communist political movements
Lobsang Denbi Gyaltsen	Third Arjia Rinpoche (1708–1768)
Lobsang Donyol	Uncle of Arjia Rinpoche (younger brother of Gyayak Rinpoche) and assistant to Serdok Rinpoche who was humiliated by the Chinese Communists
Lobsang Jamyang Gyatso	Fourth Arjia Rinpoche (1768–1816)
Lobsang Lundak Jigme Tanbe Gyaltsen	Seventh Arjia Rinpoche (1910–1948)
Lobsang Rabgyal	Positivist monk at Kumbum who triumphed over Ngawang Jimba
Lobsang Samten	Elder brother of the Fourteenth Dalai Lama who was part of the delegation that visited Kumbum in the 1980s
Lobsang Tenbe Wanshuk Sonam Gyatso	Sixth Arjia Rinpoche (1871–1909)
Lobsang Tubten Jigme Gyatso	Eighth Arjia Rinpoche (1950–); author of this book
Lobsang Tsultrim	A dopdo and younger brother of the Seventh Arjia Rinpoche
Losar	Tibetan New Year
Lumbum Gai	Father of Lama Tsong Khapa. Arjia Rinpoche is the eighth reincarnation of Lumbum Gai.
Luo Gan	Secretary of the Chinese State during the Golden Urn Ceremony
Má chin-mo	Tibetan title for the chef of high leaders
Mahayana	One of the vehicles of Buddhism; emphasizes the practice of compassion for all sentient beings
Maitreya Hall	One of the earliest temples at Kumbum. Maitreya is one of the disciples of Buddha who emphasizes the practice of compassion.
Manjushri	One of the main disciples of the Buddha who embodies the practice of wisdom

TERM OR NAME	EXPLANATION
mantra	Spiritual syllables, usually in Sanskrit, that invoke the powers of a Buddha or bodhisattva
Mao Zedong	Chairman of the Chinese Communist Party and leader of the People's Republic of China from its establishment in 1949 until his death in 1976
Master Fa Zun	Translated the *Lam Rim Chenmo*
Meido	Lobsang's wife, who escaped with Arjia Rinpoche to Guatemala and the United States
Milerepa	Tibetan yogi, famous for his meditation practice (1052–1135)
Ming Dynasty	Dynasty of China (1368–1644)
Ministry of Foreign Affairs of the PRC	Ministry in charge of protocol and policies regarding visiting foreign countries and visitors from foreign countries
Ministry of Public Security of the People's Republic of China	Communist agency that monitored security for Communist VIPs (similar to the US's CIA)
Miss Xu and Miss Zhang	Arjia Rinpoche's first-grade teachers in his Chinese school in the 1950s
Mo	Method of divination practiced by Tibetan and Mongolian lamas
Mother of All Conquerors	Supramundane Being personifying the wisdom that experiences emptiness (*Prajnaparamita* in Sanskrit)
Mount Drolma	Mountain before which Tashi Lhunpo Monastery sits; "Drolma" is Tibetan for Tara
Mr. Huang	Member of the Ministry of Foreign Affairs of the PRC; member of the Panchen Lama's party who traveled to Central and South America in 1988
Mr. Li	Chief of police for Huangzhong County, at the time of Jiang Zemin's visit to Kumbum
Mr. Lu	Friend of Arjia Rinpoche in Guatemala
Mrs. Feng	Friend of Arjia Rinpoche in Guatemala
mudra	Symbolic gesture performed by monks during religious ceremonies
Nagarjuna	Indian Buddhist philosopher (second century) who propounded the doctrines of the Middle Way school (Madhyamika)
Namgyal Tsewang Rinpoche	Abbot of Tashi Lhunpo who died in a car crash in 1988 while attending the consecration of Drashi Namgyal temple
Nartang	Monastery near Shigatse that once contained the Kangyur; its printing houses were destroyed during the Cultural Revolution. It was built in 1153.
National People's Congress	Supreme law-giving body in Communist China that directed Arjia Rinpoche to attend the 15th World Buddhist Conference in 1986 in Nepal with the Panchen Lama
Ngapo Ngawang Jigme	One of the members of the Kashag who played a role in negotiating the Seventeen-Point Agreement.
Ngawang Jimba	Positivist monk who became head of the Communist Administrative Committee that ruled Kumbum; publicly admonished by the Tenth Panchen Lama

TERM OR NAME	EXPLANATION
Ninth Panchen Lama	A lama (1883–1937) who visited Kumbum and became close to Gyayak Rinpoche. He prophesized that they would remain close.
Nori	A monk brother of Arjia Rinpoche who was with him at Kumbum
Nyingma	The eldest of the four sects of Tibetan Buddhism; the Red Hat Sect
Old Ma	Muslim who translated for Wu Jinghua in the meeting concerning the 1987 uprising
Old Wang	Friend of Uncle Chungchu Oser in Delinkha Prison Camp
Old Zhu	Cellmate of Uncle Chungchu Oser in Delinkha Prison Camp
om mani padme hum	Sanskrit mantra of the Bodhisattva of Compassion, Avalokiteshvara (*Chenrezig* in Tibetan)
Padmasambhava	Indian pandit (learned man) who brought Buddhism to Tibet in the eighth century
Panchen Lama	Along with the Dalai Lama, one of the two spiritual leaders of Tibet; reincarnation of Amitabha Buddha
Panchen Nang Makhang	Administrative area in Lhasa where monks and lay officials serving the Panchen Lama performed their duties
Panchen Shangde	A monastery of the Panchen Lama located west of Kumbum
paper hat	Punishment and stigma during the Cultural Revolution for people being shamed for their elitist roots or position. Sometimes a sufferer was required to wear an actual hat; at other times, his official papers labeled his disgrace.
paramitas	Six virtues of Buddhism: generosity, morality, patience, effort, concentration, and wisdom
the Party	The Communist Party; an elite group whose members ran the Chinese Communist government
Path of Accumulation	First path to enlightenment, during which one accumulates good karma by practicing the six paramitas
Pauline Tessler	Associate and wife of Peter Sandmann. She is a lawyer in Mill Valley, California.
Pema	Arjia Rinpoche's eldest brother
Pema Tashi	Vicious Tibetan Communist cadre who was eventually disgraced
Pema Yangchen	Sister-in-law of the Panchen Lama
Peng Dehuai	Communist right-wing hero jailed in the late 1950s for his objections to the Great Leap Forward
Peter	Friend of Arjia Rinpoche in Guatemala who assisted him in his escape
Peter and Mimi Buckley	Friends in Mill Valley, California, who gave a home to Arjia Rinpoche and his party
Peter Sandmann	Lawyer in Mill Valley, California, who assisted Arjia Rinpoche in getting legal status in the United States
Phuntsok Wangyal	A sincere Tibetan Communist, loyal to Communist ideology despite suffering many years of imprisonment by the Chinese government; a member of the Panchen Lama's party who traveled to Central and South America in 1988
PLA	People's Liberation Army—the army of the Chinese Communists

TERM OR NAME	EXPLANATION
positivist	Anyone, including monks, favorably regarded by the Communist Chinese as being receptive to reeducation
Potala Palace	A palace in Central Tibet (Lhasa) that has played a central role in the traditional administration of Tibet; includes the residence of the Dalai Lamas
PRC	People's Republic of China
Protector	Emanations of a Buddha or bodhisattva who neutralizes obstacles on the path of spiritual advancement
public accusation meeting	Public meetings where many innocent persons were denounced during the political campaigns of the 1950s and 1960s
Pure Land	Form of Buddhism practiced in the Chinese tradition
Qing Dynasty	Manchu Dynasty that ruled China from 1644 to 1911
Qinghai	Chinese name of Koko Nor (Mongolian) or Tso Ngonbo (Tibetan), the region of Amdo in eastern Tibet
Qinghai CCPPCC	Arjia Rinpoche was deputy chairman of this organization in the 1990s, a position equivalent to a deputy governor
Qinghai University for Nationalities	School attended by Arjia Rinpoche in Qinghai Province
Raku Rinpoche	Former abbot and monk who was beaten and arrested at the first public accusation meeting at Kumbum in 1958
Ramoche Temple	Temple in Lhasa, smaller than the Jokhang, also built in the seventh century
Red Book	Book of quotations by Mao Zedong that was required reading in Tibet and China during his period of power
Red Guard	A mass movement of civilians, mostly students and other young people in China, who were mobilized by Mao Zedong in 1966 and 1967, during the Cultural Revolution
Religious Reform Movement	Communist program that systematically suppressed religion and devastated monasteries throughout China and its ethnic regions
Rimé	Nondenominational Buddhism that integrates the practices of the four sects
rinpoche	An incarnate lama, or tulku; a person who carries on the spiritual lineage of his predecessor
The Romance of the Three Kingdoms	Chinese literature read by Arjia Rinpoche at Kumbum during the Cultural Revolution to improve his Chinese
Rose Boyle	Friend in New York City who gave Arjia Rinpoche and his party a place to stay upon their arrival in the United States
Round Rock Mountain	Site designated as a place to be mined
Rusar People's Commune	In the 1960s, every town was called a commune. Rusar is the town where Kumbum is located.
Sakya	One of the four sects of Tibetan Buddhism
samsara	Cycle of existence in which a being must continually be reborn due to the accumulation of negative karma
Sangha	The third of the Three Jewels of Buddhism; the spiritual community and an object of refuge

TERM OR NAME	EXPLANATION
sarira	Relics of the historical Buddha, Siddhartha Gautama
School of Mechanical Engineering	A group of young people closely trained by the Panchen Lama in the 1960s
Sera Monastery	Monastery outside of Lhasa that was partially destroyed during the Cultural Revolution. It was rebuilt in the 1980s.
Serdok Rinpoche	Boyhood and adulthood friend of Arjia Rinpoche
Shadrong Karpu	High-ranking rinpoche who was supposedly a member of the Communist Party; facilitated the marriage of the Panchen Lama
Shan Shui	Communist comrade who instructed little Arjia Rinpoche on how to denounce other monks in the 1950s
Shar Dong Rinpoche	Buddhist teacher of Arjia Ripoche at Qinghai University for Nationalities; Arjia Rinpoche's spiritual teacher during his tenure as khenpo of Kumbum
Shartse Dratsang	One of the four philosophy colleges at Tashi Lhunpo
Sherab Gyatso	Geshe Lharampa and chairman of the Buddhist Association of China in 1961 who worked to maintain the autonomy of Tibetan culture; later was tortured and passed away while under house arrest; visited Arjia Rinpoche and Serdok Rinpoche at Kumbum in late 1961
Sherap Sangbo	Second Arjia Rinpoche (1633–1707)
Shigatse	Second most important city in central Tibet, where Tashi Lhunpo Monastery is located
Shingsa Achu	Mother of Lama Tsong Khapa
Shukling Dorje Podrang	Residence of the Panchen Lama in Lhasa
Sonam Tsemo Rinpoche	Nurse in prison hospital who treated the supervisor's wife
Songtsen Gampo	Tibetan emperor and First Dharma King (seventh century), who brought writing to Tibet and built the Jokhang Temple in Lhasa
State Administration for Religious Affairs of the PRC	Communist bureaucratic organization that monitors religions in China and its ethnic regions
Stephen	Chinese-American businessman who provided a place for Arjia Rinpoche and his party to stay in Los Angeles
stupa	A monument symbolizing the enlightened mind of a buddha, usually encasing Buddhist images, mantras, sutras, and other holy objects; also a crematorium for lamas and rinpoches
Sumpa Kanchen Rinpoche	Enthusiastic positivist monk who joined the Communist revolution; later was imprisoned
Supervisor Zhao	Supervisor at Delinkha Prison Camp
Surku	Family pet name for Arjia Rinpoche
sutra	Buddhist sacred scripture
tapka	Central fire in a ger or tent
Tagtser Rinpoche	Eldest brother of the Fourteenth Dalai Lama (Thubten J. Norbu); visited Kumbum in the 1980s; khenpo of Kumbum prior to 1950; founder of the Tibetan Cultural Center in Bloomington, Indiana

TERM OR NAME	EXPLANATION
tantra	Meditation practice in Tibetan Buddhism that enables a practitioner to achieve enlightenment
Tashi Lhunpo Monastery	Monastery of the Panchen Lamas; located in Shigatse, Tibet
Tashi Rinpoche	Tibetan lama who was with Arjia Rinpoche when the Fourteenth Dalai Lama's delegation visited Kumbum
Tashi Wangshuk	Tibetan Communist who was on the Long March. He was loyal to the Party but helpful to the Tibetans.
teaching	An explanation of Buddhist doctrines by qualified lamas
Tenba Gyatso	Elder brother of Arjia Rinpoche and an attendant to Gyayak Rinpoche
Tenzin	Monk at Tashi Lhunpo whom young Arjia Rinpoche tricked
thangka	Religious artwork that features images of Buddhas, bodhisattvas, and lamas of Tibetan Buddhism. Thangkas are painted on scrolls or appliquéd and then framed in ornate brocade.
Theravadan Buddhism	Form of ancient Buddhism still practiced in Sri Lanka, Burma, and regions of Southeast Asia
Three Core Principles	One of the teachings of Lama Tsong Khapa. The core principles are renunciation, compassion, and wisdom.
Three Jewels	The Buddha, the Dharma, and the Sangha: sacred objects of spiritual refuge in the Buddhist religion
Three Red Flags	Symbols of the Great Leap Forward, socialism, and people's communes
Thubten J. Norbu	Tagtser Rinpoche, eldest brother of the Fourteenth Dalai Lama and founder of the Tibetan Cultural Center in Bloomington, Indiana
Tiananmen Square	Location in Beijing where the 1989 student revolts occurred. It is the main entrance to the Forbidden City.
Tibet Autonomous Region (TAR)	Section of Tibet recognized by the Chinese goverment as the region of Tibet
The Tibetan Book of the Dead	Guide to a person's life thread through the bardo; read to a dying person
Tibetan Buddhist College of Qinghai Province	Arjia Rinpoche was dean of this college when he left Tibet and China
Toli	Remote town where Arjia Rinpoche's and Serdok Rinpoche's relatives had been forced to relocate because the government planned to build a nuclear plant in the Dolon Nor area
Treatise on Steps toward Becoming a Bodhisattva	A teaching of Lama Tsong Khapa
tsampa	Cooked barley ground up and mixed with butter and water to make a dough
Tse Sang	Mother of Arjia Rinpoche

TERM OR NAME	EXPLANATION
Tsendor	Monk at Tashi Lhunpo who shared the rumor that Arjia Rinpoche and Serdok Rinpoche were the illegitimate sons of the Panchen Lama
Tsering	Gatekeeper of the Great Hall of Golden Tiles at Kumbum
Tsong Khapa	Learned and revered lama who founded the Gelug sect of Tibetan Buddhism (1357–1419)
Tsultrim Jongni Jung Ni	First Arjia Rinpoche (sixteenth century)
Tsultrim Lhaksem	One of the spiritual teachers of Arjia Rinpoche; also the teacher of Tagtser Rinpoche (Thubten J. Norbu)
tulku	An incarnate lama or rinpoche; a person who carries on the spiritual lineage of his predecessor
Ulan Gegan Rinpoche	A Mongolian lama who was a member of the original search committee for the Eleventh Panchen Lama
Uncle Chungchu Oser	Uncle of Arjia Rinpoche who was sent to a prison labor camp; former house manager of Serdok Rinpoche
Uncle Chungchu Yengdan	Uncle of Arjia Rinpoche who was sent to a prison labor camp, where he passed away
Uncle Tsetar	Uncle of Arjia Rinpoche—humiliated in the 1950s and sent to a prison labor camp
United Front	Short name for the United Front Work Department of the CPC Central Committee. Its headquarters is in Beijing. Each province, prefecture, and county has a branch office.
Wang Hongwen	Vice chairman of the PRC and one of the Gang of Four
Wang Houdu	Member of the Panchen Lama's party who traveled to Central and South America in 1988
Wang Zhaoguo	A minister of the national United Front in Beijing who wrote a letter to Arjia Rinpoche asking him to return to Tibet and China
Wang Zhao-yu	A leader of the United Front
Wang Zheyi	Staff person at the State Administration for Religious Affairs of the PRC
Wen Jiabao	Official sent by the central government to the Panchen Lama's headquarters at the time of his death; later became premier (prime minister) of China
World Peace Pagoda	Site in Burma where Buddha's relics were displayed during Arjia Rinpoche's visit there
Wu Bing	A businessman from Beijing invited to be the director of the liason office at Kumbum
Wu Jinghua	Party secretary of the TAR during the 1987 uprising investigation
Xihuang Si (Western Yellow Monastery)	One of the two Tibetan monasteries remaining in Beijing after the Cultural Revolution; location where the Panchen Lama established the High-Level Tibetan Buddhism College of China
Xining	Closest city to Kumbum Monastery; capital of Qinghai Province (*Siling* in Tibetan)

TERM OR NAME	EXPLANATION
Yang Ba Jian Hall	Hall in Ganden Monastery where Lama Tsong Khapa's remains had been enshrined before their desecration during the Cultural Revolution
Yang Gya Rinpoche	Tibetan lama who was with Arjia Rinpoche when the Fourteenth Dalai Lama's delegation visited Kumbum
Yang Jingren	A Muslim minister in the national United Front in Beijing who facilitated the marriage of the Panchen Lama
Yang Qing Xi	Veteran cadre who insisted that the Communist government apologize to the Tibetan people
Yar Nang Choedra	Public ceremonial courtyard at Kumbum
Yarlong Tsangpo River	The highest, major river in Tibet located near Tashi Lhunpo Monastery. It flows into India and eventually into the Bay of Bengal.
Ye Xiaowen	Minister in the State Administration for Religious Affairs of the PRC who was in charge of the search for the Eleventh Panchen Lama and the Golden Urn Ceremony
Yeshe Kalsang Kedrup Gyatso	Fifth Arjia Rinpoche (1817–1869)
Ying Ke Sheng	Secretary of Qinghai Province during the time of the selection of the counterfeit Panchen Lama
Yong He Gong Monastery	One of the two Tibetan monasteries remaining in Beijing after the Cultural Revolution. Previously, there had been 36.
Yuan Dynasty	Dynasty of the Mongol reign in China (1279–1368)
Za Marki	Town at the foot of Ahrik Mountain
Zen	A form of Buddhism practiced mainly in China and Japan
Zhang	Commissar of Huangzhong County Revolutionary Committee
Zhang Xueyi (Zhang Menpa)	Chinese doctor, a devout Buddhist, who was imprisoned for 20 years by the Communists
Zhao	Cadre of the State Administration for Religious Affairs of the PRC, who had a heart attack while presenting a report concerning the 1987 uprising and later died
Zhao Puchu	Chairman of the Buddhist Association of China in the 1980s and 1990s
Zhen Ying	Head of the United Front of the TAR at the time of the Tiananmen Square uprising
Zhou Enlai	Leading figure in the CPC and first premier of the PRC. He was born in 1898 and died in 1976.
Zhu Zi Min	Secretary of the Party committee in Huangzhong County who welcomed the Dalai Lama's delegation visiting Kumbum in the 1980s
Zon Dri Gyaltsen	Monk who complained to the Panchen Lama about the mistreatment at Kumbum by the Communists